Faculty
Development
Program
JH109

BUTLER
UNIVERSITY

Enhancing Scholarly Work on Teaching and Learning

Maryellen Weimer

Enhancing Scholarly Work on Teaching and Learning

Professional Literature That Makes a Difference

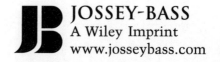

JOSSEY-BASS
A Wiley Imprint
www.josseybass.com

Published by Jossey-Bass
A Wiley Imprint
989 Market Street, San Francisco, CA 94103–1741   www.josseybass.com

Jossey-Bass books and products are available through most bookstores. To contact Jossey-Bass directly call our Customer Care Department within the U.S. at 800–956–7739, outside the U.S. at 317–572–3986, or fax 317–572–4002.

Jossey-Bass also publishes its books in a variety of electronic formats. Some content that appears in print may not be available in electronic books.

Library of Congress Cataloging-in-Publication Data

Weimer, Maryellen, 1947-
   Enhancing scholarly work on teaching and learning : professional literature that makes a difference / Maryellen Weimer.— 1st ed.
       p. cm. — (The Jossey-Bass higher and adult education series)
   Includes bibliographical references and index.
   ISBN-13: 978-0-7879-7381-0 (cloth)
   ISBN-10: 0-7879-7381-5 (cloth)
   1. College teaching.   2. Learning.   I. Title.   II. Series.
   LB2331.W365 2006
   378.1'2—dc22   2005036849

Printed in the United States of America
FIRST EDITION
HB Printing   10 9 8 7 6 5 4 3 2 1

The Jossey-Bass
Higher and Adult Education Series

Contents

Preface   ix

The Author   xxi

1. Why and How to Look   1
2. What to Look At   19
3. Scholarly Work on Teaching and Learning:
   An Overview   39
4. The Lens of Experience: Wisdom of Practice   53
5. The Lens of Objectivity: Research Scholarship   91
6. Promising Possibilities   123
7. Looking Ahead: Learning from What's Behind   141
8. From Looking to Doing: Advice for Faculty   169
9. From Looking to Doing: Advice for Academic
   Leaders   193

Appendixes

A. Discipline-Based Pedagogical Periodicals   211
B. Cross-Disciplinary and Topical Pedagogical
   Periodicals   215

References   217

Name Index   231

Subject Index   237

In Memory of My Aunt
Mary S. Robertson
1902–1990

Preface

Books grow out of personal experience—at least mine do, and this one is no exception. Even though I've held a number of different academic positions during my career at Penn State, I have done scholarly work on teaching and learning in all of them. I started publishing pedagogical scholarship because my first and finest boss expected it. But I quickly discovered that work on teaching and learning can be intellectually challenging and that my practice improved significantly as a result of it. I was hooked—one article led to another, one book to others. As the years accumulated, so has my work.

Until recently, pedagogical scholarship hasn't counted for much, if at all, in the promotion and tenure scheme of things, especially at research universities. The majority of academics who've done it have relied on other kinds of research to advance their careers. But recent interest in the scholarship of teaching has changed the way scholarly work on teaching and learning is being viewed. In my own case, after more than twenty years at Penn State, and as I worked on this book, my tenth, I made my way through the promotion and tenure process. Fifteen years ago, I couldn't imagine a dossier filled with nothing but pedagogical scholarship being successful.

It's too late for tenure to make a whole lot of difference in my career. However, new faculty at my institution and elsewhere are now being told that they can do this kind of work. There is an unprecedented openness and interest in scholarly work on teaching and learning, and a correspondingly large degree of ignorance as to its characteristics. Should the work be structured and formatted according to accepted disciplinary protocols? Should it conform to standards and rigor of discipline-based research? Do these fit when the context is pragmatic and applied? Where should the work be published—in refereed disciplinary journals only, or might it appear in other venues, some not traditionally thought of as "scholarly" outlets?

This book rests on the need to explore pedagogical scholarship more fully, in particular, to identify its defining characteristics and features as well as those standards that should apply when such scholarship counts for professional advancement. So far, work associated with the scholarship of teaching has focused on these production issues. It has been forward looking, proposing new formats and venues as part of a more positive future in which scholarly work on teaching and learning is accepted and valued. This book is committed to that vision, but it also proposes that we take to the future lessons learned from the past.

In addition to exploring the production of pedagogical scholarship, there is another, equally compelling issue that motivated preparation of this volume: the *use* of scholarly work on teaching and learning. Historically, pedagogical literature has played a minor role in the college teaching profession and in the growth and development of individual faculty. Unfortunately, this history continues as a present-day reality.

It may surprise some to learn that, although interest in the scholarship of teaching is comparatively new, pedagogical scholarship is not. Some pedagogical periodicals have been published continuously for the past eighty years. Despite this longevity, published work on teaching and learning is still read and used by only a small percentage of faculty, as Chapters One and Two document; however, most of us are not going to quibble with that fact. We all have colleagues who never or rarely infuse their thinking or practice with outside information on teaching or learning. In fact, in that fiery crucible of the classroom where I first learned to teach, I cannot recall ever consulting written material on teaching or learning. It never occurred to me that teaching could be "studied" just like the content in my discipline.

Perhaps this neglect of the literature is predictable. Most faculty still teach not having been prepared to do so, and few norms expecting growth and development of college teachers exist. So it is not surprising that many faculty remain unaware that there is much to learn about teaching and that this literature can be instrumental in developing pedagogical prowess.

I first encountered this literature when I began working at Penn State and was directed by my boss (same guy) to do a "substantive" newsletter on teaching for faculty. It was not an assignment I immediately saw as valuable. But to fill a monthly publication with "substance," I needed many more ideas than I had, so I turned to pedagogical literature: books, magazines, and articles—mostly articles and mostly in a family of discipline-based pedagogical periodicals. I looked at educational research, but I quickly learned that faculty connect more strongly with nuts and bolts material and that kind of pragmatic, applied content I found in the pedagogical periodicals.

Early on, two aspects of this practitioner pedagogical literature surprised me. First, I discovered how much I didn't know and how relevant much of the information was. I felt as though it made me a better teacher almost immediately. Second, I found that my faculty readers responded with equal enthusiasm to the short, succinct summaries of this literature that I prepared for the newsletter—which they received for free but only if they requested it. Consistently, about a third of the then–three thousand PSU faculty did. Moreover, we supplied single copies of some of the better articles to any faculty member who asked for them. One such piece was requested by four hundred faculty.

From this local, in-house publication was born a national newsletter, the *Teaching Professor*. My search to find a publisher was long and almost fruitless. I was told repeatedly that asking faculty to pay for printed material on teaching and learning was neither feasible nor financially viable, but in 1987, Magna Publications began publishing the newsletter. To our surprise, subscriptions climbed quickly, reaching a high of twenty thousand subscribers, but staying mostly in the fifteen thousand range. This is still a small percentage of all faculty in the United States and Canada (where most subscribers are located), but it is large when compared with subscriber rates for other pedagogical periodicals. I take these eighteen years of successful publication as convincing evidence that when substantive material on teaching and learning is presented in accessible formats, faculty respond positively. They subscribe, they read, and many report that they implement. There is an audience for this literature!

Despite recent interest in pedagogical scholarship, issues associated with the dissemination of pedagogical literature remain largely unaddressed. We have been so focused on the reward and recognition issues that we have barely reckoned with getting faculty to make use of the literature. This is about more than authors wanting an audience for their work. This is about a profession not having a viable literature associated with its practice—its absence a telling example of yet another way teaching continues to be devalued.

This book, then, was born out of my own experience doing and disseminating pedagogical scholarship. Doing it I discovered a host of personal and professional benefits. Disseminating it has convinced me that this literature has much to teach, that faculty have much to learn, and that the two can be connected. Previously published pedagogical scholarship has lessons to teach us that are relevant to both the production and dissemination of scholarly work on teaching and learning. Extrapolating those lessons and considering how they might help us create a better future for pedagogical scholarship are the primary objectives of this book.

Overview of Contents

The book's nine chapters fall into three different parts. The first three chapters provide the background, context, and history for the middle section. Chapter One starts where I'm imagining most readers will start: *why look* and *how to look* at previously published work. The chapter suggests three reasons that justify a review of previously published work on teaching and learning. As for how the work should be approached, the chapter makes the case for looking with an open mind and looking broadly, across disciplines, conceiving of it as the literature of a profession. Chapter Two follows by clarifying *what* this review looks at. It borders the territory and deals with issues of definition and description. It also offers a brief history of previously published pedagogical scholarship. With the stage set, Chapter Three opens the curtain and offers an overview of the next four chapters. It takes the wide view—classifying the main approaches taken in the work and explaining how each of the approaches will be analyzed in the next two chapters.

The next four chapters constitute the second part of the book, with Chapters Four and Five really being the heart of the book. In these two chapters, previously published pedagogical scholarship is analyzed. Approaches used in previously published work fall into two main categories: Wisdom of Practice (Chapter Four), in which faculty use the lens of experience to analyze instructional issues, and Research Scholarship (Chapter Five), in which faculty employ more objective frames to assess instructional issues. Chapter Four focuses on four experiential approaches: personal accounts of change, recommended-practices reports, recommended-content reports, and personal narratives. Chapter Five analyzes the three most common research approaches used in previously published work: quantitative investigations, qualitative studies, and descriptive research. Both chapters use the same five categories to analyze each of these approaches: definition, critical assessment, annotated exemplars, standards, and contribution. A detailed discussion of these categories of analysis is included in Chapter Three.

Not all previously published pedagogical scholarship uses these main approaches. Chapter Six considers a collection of promising possibilities, including literature formatted differently than the conventional journal articles, and literature, both articles and other forms, that analyzes pedagogical issues using approaches other than these most common ones. Chapter Seven, Looking Ahead: Learning From What's Behind, attempts to extract from the review and analysis of previously published work those lessons that will take us to a new, different, and better future, both as scholars of teaching and learning and as classroom practitioners.

The book concludes with two chapters that shift from looking at previously published work to doing and using pedagogical scholarship. Chapter Eight contains advice to faculty, both for those who have never done pedagogical scholarship and for those who may have dabbled but are interested in doing more and making their work better. Chapter Nine offers advice to academic leaders on advancing scholarly work on teaching and learning. It suggests ways of getting faculty connected to the literature and ways to support faculty interested doing pedagogical scholarship.

Intended Audiences

I have written this book with multiple audiences in mind. Basically, they belong to three groups: advocates committed to scholarly work on teaching and learning; editors, reviewers, authors, and potential authors; and those who do and don't use pedagogical literature. An analysis of scholarly work on teaching and learning is relevant and a useful resource to each group for different, albeit related, reasons.

Advocates Committed to Scholarly Work on Teaching and Learning

First, I'm writing to those within the higher education community who already consider themselves teaching-learning advocates and who are on board with the idea of pedagogical scholarship. I would place in this group those administrators committed to making scholarly work on teaching and learning count and who believe a viable literature would improve practice and increase the stature of college teaching as a profession. Faculty developers, those organizationally assigned to advance teaching and learning agendas within an institution, also belong to this group of advocates. Finally, there are those individuals or small groups of faculty who aspire to do what they can to change the culture for teaching within their departments and at their institutions.

Those already on board with the pedagogical scholarship agenda need resources that will help them further advance the cause. For example, to date no resource points to examples it claims illustrate what "good" scholarly work looks like. Efforts have been made to set new and broader standards for assessing scholarship generally, including pedagogical scholarship (Diamond and Adam, 1993; Glassick, Huber, and Maeroff, 1997; and Shulman, 2000), but we still don't have resources that point out examples or use the examples themselves to generate standards for specific kinds of pedagogical scholarship. At this point, the consideration of standards needs to get down and dirty. We need standards applied to pieces of work: Here's a descriptive study that analyzes student perceptions of fairness. Does it meet the kind of standards that make for credible pedagogical scholarship?

Editors, Reviewers, Authors, and Potential Authors

This analysis showcases and celebrates previously published scholarly work on teaching and learning, and even though not widely read or referenced, pedagogical scholarship does have its advocates. In this group are the editors, reviewers, publishers, and professional associations—those most responsible for the literature we now have. They have a vested interest in its future! They stand to benefit the most if this work gains more respect, if its quality improves, and if it becomes more widely read.

What I don't see this group recognizing is how much they have to learn from and with each other. Pedagogical scholarship for the most part is either deeply embedded within the disciplines or dangles free. In both cases, it is mostly created and disseminated in splendid isolation. I am hoping those who work so diligently on this literature will use this book to explore what they might learn from one another and how they might more effectively advance this agenda collectively.

Finally, in this group I include faculty authors, those who have already published scholarly work on teaching and learning and those who aspire to do so. Current and potential authors can use this resource to explore options: What approaches have others taken in their study of teaching and learning? Are there ways to write about experiential learning—those lessons learned in the school of hard knocks? Are there other approaches to systematic inquiry that might be adapted and used? They can also use the book to confront the quality of their own pedagogical scholarship or the work they aspire to create: What aspects make some work on teaching and learning exemplary? Mostly, I hope the book will inspire faculty authors, convince them that this kind of scholarship is worth doing—that it can stretch intellectual muscles at the same time as it develops prowess in the classroom and advances the profession.

Those Who Do and Don't Use Pedagogical Literature

Finally, I am writing this book for those who may read some pedagogical literature but not a lot, and those who may not read it at all. Here I am also imagining an audience broader than just faculty. Academic leaders, be they department chairs, division heads, deans, or provosts, who care about teaching and wish to create institutions known for genuine commitments to instructional excellence, need to realize that pedagogical literature can and should play a vital role in improving practice and creating climates that value teaching and learning. To cultivate that awareness, I invite these academic leaders to join faculty in sampling the literature.

Some faculty and academic leaders do read pedagogical literature. Usually, they don't read a lot and they mostly read material written by colleagues in their discipline. That's a fine place to begin, but the potential of pedagogical reading to increase instructional effectiveness is more broadly based. Some of the lessons it has to teach are best learned by reading outside the discipline. As essential as they are, disciplinary perspectives can blind faculty to larger, different, and sometimes better views of instructional issues. If a testimony might be persuasive, see Yakura and Bennett (2003); here are a social scientist and a mathematician, respectively, who offer a detailed description of insights gained during their cross-disciplinary collaboration. However, I think that faculty who do not sample the literature widely or collaborate with colleagues outside their discipline are more likely to be persuaded when they experience the benefits firsthand. They need pieces of good pedagogical scholarship with relevant content from other fields put in their hands. Until I started reading the *Journal of Engineering Education*, I would not have believed it contained content meaningful to my instructional practice.

Those who don't read pedagogical scholarship and are unconvinced of its merit need resources that will convince them of two facts. First, that valuable lessons about teaching and learning can be acquired by reading. That's not a tough sell because the higher-education community is filled with people who read and rely on reading for a significant part of their learning. Second, that valuable information on teaching and learning is available. Here, the point is the same as it was with those who already read the literature. They don't need to be told that good literature exists—they need materials put in their hands, offered with an invitation to read and make judgments for themselves. We need resource collections that provide compelling examples—ones where the content itself convinces and motivates.

Other Details

Two other topics merit mentioning here at the book's outset. First, I want to underscore the importance of the exemplars showcased in Chapters Four and Five and referenced throughout the book. When first considering a book on pedagogical scholarship, I envisioned an edited collection of exemplary articles drawn from a wide range of sources. Despite less-than-supportive conditions, some truly outstanding scholarship on teaching and learning has been completed by practitioners. It deserves recognition as credible scholarship and as literature able to contribute much to instructional practice and professional recognition. You don't have to take my word for it; this book references and describes specific examples.

As I started assembling a collection of exemplary work, I realized how many issues related to previously published work merited review and analysis. I thought I might be able to reprint some examples or excerpts in the book, but realism about book length prevailed. Given the pedagogical reading habits of most in the higher education community, a nine-hundred-page manuscript would end up with neither a publisher nor an audience. So this book reprints no examples, although it references many. My worst fear is that people will read the book but never get to the exemplars. Please don't let this happen! Please read the exemplars—all of them if you wish to understand the range of work that appears in previously published scholarship, most of them if you wish to assess the lessons drawn from the scholarship, or at least some of them if you are ambivalent about the real and potential quality of scholarship on teaching and learning.

Second, there is a matter of nomenclature. Because I am dealing with already published work, a great deal of it completed before the phrase "scholarship of teaching" entered our vocabulary, I have chosen to refer to it as "scholarly work on teaching or learning" or "pedagogical scholarship." I have avoided the "scholarship of teaching" moniker for a couple of other reasons unrelated to when the work was completed. Virtually everyone agrees that, despite its significant contribution, Boyer's monograph, *Scholarship Reconsidered* (1990), did not clearly and precisely define what was meant by the scholarship of teaching. Despite this omission, the idea resonated and gained notoriety. Minus a clear definition, the term became a trendy moniker that included almost any endeavor that supported and valued teaching. It came to mean everything, anything, and nothing.

As a consequence, multiple efforts ensued to define the term and the kinds of scholarship it included, resulting in a kind of definitional morass from which we are still working to escape. I worry that as we wallow around seeking to differentiate between "excellent" teaching, "scholarly" (or informed) teaching, and the "scholarship of teaching"—be it some combination of scholarly teaching and published outcome or some kind of pedagogical content knowledge linked to learning but embedded in the discipline—the door of opportunity opened by Boyer's notion that we can define scholarship differently will close before pedagogical scholarship manages to move inside. In the interest of regaining lost momentum, I have opted for different terminology that I work hard to define clearly and use precisely throughout the book. Perhaps this sidesteps the issue, but I agree with Healey (2003), who believes it is "unrealistic to expect a single definition to emerge" (p. 20). More significant, time spent seeking to settle definitional details takes us away from important advocacy that still needs to occur. The idea that scholarship and teaching can be linked is still far from universally accepted.

Acknowledgments

One writes alone, but no book happens without the help of many. Thanks to trusted colleagues and dear friends Dave Ackerman, Dave Bender, and Chuck Walker, who read and helped me with various parts of this book. My brother, Mark Robertson, helped with references. Thanks to Larry Spence and Chris Knapper, who challenge my ideas over breakfast and wine, respectively. Nothing has shaped my views on pedagogical scholarship more than monthly preparation of the *Teaching Professor* newsletter. I am deeply indebted to Bill Haight for his willingness to undertake its publication. He and the rest of my colleagues at Magna Publications continue to support this cornerstone of my professional career. Many of my campus colleagues support my work—among those deserving special thanks are Maureen Bokansky, Deb Guy, Deena

Morganti, and Ike and Lisa Shibley. My academic dean, Carl Lovitt, did much to create conditions conducive to my productivity. My superb Jossey-Bass editor, David Brightman, makes my books better; I so enjoy working with him. And there continues to be Michael, my wonderful spouse, who doesn't read my books but endorses them anyway.

Following the tradition of my previous books, I have dedicated this one to yet another of my aunts: Mary S. Robertson, the aunt I took for granted growing up. She was with us for every holiday. She never missed a birthday. I felt her interest in every aspect of my life, but most especially my education. Mary was a high school teacher; seldom has education had a more ardent advocate.

I cannot remember when I decided to teach. I don't think it was a conscious decision, more like slowly waking and reckoning with the day's tasks. I think Aunt Mary made teaching the task of my days without either of us noticing. We had our last coherent conversation in the Seattle airport on my way home at the end of my first year in grad school at Penn State. Over coffee, she peppered me with questions—literally, about every class I'd taken. I don't remember asking her anything. Her loving presence has loomed large and lingered long over my life.

January 2006   Marsh Creek, Pennsylvania
                          Bluff Island, Tupper Lake, New York

The Author

Maryellen Weimer teaches beginning students introductory communication courses full-time at Penn State Berks, where she is a professor of teaching and learning. In 2005, Weimer received the Milton S. Eisenhower Award for Distinguished Teaching, one of Penn State's university-wide teaching awards.

Weimer received a Ph.D. in speech communication in 1981 from Penn State. Spending most of her career at Penn State, Weimer has held several different positions at the university. For ten years she directed the university's Instructional Development Program. She also served as a senior research associate in Penn State's Center for the Study of Higher Education, where she was an associate director of the National Center on Postsecondary Teaching, Learning, and Assessment, a U.S. Department of Education Research and Development Center funded for five years.

Over the past twenty years, Weimer has consulted with more than 275 colleges and universities in the United States and Canada as well as overseas on a variety of instructional issues. She regularly keynotes national conferences and regional meetings.

Since 1987, Weimer has edited *Teaching Professor,* a monthly newsletter on college teaching. She has authored or edited nine books, including one on faculty development, one on teaching for new faculty, and an anthology edited with Robert Menges, *Teaching on Solid Ground: Using Scholarship to Improve Practice* (Jossey-Bass, 1995). Her most recent Jossey-Bass book, *Learner-Centered Teaching: Five Key Changes to Practice*, was published in 2002.

Enhancing Scholarly Work
on Teaching and Learning

1

Why and How to Look

I didn't start out planning to write a book about pedagogical schol-arship. I began with some favorite articles—ones that had im-proved my practice, made me think, and deepened my devotion to teaching. I had collected them across the years from discipline-based pedagogical periodicals in fields far removed from my own. I thought that more faculty should benefit from their very relevant content. But as I began assembling this collection (most end up in this book as the exemplars cited in Chapters Four and Five), larger questions kept emerging: What makes these articles so good? What features define them, and how are they different from other work in the body of previously published pedagogical literature? Does this pre-viously published work hold lessons relevant to current interest in the scholarship of teaching? Is this work scholarly? Why don't more faculty read more pedagogical literature? The questions kept side-tracking me until I realized a collection of noteworthy examples was much less valuable without considering these larger issues. Previ-ously published practitioner pedagogical scholarship needed criti-cal review and analysis. It needed to be looked at as a body of literature. As work on the project proceeded, the questions solidi-fied into three reasons that this previously published work merits review, which are presented in this chapter.

From the start of this project, I also struggled with the question of approach—how this previously published work should be looked at. I wanted readers to look at the work with open minds, to see this review as an opportunity to examine pedagogical scholarship with fresh eyes, to ask old questions but consider new answers—in essence, to look in ways that make learning possible. But a conundrum presented itself. I was not looking at the scholarship for the first time. I had formed opinions about it. Truth be known, I am passionately committed to the need for scholarly work on teaching and firmly convinced that it can be credible scholarship and a viable literature for professional practice. Could I challenge readers to make up their own minds and at the same time fill the book with my ideas about what this scholarship is and could be?

I decided it might work as long as I kept before readers the need to approach the work with open minds and press them to look at it broadly. To help keep minds open and perspectives broad, I use questions as honest queries—because even though I may think I have answers, at this juncture those responses should only be used as starting places, points of departure from which readers should develop their own theories, test their ideas, and form conclusions for themselves. As writer and reader we commit to the same goal: a different and better future for scholarly work on teaching and learning completed by practitioners.

Before considering why and how to look at this literature in more detail, I need to establish the parameters of this review. A simple definition will get us started; Chapter Two explores matters of definition in depth. For now it is sufficient to know that this book considers previously published work on teaching and learning authored by college faculty. It is not the same as what I will refer to as educational research, the product of those fields devoted to the exploration of a range of issues for all educational levels, but a practitioner scholarship that explores postsecondary teaching and learning and is completed by faculty in disciplines other than education.

Why Look?

Why look at previously published scholarly work on teaching and learning? Three reasons justify the review and can be previewed briefly. The first is easy and straightforward: the time is right, and no one has taken a serious and comprehensive look back. The second two reasons emerge out of what scholarly work on teaching and learning most needs in order to advance as scholarship and from what college teaching most needs in order to improve.

First, practitioner work on teaching and learning must be credible scholarship. It needs to count, to be taken seriously, and to be of a caliber that merits reward and recognition. Second, college teaching desperately needs a viable literature associated with professional practice. Only doing the first, making pedagogical scholarship credible, will serve important but limited ends. However, addressing both accomplishes a larger objective. Pedagogical literature has the power to improve the practice of individuals as well as that of the profession. For teachers, it identifies ways to teach that promote more and better learning. For the profession, it helps to establish benchmarks and best practices. During this time of opportunity, we look back to see what the past might teach us about credible scholarship and viable literature. Each justification merits fuller exploration.

The Time Is Right

Interest in the scholarship of teaching, one of four kinds of scholarship identified in Boyer's (1990) work, has created a window of opportunity for pedagogical scholarship. As already noted in the Preface, attempts to define more precisely what Boyer meant by the scholarship of teaching have been multiple (see Kreber's Delphi study of definitional issues, 2001b) and are indicative of widespread interest in scholarly work on teaching and learning. These efforts have been accompanied by attempts to illustrate the scholarship of teaching via individual faculty work and programmatic initiatives. Most notably in the United States, the Carnegie Foundation has funded the Carnegie Academy for the Scholarship of Teaching and Learning (CASTL) in conjunction with the American Association of Higher Education (AAHE). There have also been programs promoting the scholarship of teaching worldwide. For an excellent summary of them as well as extensive references, see Healey (2003). Many of these initiatives call for new forms of scholarship and new venues for dissemination.

While funded projects have pushed the envelope, at most institutions that are not part of those projects the interest is less cutting edge but still present. There is an openness, a willingness to consider how scholarly work on teaching might count for professional advancement. The extent of openness, of course, depends on the type of institution. At places with teaching missions, there has always been more openness, but encouragement and expectations for pedagogical scholarship have been missing or modest (Weaver, 1986). However, recent years have seen an increase in these venues in both research expectations for faculty and the value placed on pedagogical scholarship. At other places, most notably the research universities, there has not been openness to pedagogical scholarship; in fact, the encouragement has been to *not* complete it. Even at these universities, however, interest in the scholarship of teaching has opened doors, not widely, but enough for some of us to get a toe in.

As these initiatives challenge us to consider new forms of pedagogical scholarship, a look at already completed work balances the calls for change. There is about this previously published pedagogical work a comforting familiarity. It exists most commonly as articles in refereed journals, books, reports, and monographs—those formats for disseminating scholarship that have stood the test of time. They are known and accepted within the academic community. Yes, there is room and need for new formats and venues, but for an academic community inexperienced with and still only modestly supportive of pedagogical scholarship, this is a safe and sensible place to build further understanding and commitment. A promotion and tenure committee may question the merit of scholarly work on teaching and learning, but if the work is published as an article in a refereed journal, at least the format and venue are familiar and credible.

More important, those calling for new forms of scholarly work should be made cognizant of those used in the past. Better decisions about the future are the likely result of having looked carefully at what's behind, and so far, little retrospective analysis has occurred. Without it, we cannot say if it makes sense to dig new foundations or build new work on these existing foundations. Without it, we cannot prevent the remaking of old mistakes. Despite a history of growth in an unfriendly, sometimes hostile, environment, the body of previously published work on teaching and learning does have lessons to teach us. As we consider alternative forms, formats, and functions for pedagogical scholarship, we move to a more enlightened future if the lessons of the past accompany us.

Credible Pedagogical Scholarship

More important than the timeliness and appropriateness of looking back is the second justification for this review of previously published scholarly work on teaching and learning: we need credible pedagogical scholarship. Historically, work on teaching and learning done by faculty practitioners has not been seen as robust, reward-worthy work. It is still not a preferred or assured path to professional advancement, despite recent interest. Based on the survey response of 1,424 faculty at five different types of colleges and universities and from four different disciplines, 75 percent of the sample listed no publications in the scholarship of teaching domain for the previous three years (Braxton, Luckey, and Helland, 2002). These levels of non-publication were consistent across institutional type and academic discipline.

Why don't more faculty do pedagogical scholarship? It may not be of interest. That is probably true for some faculty, but it seems more likely that others potentially interested do not see the work being rewarded or recognized. They do not view it as a viable path to professional advancement.

Most of us need not look at national surveys for compelling evidence that pedagogical scholarship still counts for little. Consider the full professors at your institution and another cohort of the recently tenured. How many reached the rank of full professor because of their research productivity? How many were promoted to this level on the basis of their pedagogical scholarship? How many of the recently tenured acquired that status with a dossier containing mostly or exclusively pedagogical scholarship? Even at places where faculty are promoted on the basis of teaching excellence, how often is pedagogical scholarship regularly part of the equation?

The diminished value of pedagogical scholarship is also apparent with the academic disciplines. In Huber and Morreale's work (2002) on disciplinary styles in the scholarship of teaching, the chapters written about the fields of management, engineering, history, chemistry, and communication all confirm the second-tier status of work on teaching and learning. I would be surprised if there is any academic discipline where pedagogical scholarship merits the same reward and recognition given research work in the field.

Out of this longstanding lack of credibility emerges the first of two central questions explored throughout this book: What would make pedagogical scholarship credible? Obviously, gaining this respect involves more than the scholarship itself. It will take changes in the value placed on teaching within both higher education and society at large. But the question as it is explored here relates to the literature itself. What characteristics of scholarly work completed by practitioners would make it credible? What features indicate rigor and intellectual integrity? How is this kind of scholarly work alike and different from discipline-based scholarship? With a better future for pedagogical scholarship the objective, the look back is about identifying characteristics and features of previously published work and then assessing their potential as characteristics and features of credible scholarship. That's the second reason that a look back is justified.

Viable Pedagogical Literature

In addition to the need for credible pedagogical scholarship, a second, equally compelling, need exists. If practice is to improve and college teaching is to develop respect as a profession, there must be a viable literature associated with it. The future of scholarly work on teaching and learning involves more than its production, as central and necessary as this consideration is. Most faculty still teach with no or very little formal training. Their further growth and development as teachers are stunted when their learning derives only or mostly from what they experience. There are important insights to be gleaned from the experience, wisdom, and research of others and a deeper, more reflective analysis of one's own. A viable pedagogical literature affords the opportunity for this larger learning.

However, to improve practice and have an impact on the profession, pedagogical literature must be seen as a valuable repository of information. It must be read; currently only a very few do so. The evidence that supports this fact is easily summoned: look at the subscription rates for a given pedagogical periodical and compare it to the number of faculty teaching in the field. The periodicals reviewed in this book have circulations that range between five hundred and ten thousand, but they belong to disciplines with thousands—in some cases tens of thousands—of faculty members. To illustrate specifically, the cross-disciplinary publication *College Teaching* has about 1,400 subscribers (Statement, 2005, p. 13); there are almost 620,000 faculty members in the United States (U.S. Department of Education, 2001–02).

Further evidence exists in the research literature as well. Quinn (1994) reports on the reading habits of a group of full professors, all recipients of teaching awards—a group the researchers expected to be "the most curious and experimental of teachers, precisely the ones who would consult the literature as they develop pedagogical refinements and innovations" (p. 64). They found that only 35 percent of this cohort reported that they got fresh ideas about teaching from reading. Thirty percent reported that they spent no time reading about teaching. Those who did most often reported that they spent one to two hours a month on such reading. Few reported any systematic, substantive reading of pedagogical literature in their field or elsewhere.

I don't have any trouble believing these findings. In my workshop activities with faculty I regularly ask, "What are you reading about teaching?" "What have you learned recently from the literature?" The silences are frequently just as prolonged and awkward as when I query my beginning students about what they've been reading.

My experience is neither isolated nor exceptional. Writing about their field, Wankat, Felder, Smith, and Oreovicz (2002) observe, "Most engineering professors do not read the literature that demonstrates the advantages of student-centered instructional methods and continue to insist on lecturing exclusively" (p. 231). The failure to implement any number of instructional approaches known to promote more and better learning attests further to the neglect of the pedagogical literature by faculty in most fields. Huber (2002) succinctly sums up the point: "Academics are not in the habit of reading about teaching and learning: Thus, when a problem turns up, they are more likely to ask advice from an old friend or colleague than to go to the library" (p. 29).

So, pedagogical literature is only read by a few. But there is also a second sense in which pedagogical literature is not widely read. In this case, it is the matter of what faculty read when they do access the literature. They favor pedagogical material from and within their disciplines. Here the evidence exists in the pedagogical periodicals themselves, specifically the reference lists at the end of the articles. In the majority of cases, the most frequently cited sources are previously published articles from that same pedagogical periodical. Writing at the conclusion of her editorship of the *Journal of Social Work Education*, Gambrill (2003) observes, "One striking feature of the many manuscripts submitted to the *Journal* during this three-year period was the confinement of literature reviews to material in social work, neglecting rich areas of related inquiry in other fields" (p. 3). Or consider the book review sections of these periodicals (almost all of these journals have one). The bulk of books reviewed are textbooks in the discipline. Rarely will you find books reviewed that distill and integrate educational research, or books that address pedagogical issues generally. An actual survey of forty-five members of the *Teaching of Psychology* editorial board asked them to list up to ten general books and articles they considered essential pedagogical reading. Despite the fact that they were also asked to list essential sources on teaching psychology, three of their top five generic recommendations were sources authored by or written for psychologists (Saville and Buskirk, 2004). The literature is not widely read, meaning few faculty read it, and few read pedagogical materials outside their disciplines.

The cost of not having a viable literature associated with instructional practice is high. Because norms do not expect systematic growth and development for college teachers, classroom practice rests unevenly on what has been well established experientially and empirically. The less-than-perfect understanding of both can be seen in how faculty think about what they do, or, more accurately, how they don't reflect on what they do. Many teach from habit, blind to the premises and assumptions that ground the practices they routinely use. Further evidence can be found in faculty conceptions of teaching. Teaching does involve skills, instructional nuts and bolts, strategies and techniques. It is related and inextricably tied to content. But these simplistic conceptions trivialize the complexity that is inherently a part of teaching. Classrooms are dynamic venues where what happens one day never guarantees what will happen the next. In that kind of environment power lies not in having many techniques and a good grasp of content, but in the ability to select and adapt so that techniques and content serve changing learning needs.

How faculty view the teaching-learning relationship also leads to some uninformed instructional decision making. Faculty's continuing fixation with teaching prevents them from seeing that teaching has no purpose unless it can be directly and explicitly connected to and with learning outcomes. True, most teaching does result in learning. But faculty views of learning should be much more precise than that. What students learn and how they learn are fundamentally functions of how they are taught. Instruction that is didactic, lecture-based, and content-driven produces one kind of learning. Instruction that is facilitative, interactional, and experiential produces another kind of learning. (Kember's research work most convincingly illustrates this effect, starting with his 1994 study with Gow, but their findings are being corroborated by others, such as Church, Elliot, and Gable, 2001.) Instructional practice suffers because many faculty fail to think, conceive, or view teaching and learning cognizant of the knowledge base on which it rests.

In addition to these costs to individual practice, there is the price paid by the profession. What other profession exists without a viable literature supporting its practice? In what other profession can those who practice do so for years without expanding or updating their knowledge or skills? What other profession fails to use its literature to set benchmarks, identify best (or at least preferred) practices, and exert at least some pressure on those professionals who fail to meet standards? That college teaching has no viable literature associated with its practice illustrates one of the most significant ways in which teaching and learning have been devalued.

The need for a viable literature for the profession can be framed as a second question that justifies a look back: What would make pedagogical literature viable? Are there lessons to be extracted from the previously published literature itself? Do some features make it readable? Do some characteristics motivate change and the implementation of findings? What of this literature could be used to benchmark best practices? With a better future for pedagogical scholarship the objective, the look back is about identifying characteristics and features of previously published work and then assessing their potential as characteristics and features of a viable pedagogical literature. That's the third and final reason justifying a look back.

How to Look

As important as understanding *why* we should look at previously published pedagogical scholarship is considering *how* to look at it. How previously published scholarly work on teaching and learning is viewed will influence what is seen and ultimately what is learned. To gain the most insights, I believe it is necessary to look at the work with an open mind and to consider it broadly, across disciplines.

Looking with an Open Mind

Few will begin the review having no opinions, even though most will not have read widely in previously published pedagogical literature. The circumstances surrounding previously published work on teaching and learning are well known and have obvious quality implications. Given that the work has not counted for scholarly advancement and is not well known, widely read, or highly regarded, it's easy to conclude (as some may already have) that no or very little quality work has been completed.

But does that view rest on valid assumptions? Could other assumptions offer a more viable explanation? It may be that the work is not widely read because there are no norms expecting that faculty keep current of pedagogical developments. It may be that the work is not highly regarded because teaching itself continues to be devalued. In a proposal for broader and more precise definitions of scholarship in psychology, Halpern and others (1998) describe the effects of prejudicial thinking about teaching: "Despite public statements to the contrary, a de facto prejudice against teaching continues to characterize higher education, a prejudice that has been labeled 'teachism' to symbolize its similarity to other prejudicial 'isms' such as sexism, ageism, and racism. Like other prejudices, it can be subtle or overt, and its effects are pervasive because it influences almost every aspect of academic life" (p. 1,294). If the work isn't read because faculty aren't expected to use literature to grow and develop as teachers, or if the work isn't read because teaching continues to be devalued, those are quite different reasons from assuming previously published work isn't read because it isn't any good.

Quality issues as they relate to the overall caliber of previously published work cannot and should not be ignored. Given the value of proceeding into the review with an open mind, let me propose a sensible stance to take on quality—one that reckons with reality at the same time as it balances the issue of merit against the questions of what is needed to advance pedagogical scholarship and literature.

First, work of questionable quality has certainly been published. There is no dodging this fact. I do not intend to commit professional suicide by listing examples, but trust me, they are easy to find. However, documenting the number serves no real purpose. This is published work, water passed under the proverbial bridge—it cannot be unpublished. Instead, we can use it to mark the place from which we begin and from which our motivation to improve springs. Let us opt to take from it lessons that will enhance scholarly work on teaching and learning.

The second fact explains the first: given the conditions under which it has been created, flaws in this literature are not unexpected. This fact does not excuse the flaws in the literature but it does help to explain why they are there. Moreover, the presence of flaws in general is not particularly troubling. What body of work in any field is without them? Of more concern are the flaws themselves. Two questions will be relevant when we consider such flaws in Chapters Four and Five: How widespread is the flaw? Do we have a fixable flaw or an inherent defect? We will discover we have some of both.

The third fact tempers the first: the quality of previously published pedagogical scholarship varies. Its quality is not uniformly awful. It varies across many dimensions over the years, with some tangible signs of improvement appearing in recent changes and explored in Chapter Two. It varies within disciplines and across them, as it does within given issues of a journal and across the different journals in this family of publications. It varies depending on the type of scholarship. Some approaches are consistently stronger than others. In sum, a comprehensive look at previously published pedagogical scholarship reveals a continuum of quality.

Finally, the fact that counterbalances the first: some scholarly work of high quality has been published. Yes, you may at this point say, that's my opinion, but it is an opinion that will be substantiated by examples, many cited in Chapters Four and Five, as well as others throughout the book. And yes, the criteria being used to make that determination have not yet been articulated, but they will be subsequently, also in Chapters Four and Five.

Looking at previously published pedagogical scholarship with an open mind means expecting to see work that ranges across the quality continuum but not being preoccupied with the relative proportion of fine or flawed work. Troublesome characteristics and features of previously published work are identified and discussed subsequently, but the more central focus of the book is on using good examples to find our way to a kind of scholarly work on teaching and learning more likely to be valued and read, that is, credible pedagogical scholarship and viable pedagogical literature.

Looking Across Disciplines

To learn the most from this look back, one also needs to approach the work broadly, viewing it as a collective entity and considering it outside disciplinary boundaries. The goal here is not to relocate this scholarship to some generic place but to look at previously published work with fresh eyes, to see it in different ways and from different perspectives. Consider four benefits likely to accrue when the work is approached from this broad, inclusive perspective.

The first builds on a lesson learned in faculty development work. We have discovered time and again across the years of working with faculty on implementing a wide range of instructional initiatives that they learn much from and through collaboration with faculty from disciplines other than their own. Faculty gain from colleague collaboration when the objective is individual efforts to improve teaching, so the disciplines stand to learn from and with each other when the topic is pedagogical scholarship. Huber (2002) elaborates, "There are certain questions that come more naturally to some disciplines than others, problems that call for different methods, issues that lend themselves to different explanatory strategies, and audiences that respond to different forms of address" (p. 20). Consider one very specific example: Calder, Cutler, and Kelly (2002), writing about the scholarship of teaching in history, note, "There is a great need to know about the state of practice. How do history teachers teach? Who uses textbooks, document readers, and the like, and how do they use them? What is the state of cognition among teachers themselves, what do they think history is, and what are their instructional goals for students?" (p. 60). An impressive amount of state-of-practice descriptive work has been completed in the fields of psychology, sociology, and marketing, reported respectively in *Teaching of Psychology, Teaching Sociology*, and the *Journal of Marketing Education*. Not only would history find models, methods, instrumentation, and approaches to data analysis, all fields would benefit from replicating these valuable inquiries.

The example should not be taken as evidence that the fields of psychology, sociology, and marketing do better pedagogical scholarship than history. Rather, this kind of descriptive research grows naturally from how psychologists, sociologists, and marketers— and others in the social sciences—study behavior. The pedagogical knowledge base is enlarged and enriched by various methodological approaches. But if pedagogical scholarship only uses the methods and approaches of the discipline, this benefit is diminished, to say nothing of liabilities incurred when those methods don't fit the nature of teaching and learning phenomena.

The second benefit of this broad view comes not from these different approaches to scholarship but from findings that are the same: power resides in well-established findings. Again, I can be specific. Over the last ten to fifteen years, virtually all of the pedagogical periodicals have published articles that report on the inclusion of group work (of various types) and the almost uniformly positive impact of those strategies on a number of different learning outcomes. In this case, the experiences and findings reported by practitioners are consistent with results well established in educational research. It is true that the quality of these practitioner analyses varies (as does some of the educational research), but even discounting a significant number of them, a convincing amount of evidence still supports the proposition that students can and do learn from and with each other. Yes, it is important to have evidence documenting that conclusion within a particular field, but the power of what is known about how groups facilitate learning in one field is strengthened by similar findings from many fields. Here's a reason that a collective literature can better serve the profession: It enables us to challenge faculty in our own and other disciplines who ignore approaches to teaching that promote learning. It enables us to establish benchmarks, to identify practices that really are best, and to begin to gain respect for the profession by addressing issues of standards.

In addition to benefiting the study of teaching and learning within a discipline, looking broadly at pedagogical scholarship can support the efforts of teaching advocates. Pedagogical scholarship has a long history of being dismissed or marginalized in virtually all our fields and at most of our institutions. Interest in the scholarship of teaching has started to change some of this situation, but those who advocate for pedagogical scholarship are still not a majority. They can advance their cause more effectively if they know how issues are being handled in other fields and can draw examples from what's being done across disciplines. There is still a considerable amount of "aping" behavior among disciplines, just as there is between institutions. New approaches have more appeal if they are perceived to be part of the latest trend—if they are being implemented in those fields and at those institutions we respect and aspire to be like.

And finally, possibly difficult to accept at the moment, is the benefit that faculty can improve their individual practice by reading pedagogical scholarship in fields other than their own. Of course, this does not rule out disciplinary colleagues as sources of instructional information—I would happily let them remain the primary source. But it does assert that some important pedagogical knowledge transcends disciplinary boundaries. The examples come easily. Learning problems that result from poor time management and low self-confidence are not discipline-specific. They plague students everywhere. Classroom management problems do not belong to one or two fields. They perplex faculty, especially new ones, everywhere. Does this deny the validity of discipline-specific pedagogical knowledge? Not at all. Understanding differential equations does make it easier to select the instructional strategies most effective in teaching that particular math content successfully. Content knowledge is one, but not the only, kind of pedagogical knowledge.

If personal testimony is persuasive, I have been reading pedagogical scholarship from a wide range of disciplines since the early 1980s. In my own teaching, most of what I believe and do has come from and been informed by the scholarship of faculty in fields other than my own. The five pedagogical periodicals I have learned the most from (in no particular order) are the *Journal of Chemical Education, Engineering Education*, the *Journal of Management Education, Teaching Sociology*, and *Teaching Psychology*—and my field is speech communication. Am I proposing that faculty read all the pedagogical periodicals? Of course not; I'd be happy if they regularly read one! What I'm after here is the more fundamental recognition that disciplinary pedagogical knowledge can have relevance to others. Am I claiming that all pedagogical scholarship is useful in all contexts? Of course not! There are lots of articles and examples appearing in the *Journal of Chemical Education* that I don't understand, but if I had to list the five pedagogical articles that have most influenced what I do in class, "What Do You Do When You Stop Lecturing," by Black (1993), published in the *Journal of Chemical Education*, would definitely appear on that list.

The point may not have been made convincingly yet, but it stands no chance of being established unless pedagogical scholarship is approached broadly, unless an open mind allows for the possibility that work worth reviewing has been done in other fields. The chapters to come showcase pedagogical scholarship from a wide range of disciplines. I think it is exemplary work, widely applicable and relevant. But my views are offered here in the hope they will encourage others to look and decide for themselves.

A broad look at pedagogical scholarship potentially accrues four benefits: lessons about pedagogical scholarship for the disciplines to learn from each other; the power of well-established findings to advance the profession; more effective advocacy for those working to advance the teaching-learning agenda; and the power of reading widely to improve individual practice. I think these four benefits make a strong case for looking broadly, and the need to do so is further cemented when subsequent exploration uncovers problems that result when pedagogical scholarship is viewed exclusively from the disciplinary perspective.

To sum the issues of why and how to look at previously published pedagogical scholarship: given the importance of the three reasons that justify taking a look back, I'm glad that this book ended up being more than an anthology of exemplary articles. A unique opportunity presents itself. Reward and recognition for scholarly work on teaching and learning has started to occur, but what has only begun must be cultivated and nurtured. We need to identify and explore specific features that will establish the credibility of this practitioner scholarship. Looking back may lead to answers. Long-absent respect for college teaching as a profession can be attributed in part to the lack of a viable literature associated with its practice. During this time of opportunity we need to push the door open wider and explore what kind of literature practitioners need in order to develop their instructional skills and knowledge and what features could establish its viability as the literature of the college teaching profession. Looking back may lead to answers.

Equally as important as the reasons that justify a review of previously published scholarly work on teaching and learning is the matter of approach—how the work should be viewed. To learn all that it has to teach, the work needs to be approached with an open mind, and it needs to be looked at broadly—in new places and in new ways. With a justification and approach now in hand, we stand ready to survey the territory we are about to explore.

2

What to Look At

This chapter aims to introduce the pedagogical literature and to clarify precisely what it is that we are looking at. Like good introductions to new people, this one seeks to provide enough background information and intriguing details so as to pique interest in learning more. To that end, for previously published work on teaching and learning the chapter considers the following issues:

- Definition: What are we looking at?

- Location: Where is it to be found?

- Features: What defines and characterizes it?

- Content: What topics does it cover?

- History: What of its past?

- Recent changes: What of its future?

Definition: What Is It?

Chapter One introduced a simple definition for pedagogical scholarship: published work on teaching and learning authored by college faculty in fields other than education. But even straightforward definitions are not necessarily uncomplicated.

Pedagogical scholarship is related to the scholarship of teaching, and definitions for that are neither simple nor straightforward. As already noted, because the scholarship of teaching was not clearly defined, all sorts of questions and ambiguities emerged as a variety of initiatives got under way. Does the scholarship of teaching involve practice or publication, or both? Is it a new form of scholarship or an adaptation of something done before? For a more complete list of questions, see Cunsolo, Elrick, and Middleton (1996). For summaries of the various definitions, see Kreber and Cranton (2000), Kreber (2001b), Braxton, Luckey, and Helland (2002), and Healey (2003). Unfortunately, this definitional dilemma continues to keep us focused on hairsplitting details. Now there is debate about whether we can handle multiple definitions (Healey, 2003) or need to settle on one (Braxton, Luckey, and Helland, 2002). Using different terminology and defining it clearly allows us to sidestep this quagmire and establish clear parameters for this review, but it does not settle the definitional issues of scholarship of teaching or say how scholarly work on teaching and learning should be defined in the future.

In addition, it is necessary to differentiate the literature under review here from that generated by educational professionals, those faculty in various disciplines, but mostly education, educational psychology, and higher education, whose research focuses on various aspects of postsecondary teaching and learning. These fields have their own research journals, specialized language, professional associations, and all the accoutrements of any academic discipline. Some of us believe strongly that the disconnect between educational research and classroom practice impoverishes teachers and diminishes learning. This research knowledge should be part of what informs classroom practice.

For the most part, when faculty turn to pedagogical literature they do not look at educational research, even those specialty subfields that now marry education to the disciplines, such as math education or chemistry education. There are a variety of reasons (most of them not very good) that explain this neglect. I have written about those reasons elsewhere (Weimer, 2001), and to digress further into this related but different problem takes us away from an exploration of pedagogical scholarship completed by faculty in disciplines other than education.

Before leaving the topic, however, I do want to suggest that at this early juncture it is not appropriate to assume that practitioner pedagogical scholarship is more desirable than educational research, or that educational research is better than practitioner pedagogical scholarship. The two literatures are different, distinct, and at this point separate in their existence. Because both study teaching and learning phenomena, the two are inherently related, but that relationship has never been described. The educational research knowledge base for teaching and learning has never been integrated with or studied in relation to the applied knowledge base as it exists in the practitioner literature we are about to analyze. This lack of relationship and its many implications will be revisited at various points in the chapters ahead.

Location: Where Is It?

Unlike scholarship in a discipline that finds outlet in a discrete number of journals associated with the field, pedagogical scholarship has been published in many different places, although most of it does reside in the discipline-based pedagogical periodicals listed in Appendix A. Actually, Appendix A contains two lists. The first identifies pedagogical periodicals (mostly journals, but some magazines) written exclusively for a higher education audience. The second list identifies discipline-based pedagogical periodicals written for educators at a variety of levels—not just college. Originally I planned to include on the second list only those journals where at least 50 percent of the content was written for college-level educators. But audience is not always specified, and some articles address issues relevant to all educators. So I opted to list all the pedagogical periodicals with content for college teachers. In a few of the periodicals, fewer than 10 percent of the articles contain content exclusively relevant to college teachers. In others, that percentage would be closer to 90. The amount ranges widely and is difficult to determine precisely.

A review of the periodicals listed in Appendix A reveals that most, but not all, major disciplines have pedagogical periodicals. Some have more than one. Some small and highly specialized fields also contribute a periodical to this family of publications. Several other lists of these pedagogical outlets have been assembled, a number now appearing on institution-based teaching centers or scholarship-of-teaching Web sites. On most I found more than a fair share of errors—partly due to the evolution of publications (name changes, mergers, and new additions). But some of the discrepancies between lists are the result of not having clear or agreed-upon criteria to use in determining if a journal is a pedagogical periodical. I was less critical of others when I started compiling my own list.

Other pedagogical periodicals exist as well; they appear in Appendix B, which contains three lists. The first identifies generic pedagogical periodicals. Articles are written for and by faculty in multiple fields or, in a few cases, sets of related fields, as in the *Journal of College Science Teaching*, for example. These are cross-disciplinary publications. The second lists periodicals written about higher education generally in which articles on teaching and learning appear regularly. Finally, there is a list of theme-based or topical pedagogical periodicals written by and for postsecondary educators.

What periodicals are *not* listed in Appendixes A and B? The research journals of education and its related fields—excluded by virtue of how pedagogical scholarship is being defined for the purposes of this review. Also not listed are some non-pedagogical, discipline-based periodicals that regularly or occasionally include articles on teaching and learning. I did not include this pedagogical scholarship in this analysis because it is difficult and time consuming for a disciplinary outsider to locate and because I opted in this first analysis to stay where the bulk of the literature exists. Also not listed are a group of quasi-journals, mostly published by institutions for faculty at that institution and mostly electronic in format. Some of these are available to anyone online and contain articles written by faculty not from that institution, but they are not being purposefully marketed or disseminated to a national audience and do not constitute a significant portion of the previously published scholarship. Finally, I chose not to list journals that only include pedagogical content knowledge. Arguably, they are pedagogical periodicals, but in a book on pedagogical scholarship, generally little can be learned from scholarship that can only be understood if the disciplinary content is known. More details on the rationale behind this decision follow shortly in the section on these journals' content.

Some bounding of this territory is also necessary because beyond the domain of periodical literature exists still more published work on postsecondary teaching and learning. It appears in books—some discipline-based, others written for anyone who teaches college students, some directed toward or about a specific audience, such as new faculty or adult learners, and many covering specific aspects of teaching or learning, such as assessing learning, using active learning, or developing critical-thinking skills. Still more pedagogical literature may be found in other published forms, such as newsletters and magazines; some of these are distributed nationally while others are local, in-house publications. Finally, work on teaching and learning now exists in a variety of online sources: electronic journals, resource collections provided by publishers or professional associations, and Web sites sponsored by professional organizations or the journals themselves, for example.

Most of the review and analysis that follows focuses on the pedagogical scholarship that appears in Appendixes A and B, with special attention paid to discipline-based pedagogical periodicals. In addition to most of the literature being located in those sources, some other pragmatic purposes are served by scrutinizing this scholarship the most intensely. If more faculty do start reading material on teaching and learning, evidence suggests that this will be the place most will turn first. If more faculty start doing this kind of scholarship, this will likely be their first venue of publication. As pedagogical scholarship starts to count toward promotion and tenure decisions more regularly, this will be the family of publications first assessed in terms of quality issues.

Previously published pedagogical scholarship has appeared in many published venues and for many years. It is a large and diverse literature. To expedite the review process, I have chosen to focus primarily on the practitioner scholarship that appears in a family of pedagogical periodicals—mostly those associated with the disciplines but some cross-disciplinary and topical publications as well.

Features: What Defines It?

It almost doesn't matter what collection of features are selected for review; the enormous diversity within this family of publications evidences itself immediately. Exceptions regularly outnumber rules.

Editorial Policies and Practices

Editors of these journals are usually faculty who mostly serve on a rotating basis, although some rotate through the position very slowly. Almost all the journals have editorial boards, and college faculty dominate them. This is true even of those journals where much of the content addresses basic educators. Sometimes these board members function as reviewers; in other cases they establish publication policies, with article reviewers a separate group.

The majority of these pedagogical periodicals select articles via some sort of blind review process, with reviewers most often being faculty from the field where the periodical is based. Review processes mirror those used for discipline-based research journals. For the most part, they are substantive. *Issues in Accounting Education*, for example, assigns each manuscript an associate editor who

oversees the review process. Each manuscript is sent to two reviewers, who return it with recommendations to the associate editor, who
then makes a recommendation to the editor, who makes the decision.
Authors receive reviewer feedback and revise-and-resubmit papers
are returned to the same associate editor and reviewers. Rejection
rates for this family of periodicals also vary; most are above 50 percent, and the number with rates above 80 percent continues to grow.

Some of these journals are published monthly or bi-monthly,
some four times a year, some twice a year, and a few only once a
year. Issue size varies across an equally wide continuum.

Most of these publications look like journals, although a few
called journals are formatted more like magazines, such as the *Journal of College Science Teaching*. More noteworthy are the ways these
periodicals reflect the protocols and conventions of the discipline.
For example, articles in *Journalism and Mass Communication Educator*
appear in newspaper-column form, with short paragraphs and tight,
clean journalistic prose, while articles in *Microbiology Education* all
begin with abstracts and follow a prescribed research article format.

Organizational Arrangements

Frequently, the discipline-based journals (and sometimes the cross-
disciplinary ones as well) have some sort of relationship with a professional association or organization, although the nature of these
relationships varies significantly. In some cases the association financially supports the journal; sometimes the subscription price is covered by membership dues. Some of the journals are published by the
association; others are marketed by commercial publishers. If this link
with a professional organization exists, the journals communicate the
news and business of the association, including details about and
from national meetings. The majority of these periodicals include
advertisements that offer a wide range of items—employment opportunities, lab equipment, textbooks, related publications, and other
instructional support materials.

Kinds of Articles

Most of these pedagogical periodicals include a variety of different sections within the journal, each featuring different types of articles. See the box at the end of this chapter for examples that illustrate the range of options. Many creative alternatives and combinations can be found. A sampling is highlighted in Chapter Six, where promising possibilities contained in the journals are reviewed.

A number of the journals have regular monthly columns usually authored or edited by the same person. Content of these column features varies dramatically—it might be directed toward a particular audience, such as advice for new teachers, or it might focus on content like "The physics trick of the month," or it might address political issues relative to pedagogy and the discipline.

The way these journals organize their content does not reflect the main approaches used by authors to analyze pedagogical problems and issues. Many journals lead with a section of "main" or "featured" articles. Generally, that means that the articles are longer and more substantive than what appears in the rest of the journal. That section may contain articles that use several of the approaches I introduce in Chapter Three and analyze in Chapters Four and Five. Nonetheless, where a journal locates a certain kind of article often contains hints as to the perceived value and importance of that particular kind of scholarship. It is here one finds evidence of the increasing value placed on pedagogical research work.

Audience

One common and unique feature these discipline-based periodicals share involves the matter of audience. They are written for teachers at various levels, not just college educators. The lists in Appendix A illustrate the proportion of those written exclusively for college faculty versus those written to a broader audience of educators. In the beginning, this extended audience only included basic educators, though it expanded to high school and junior high teachers in the case of the *Journal of Chemical Education* and to teachers from kindergarten through college in the case of the *Physics Teacher*. Now, with some of the new publications, such as *Academy of Management Learning and Education*, the audience is broadened to include others who teach, such as those in training, development, and corporate education.

In the articles themselves, the subject of audience is not always addressed. Neither the article's title nor opening paragraph indicates whether it's for high school teachers or college faculty. In fact, in carefully reviewing all these journals as preparation for writing this book, I was surprised to discover that some of my favorite journals, such as *Teaching of Psychology*, were intended for these larger audiences. I was unable to determine the proportion of college faculty readers versus basic educators for any of the journals, with one exception. In a survey of its readers, the *Journal of College Science Teaching* found that 56 percent were faculty compared with 15 percent who were secondary school teachers (Druger, 2003).

Given the goals of making pedagogical scholarship credible and establishing a viable literature associated with college teaching, is it a problem when a periodical addresses the needs of all educators? One could argue yes: college faculty are a persnickety, credential-conscious bunch who tend to think that college teaching is unique. The issues faced in the college classroom are not the same as those high school teachers confront. The veracity of these assertions could be debated but the fact remains that, functionally, college faculty and basic educators occupy different worlds unless some special program unites their efforts. So how likely are faculty to turn to a publication not written exclusively for them? Could this be another way teaching is devalued—the concerns of college teachers get commingled with those of other kinds of educators? Is scholarship that appears in this kind of publication likely to be deemed less credible? As we look to a different future, is this a feature that should continue?

On the other hand, one could argue no—it does not matter whether the intended audience is college faculty or all educators. If the audience of a particular article is not specified, how likely are faculty to even notice its relevance to other educational settings? Given their dominating presence on editorial staffs, boards, and as reviewers, college faculty control the content of these publications anyway. Besides, there is merit in quietly demonstrating that educators everywhere do share many concerns and issues.

As far as I could discover, no one has systematically assessed the impact of this feature of the pedagogical literature. Given its relevance to the issues of credibility and viability, it certainly should be considered. In fact, a review and assessment of the various editorial policies and practices, organizational arrangements, kinds of articles, and other features of these publications has never been undertaken and much could be learned from that as well. I'm not advocating for this kind of assessment and collaboration because all pedagogical periodicals need to be the same. The diversity of this literature is a strength; it could also be a source of learning.

Content: What Topics Are Covered?

As for content, every imaginable aspect of teaching and learning has been covered by the articles in these periodicals. To list them all would take the rest of this book. In addition to coverage of all the expected topics, there is some content that surprises. *The Journal of Chemical Education* showed that some issues in education don't change, with a piece that highlighted still-relevant content from its first issue published in 1924 (Lagowski, 1998). The prize for consistently covering the most unusual topics probably goes to *Teaching of Psychology*. To illustrate: on the one-hundredth anniversary of the publication of the first book on teaching psychology, the journal featured a special section with four retrospective analyses of the book (Brewer, 2003; Wight, 2003; McKeachie, 2003; and Korn, 2003). Another issue (Perlman, Marxen, McFadden and McCann, 1996) contains an article that analyzes candidates' letters of application for evidence of "teaching awareness"; this insightful study documents how extensively candidates focus on their research prowess. Other unexpected topics covered by other journals include a *Journal of Management Education* analysis (Burke, 2004) of high-maintenance students, those who sap instructors' energy with their seemingly unending complaints and anxieties, and the identification and assessment by Beatty (2004) in the *Academy of Management Learning and Education* of the counterproductive ways grades function like money.

Some journals, often in editorials, tackle the political issues associated with the lack of reward and recognition for teaching generally and for pedagogical scholarship specifically. For some samples, see Matthews (2002) in the *Journal of Geography in Higher Education*; Lucal and others (2003) in *Teaching Sociology*; and Druger (2001) in the *Journal of Natural Resources and Life Sciences Education*.

A number of the journals regularly or intermittently publish issues on special topics, in which a particular aspect of education is explored at length. For example, the August 2004 issue of the *Journal of Marketing Education* is devoted to articles on teaching the principles of marketing, the October 2004 issue of the *Journal of Management Education* focuses on problem-based learning, and the Spring 2004 issue of *College Teaching* includes a collection of articles on grading issues, specifically grade inflation and self-grading. In some cases, the topic is announced in an earlier issue and submissions solicited; in other cases, the articles are invited. Sometimes the entire issue is devoted to one topic; other times a group of articles exploring aspects of a topic is featured in the journal.

As with the editorial features of the journals, however, no systematic content analysis of the literature as a whole has been undertaken, and few such analyses have been done for individual periodicals. Daniel (1992), writing about the content in *Teaching of Psychology*, points out that some have tried to analyze it but found the task impossible, given the range of topics covered. Without good content analysis work, we cannot say if group work (or any other instructional method) is written about more often than classroom assessment (or any other evaluative method). Some assessments of individual discipline-based journals have been published (see Daniel, 1992; Wankat, 1999; Wankat, 2004; Whitin and Sheppard, 2004; Baker, 1985; and Chin, 2002 for examples), but the analysis of these journals' content coverage occurs inconsistently and not in any way that makes the results comparable. However, analyses by Wankat (1999, 2004) and by Whitin and Sheppard (2004) of the content in the *Journal of Engineering Education* model how these analyses can be conducted as well as demonstrate how much can be learned by looking at a journal's content systematically.

I would say, based on my regular reading of these journals, that the number of times a topic gets written about reflects current trends and interests in higher education. When I first started reading these journals, there was only an occasional article on group work. Now the topic is covered regularly. Few articles directly dealing with learning appeared in these journals prior to the mid-1990s.

The journals also vary in the extent to which the material in them covers discipline-specific content knowledge versus general teaching and learning issues—what I would call pedagogy. A few are entirely embedded in the content of the discipline, meaning the articles address content-related issues—what content to include (in a particular course, for example) or how to teach that content, not via what method, but what explanations, examples, or demonstrations best convey that material. These are the journals I have opted not to list in Appendix A. In some fields, that content focus is on what problems or lab exercises students should complete to learn a concept or principle. Other journals balance the focus on content with articles that address the mechanics of teaching—that is, what methods, techniques, and strategies best promote learning. And some journals include content that covers all aspects of teaching and learning—content, methods, assessment, classroom management, teacher preparation, and faculty development, as well as political issues, such as reward and recognition for teaching.

Obviously, those journals heavily embedded in content topics are less useful to readers outside the discipline, but that is not their intended audience. However, they do raise a couple of interesting questions. Should a journal be considered a pedagogical periodical if it never or only rarely addresses issues other than content? Less philosophical and more pragmatic is the question of balance: Is there a desired proportion between content coverage and pedagogical issues that a journal should aspire to reach? Are there liabilities when a journal exclusively covers one and not the other? More bluntly, does the focus on content at the expense of pedagogy diminish the importance of teaching?

To sum, then, it is safe to say that coverage of instructional topics is broad. Beyond that it is difficult to be more specific. Across the literature we cannot say how often a topic is covered or whether the amount of coverage is increasing or decreasing, despite the fact that knowing this would provide a valuable gauge of how important certain topics are to practitioners. How often a particular finding, experience, or outcome is reported would help establish its significance. From information like this we could begin to formulate an applied knowledge base for teaching and learning. The journals also vary in the degree to which they address content knowledge and pedagogical issues, but beyond that we can say little as to the impact or desirability of these respective foci. Even a cursory content analysis like this reveals how little we know and have thought about the nature of practitioner pedagogical knowledge.

History: What of Its Past?

Given our aim of reviewing and analyzing the scholarship itself, a comprehensive, definitive history of pedagogical periodicals is not in order. Unfortunately, there are no general references to which an interested reader might be referred. Some fairly complete histories of individual journals have been published and this brief introduction draws on those sources. But the point made about content bears repeating: A more complete historical analysis would be supportive of our efforts to develop pedagogical scholarship.

If the *Journal of Chemical Education* is not the oldest pedagogical periodical, it is certainly one of the oldest, having now been published continuously since 1924. *College Teaching* is one of the oldest cross-disciplinary pedagogical periodicals, beginning publication in the early 1950s. Many more of these journals started publication in the 1970s.

Many began very informally. Gallos (1994), then its editor, describes the birth and growth of the *Journal of Management Education*: "From its informal beginning in 1975 as a hand-typed newsletter about OB [organizational behavior] teaching to colleagues at fifteen institutions, *JME* has matured into a respected academic journal, one of Sage Publication's fastest growing professional periodicals, and a leading voice in the field of innovative management education" (p. 135). Similarly, Daniel (1992), the first officially appointed editor of the journal *Teaching of Psychology*, reports that that journal was preceded by fifty-nine issues of a newsletter that was launched in 1950. The first issue of the journal, forty-eight pages, appeared in October 1974.

Many also began publication with no formal publisher and with editors who literally did everything from opening the mail to renewing subscriptions and sending out the issue. Often these editors were individuals who first proposed the idea of the journal and then labored to make it happen, generally without reward, recognition, or payment. Daniel (1992) writes with some humor about issues of *Teaching of Psychology* being delayed at the post office during the 1970s because of bomb threats, elevators overloaded with issues ready for mailing getting stuck between floors, and ink color changing after printing. Jenkins (1997) poignantly describes being denied promotion repeatedly, despite acknowledgments of his work as founding editor of the *Journal of Geography in Higher Education*.

What history we have of pedagogical scholarship is rich with detail that attests to a long-standing and deep-seated commitment to advancing knowledge about teaching and learning. There are faculty in most fields who laid the foundations for scholarly work on teaching and learning under difficult circumstances. We owe them much. Our work today does widen the road, but these early pedagogical scholars hacked out that first path when the forest was much denser.

Recent Changes: What of the Future?

Practitioner pedagogical literature is changing; most of those changes do positively implicate its quality. For starters, new journals are being launched; for example, the *Academy of Management Learning and Education* was launched in 2002, following *Cell Biology Education*, launched in 2001. Next, a significant number of the already existing journals now publish more often and have increased their issue size. For example, the *Journal of Management Education* went from four to six issues annually in 1998, and Wankat, Felder, Smith, and Oreovicz (2002) report that "the *Journal of Engineering Education* increased 26 percent, from 405 pages in 1995 to 509 pages in 2000" (p. 225), having jumped from forty-seven pages in 1996 to ninety-six in 2001 (Whitin and Sheppard, 2004). Correspondingly, rejection rates have gone up in many of the publications. Brewer, long-time editor of the *Teaching of Psychology,* reports in an interview that the rejection rate of that periodical climbed to 85 percent during his editorship (Saville, 2001). If the number of periodicals is on the rise, along with their size, and at the same time rejection rates are also increasing, these changes should affect the quality of the literature in synergistic ways.

In addition, there is almost universal recognition among all who care about this literature that standards and rigor are key issues, especially in light of the attention now being focused on this scholarly work by the scholarship-of-teaching movement. Journal editors write about standards. Prados, in a series of three editorials (1996, 1999, and 2001) in the *Journal of Engineering Education,* is adamant and specific: "The essential question that should be asked by anyone who considers submitting a manuscript to the *Journal of Engineering Education* is, 'If this were a technical paper, would I be comfortable submitting it to a leading publication in my engineering specialty?' If the answer is 'yes,' please send us the paper right away! If the answer is 'no,' think what revisions might enable the manuscript to meet high standards of scholarship" (2001, p. 169).

Those who have looked at scholarship in their disciplines also write about standards. Chin (2002) writes in his analysis of *Teaching Sociology*, "I feel that setting the highest possible standard insulates the scholarship of teaching and learning from the criticism that it is evaluated according to more lenient standards than basic research" (p. 55).

Admittedly, calling for high standards and implementing those standards are separate steps, but higher-quality standards are rarely implemented without first calling for them. Moreover, some creative attempts to illustrate and promote quality pedagogical scholarship have already occurred. For example, Frost and Fukami (1997) edited a research forum in the *Academy of Management Journal*, one of the leading research journals in this field, that included articles chosen to demonstrate how scholarly work on teaching and learning could be a serious academic endeavor and could match the quality of research regularly published in this respected publication.

Matthews (2002), editor of the *Journal of Geography in Higher Education (JGHE)*, sought to establish the status of the journal using two different statistical measures. First, he used something called the *impact factor*. "This is a measure of the frequency with which the 'average article' in a journal has been cited in a particular year. The Impact Factor is calculated by dividing the number of current citations to articles published in the two previous years by the total number of articles published in the two previous years" (pp. 5–6). The article provides more detail on sources used to compile the factor. *JGHE*'s Impact Factor increased each year between 1996 and 2000, reaching a score of 1.148 in 2000. Scores above 1 are "especially revered," according to Matthews (p. 6). Matthews also used a calculation called the *cited half-life* to ascertain the journal's standing among other journals in the field of geography. A combination of these two measures position *JGHE* eleventh out of twenty-one geography journals, a number that includes the discipline's research journals.

The *Journal of Geography in Higher Education* has been consistently concerned with quality issues—more so than any of the other journals reviewed. Articles by Jenkins (1997), Brown, Bucklow, and Clark (2002), Bullard (2002), Burkill (2002), and Matthews (2002) show the kind of role a journal can take in supporting and advancing teaching and learning causes within a discipline and beyond.

In yet another attempt to promote quality, several journals now have awards recognizing outstanding published work. In 2001, as Bullard (2002) reports in an editorial, the *Journal of Geography in Higher Education* "launched a biennial award for the best academic paper promoting excellence in teaching and learning in geography or closely allied subjects at the higher education level" (p. 209). Bullard elaborates on the details of the award first won by Livingstone and Lynch (2002a). Ironically, though, in a short reflection piece about their winning paper, Livingstone and Lynch (2002b) report that the paper was not considered in their professional review. The *Journal of Engineering Education* selects one paper per year to receive the William Elgin Wickenden Award, and an editorial (Lewicki, 2004) in *Academy of Management Learning and Education* announces recipients of a newly created Best Paper Award. Selection of outstanding papers operationally defines what a journal considers excellent pedagogical scholarship. It is part of the process of establishing credibility for scholarly work on teaching and learning.

In terms of definition, location, defining features, content, history, and recent changes, we begin this review and analysis recognizing that pedagogical scholarship has a past, although few aspects of it have been studied systematically. This book sets our sights on a review and analysis of the scholarship itself, but this broad overview of the pedagogical literature domain should provide background helpful in more fully understanding the closer and more detailed analysis that's to come. However, it does leave for other times and persons the important and necessary work of systematically analyzing its features, content, and history.

Sections from Selected Pedagogical Periodicals

The Academy of Management Learning and Education

> *Research and Reviews:* Quantitative and qualitative empirical papers, theoretical discourses and models, and general or specific appraisals and descriptions of effective approaches to individual learning and management education

> *Exemplary Contributions:* Invited from prominent scholars and practitioners

> *Essays, Dialogues, and Interviews:* Commentary, critique, discussion, and debate on current and future trends in teaching, learning, and management education

> *Books and Resource Reviews*

Journal of Nursing Education

> *Major Articles:* Reports of studies on nursing education, integrative reviews of the literature, philosophical analyses or analyses of political, social, economic, professional, pedagogical, and technological trends and issues influencing nursing education

> *Briefs (Research Briefs, Educational Innovations, Faculty Forum):* Small-scale studies, educational innovations, and editorial opinion, commentary, and political analyses; de-

scriptions of innovative approaches to issues of relevance, such as tenure, academic freedom, and faculty evaluation

Syllabus Selection: Innovative Learning Activities—Two-page descriptions of strategies, methods, or case examples used to help students learn nursing concepts and content

Teaching of Psychology

Topical Articles: Pieces from twenty-five hundred to seven thousand words on a range of content

Methods and Techniques: Papers of one thousand to two thousand words describing demonstrations, laboratory projects, and other learning-teaching devices or instrumentation

Faculty Forum: Commentaries, criticisms, or opinions of fewer than twelve hundred words on the full range of journal content

Computers in Teaching: Articles examining the integration of computer technology and the teaching of psychology

News from ToP and the Society for the Teaching of Psychology

Journal of Chemical Education

Chemical Education Today: News, commentary, reviews of books and other media, letters to the editor

Chemistry for Everyone: Applications, history, interdisciplinary activities, and public understanding

In the Classroom: Teaching tips, methods, demonstrations, content, and principles

In the Laboratory: Experiments and safety

Information, Textbooks, Media, other Resources: Textbook forum, technology and multimedia applications, and information technology

Research: Science and Education—Papers that interpret a specific aspect of chemistry for teachers; science education research

Journal of Geography

Articles on Research and Instruction: Manuscripts that make new and important contributions to geography instruction or geographic education research

Teacher's Notebook: Short articles outlining innovative teaching strategies for the geography classroom in grades one to twelve

Comments: Essays addressing current issues in geographic education

Symposium: A group of commentaries by different authors

Reviews: Book and multimedia reviews

Letters: Responding to articles, comments, reviews, or editorials

3

Scholarly Work on Teaching and Learning: An Overview

Having considered *why* we should look at previously published work on teaching learning, *how* we should view it, and *what* precisely it is that we are looking at, now we can turn our attention to the scholarship itself. Chapters Four, Five, and Six offer an up-close and much more detailed view of it. However, because practitioner pedagogical scholarship has never been looked at as a collected body of work, the goal for this chapter will be to describe its overall structure. To help do that, I introduce a classification scheme that identifies the major approaches used by practitioners to analyze teaching and learning in this literature. The chapter concludes with an assessment of what this categorization scheme can and cannot be used to accomplish.

Classifying the Approaches

Let me begin with the basis for this particular categorization of the literature: it emerged out of my reading and analysis. I read a lot of pedagogical literature and have done so for many years. These are the approaches I see used most often in the literature. Others may look and see a different landscape. In fact Nelson (2003) has proposed another set of categories that can productively be compared with these. To advance our understanding of scholarly work on teaching and learning, we need many thoughtful perspectives on its structure.

As I see it, published practitioner pedagogical work can be separated into two major categories: wisdom-of-practice scholarship and research scholarship. Each of these large categories contains a number of different approaches, which are covered individually in Chapters Four and Five. A brief overview of each now will set the stage for the detailed analysis that comes in the next two chapters. Chapter Six looks at alternatives, promising approaches, and formats that also appear in the pedagogical literature but are not as commonly used as these major approaches.

Wisdom-of-Practice Scholarship

This category contains the experience-based pedagogical scholarship of practitioners. Faculty learn about teaching as they teach. Sometimes that learning happens by trial and error without much conscious awareness. In other cases, the learning is intentional and systematic. I believe the "wisdom" label is justified because there is valuable knowledge embedded in practice. Often these understandings are intuitive, but with systematic review and reflective analysis they can be made explicit and beneficially shared with others. The experience base makes this work personal, practical, and usually very applied. I would characterize it as the how-to literature of teaching. Four different approaches dominate this major category.

Personal Accounts of Change

As the name implies, when using this method of analysis, faculty report on experiences associated with implementing an instructional policy, practice, technique, method, or approach. Almost always, the literature reports on the implementation of something different, a change. The extent of change reported varies. It may be a single technique (such as student-generated exam questions), a collection of strategies (such as cooperative learning), or a whole approach to teaching (such as critical pedagogy). Furthermore, these changes derive from different sources. They may be original with the author or they may be adaptations, applications, or replications of something developed or used by others.

Recommended-Practices Reports

This is advice-giving literature. It recommends what should be done about a single, several, or many aspects of instruction. This advice-giving feature is differentiated in two important ways: what the advice is based on, and the qualifications of the person offering it. The advice contained in this literature rests on experience (sometimes individual, sometimes collective), research evidence (sometimes a single study, more often a collection of them), or some combination of the two. The qualifications of those offering the advice also range from novice to expert.

Recommended-Content Reports

Work in this area differs from the previous one only in focus—what the advice is being given about. In these analyses authors propose ways of teaching particular aspects of content; not how they should be taught pedagogically, but what devices should be used to explain, illustrate, demonstrate, and otherwise support the acquisition of course content. They also make recommendations as to content that should be included in a course as well as content and skills that should be appropriate parts of particular degree programs. Much of this work is pedagogical scholarship embedded in the discipline, what Shulman (1987) first identified as pedagogical content knowledge. This work is meaningful only if the content is familiar. Exercises that help students understand the concept of sidereal time and distance aren't meaningful unless you teach astronomy, but they can help a lot if you do.

Personal Narratives

More diversity exists with this approach, where the method of analysis is generally reflective and critical. It is distinct from the first three approaches in that it does not generally focus on specific aspects of instruction that have been changed and it does not usually offer advice. In this work authors look inward, relying on their own ideas, insights, and judgments. The perspective is personal and often includes an emotional dimension. Examples of work in the personal narrative category include accounts of personal growth that track development or the evolution of pedagogical thought, individual statements of teaching philosophy, and work that expresses a particular point of view (faculty should not have to teach college students basic skills), argues for one side of an issue (students are not customers), takes a position (grading on a curve is wrong), or advocates for a change in more broadly based policy issues (more outcomes assessment would improve academic quality).

Research Scholarship

Research inquiries of various sorts have been conducted by practitioners. They differ from traditional educational research in some ways, although many of the methods are borrowed. For example, the empirical questions addressed are mostly pragmatic, applied, and often relate directly to the instructional practice of the person asking the question. Because personal interest motivates the questions, analysis of them tends to be atheoretical. Practitioner research does not generally build on previous or related work in systematic ways. It is more often an isolated inquiry than part of an organized research program.

Because modes of inquiry for practitioner pedagogical scholarship have never been specified, practitioners who use research approaches to study teaching and learning opt for those methods they know—the research paradigms of their discipline—or they import and sometimes adapt traditional social science modes of inquiry.

This use of established research protocols means that pedagogical research work falls into categories to which familiar names can be attached.

Quantitative Investigations

Scholarly work using this approach relies on experimental designs that involve treatment and control groups, with some manipulation of variables across or between them. This is the kind of analysis traditionally equated with educational and social science research. Early pedagogical literature contains almost no quantitative analyses, but now the approach is more common and there is a push to move pedagogical scholarship more in this direction.

Qualitative Studies

Here the work borrows methods developed and used in disciplinary work, again, mostly in the social sciences but also the humanities. Qualitative methodologies are multiple and diverse, but they share a commitment to study phenomena in naturalistic settings and to analyze results interpretively. Within previously published pedagogical literature, this is the newest and smallest category, which reflects the recent advent of its use and reluctant acceptance given these methods by the disciplines.

Descriptive Research

Work using this approach does as the name implies. It describes, most commonly by collecting and then analyzing survey data. Of the three kinds of research scholarship in previously published work on teaching and learning, this is the largest and most well-developed kind of practitioner pedagogical research. The approach has been used to study many aspects of college teaching and learning, such as the prevalence of certain practices, student attitudes and perceptions on a range of topics, or faculty beliefs and opinions about students. Collected results are analyzed using either quantitative or qualitative methods and sometimes a combination of the two.

Up to this point, when it has been considered at all, all the kinds of pedagogical scholarship have tended to be lumped together. Even experience- and research-based works have not been looked at separately. I'm hoping that dividing the work into these two domains and then establishing subcategories within each will showcase the diversity that exists within this body of work at the same time that it allows us to consider a range of options. Which of these kinds of pedagogical scholarship is the most credible? Which is most consistently done well? Which is most likely to be read by faculty? Which best supplies the information needed to improve instructional practice and student learning?

Areas of Analysis

In many respects, Chapters Four and Five are the heart of this book—the centerfold that showcases and analyzes scholarly work on teaching and learning previously published. The experience- and research-based approaches described in each chapter, respectively, are analyzed using the same five areas: description, critical assessment, exemplars, standards, and contribution.

The analysis begins with a detailed description that further defines and establishes the basic characteristics of each approach. That is followed by a critical assessment of quality issues—those identified by others and my own. Because this literature has not been valued and there are legitimate questions as to its merits, it makes sense to tackle the quality issues head-on: What makes literature that uses this approach troublesome? After identifying the quality concerns, I ask two follow-up questions about each: how widespread is the problem, and how serious is it (fixable flaw or inherent defect)?

For each approach there is a continuum of quality that allows the identification of exemplary work. For some approaches exemplary work is easier to find than for others. For each, an annotated bibliography within the text names *exemplars*. In the Preface, I've

made as passionate a case as is professionally appropriate for reading these examples. The analysis of each approach makes much
more sense with concrete examples in mind, to say nothing of all
that can be learned from their content. In assembling the examples
for each approach, I opted not for an exhaustive listing but for a
group of those that, first and foremost, are exemplary—I wanted
each collection to illustrate what is possible when the approach is
used well. Then I tried to include examples from a range of pedagogical periodical sources on a variety of substantive instructional
topics and that use the same approach but in different ways.

Throughout the discussion of each approach, I have included
references to other excellent examples that are not included in the
exemplar list because they don't meet the criteria just discussed or
because they combine approaches. As discussed in this chapter's
final section on caveats, these categories are being superimposed on
an eclectic collection of work, which means there is much blurring
between the two main categories as well as between the approaches
within each. None of this work was created with this typology in
mind. Examples that clearly illustrate the approach are not pre-
sumed to be "better" scholarship, but in this first attempt to organize and provide an overview of this literature, it seemed propitious
to choose exemplars that clearly illustrate these most common
approaches.

Each list of exemplars is followed by a discussion of standards
relevant when that particular approach is used. As I considered a
broad collection of articles that use the approach, I tried to identify
those characteristics that set the best work apart from the rest. In
cases where the approach borrows methods from education or other
disciplines, some of the standards for exemplary work have already
been established and can be applied to pedagogical scholarship that
uses the approach. I offer standards in the interest of starting a more
substantive and specific exchange about credible pedagogical scholarship and in the interest of demonstrating the kind of concrete
assessment criteria needed when individual work is assessed.

The analysis concludes with a contribution section that considers what we have learned from this approach to scholarship. What has each approach contributed to our understanding of teaching and learning? This analysis foreshadows subsequent exploration of the extent to which the scholarship we have relates to what is needed.

An early analysis of practitioner pedagogical literature like the one offered in this book precludes definitive answers. It barely suggests tentative ones. Even those raise yet another set of questions—the kind of queries that prompt more reflection, analysis, and critique, the kind that show how much there is about scholarly work on teaching and learning we have yet to figure out.

Benefits of Categorization

With previously published work on teaching and learning organized into these categories and approaches, what can we do with the typology? Does it allow us to accomplish some objectives that couldn't be realized without it? I think it does. Let me share five goals the typology can be used to help achieve.

Beginning broadly, a classification scheme like this enables us to better understand pedagogical scholarship. If we think about this collection of work on teaching and learning as a relatively uncharted territory, the typology functions as a map that enables us to explore more efficiently. We start developing an understanding of pedagogical scholarship by first getting a lay of the land, seeing its distinguishing features and natural borders. I also hope that early attempts to map this unexplored landscape will pique interest and encourage others to examine the territory so that we can name more places and more accurately characterize its distinguishing features.

This characterization of basic approaches can also be used as a sort of operational definition of pedagogical scholarship. This kind of definition-in-action is not theoretical or abstract—which is not a covert indictment of those definitions that are. They are just as necessary as operational ones. However, at the current time we have plenty of theoretical and hypothetical definitions of the scholarship linked to teaching but few concrete, specific ones that can be applied to individual products: Is this piece of work pedagogical scholarship?

However, this classification system does not provide the most needed definition. It's definitely concrete and specific, alright; it grows out of the literature itself. But that makes it a definition based on what is, which may not be what pedagogical scholarship should be. The value of a detailed definition of what is emerges when the impetus is to redefine or better define pedagogical scholarship. Now that new and needed definition can be constructed taking into account the adequacies and inadequacies of the old one.

Third, classifying the literature enables us to use it for comparative purposes. This early on I don't think the comparative emphasis ought to be evaluative in the summative sense—how pedagogical scholarship compares with research work in the discipline, for example. In the beginning the focus ought to be on similarities and differences within the pedagogical scholarship domain: How do these various approaches compare to and with one another? Should one or several of these types of scholarly work on teaching and learning be valued more than others? That kind of formative analysis of differences and similarities within the pedagogical scholarship domain will lead to its comparison with disciplinary research and one final, perhaps most important, question: Do the differences between pedagogical scholarship and disciplinary research justify defining pedagogical scholarship as a discrete entity?

In a bit of a different direction, the identification of different approaches enlarges the range of options open to those interested in doing pedagogical scholarship. Because the frame for scholarly work on teaching and learning is often discipline-based, would-be authors usually see only those methods and approaches used in their discipline. All of the approaches identified can be used by all disciplines to explore teaching and learning topics. Most disciplines use these various approaches, but in some disciplines, certain of the approaches are used with more sophistication than they are in other fields. So, individual authors and whole fields can use a detailed characterization of the literature to enlarge their understanding of the various approaches. With that point, we've yet again underscored the value of looking at pedagogical scholarship and literature broadly, across disciplinary boundaries.

Finally, a typology like this establishes a foundation for assessment criteria. When scholarship is evaluated, as in an annual performance appraisal or as part of the promotion and tenure process, evaluators look at individual pieces of work or a collection of them completed by one faculty member. They need specific criteria as well as detailed definitions. Recent years have seen a variety of attempts to articulate more clearly criteria for all kinds of scholarly work, including the new forms of scholarship (Diamond and Adam, 1993; Glassick, Huber and Maeroff, 1997; Shulman 2000). These establish necessary and useful general guidelines. In addition to these, those evaluating pedagogical scholarship also need specific criteria that might enable them to make distinctions between a collection of wisdom-of-practice pieces of work, for example. A first analysis like this one should not be used to accomplish this objective, or it should be used tentatively. Early on, the focus should be descriptive. Making evaluative distinctions between pieces of scholarship on teaching and learning depends on being able to define and characterize the work overall first.

Caveats

As important as I believe it is to develop a more complete and concrete understanding of previously published pedagogical scholarship, and as much as I think categorizing the literature can contribute to that goal, several caveats must be part of our thinking as we use this typology to delve more deeply into already completed work. For starters, in all likelihood this set of categories and approaches is not totally accurate. As already noted, the territory of pedagogical literature has not been extensively explored. Few other maps exist, and this one is not based on detailed satellite imagery. Clearly, it will benefit from further refinement.

Second, some overlap between the major approaches identified does exist. The major categories themselves look fairly discrete, but when one moves from the categories to specific articles, the fuzziness of these boundaries becomes clear almost immediately. For example, some research work does offer advice on applying those findings. Is that piece of work research or is it a recommended-practices report? I would answer that it depends on what the article emphasizes. If it reports a research investigation and offers advice about its findings, I'd call it research. If it offers advice and bases those recommendations on research work, I'd call it a recommended-practices or recommended-content report. In addition, often the research application recommendations are offered in terms of possibilities—what *might* be done about the results. Recommended-practices reports tend to be less tentative: they propose what *should* be done. But overlap between several of these categories does exist regardless of clear theoretical distinctions.

Next, not all published work fits into this typology. As already noted, none of the work being reviewed was created with these categories in mind. The work came first. Now, after the fact, we are trying to identify major categories and approaches that we can use to help us understand how this knowledge is structured. Even a small collection of pedagogical work will contain articles that are interesting hybrids of the two major categories, others that sort of illustrate one of the major approaches or a combination of several, and some that just plain don't fit anywhere. At this point the categories and approaches are most helpful if they are loosely defined. Think of them as representing the most common approaches taken but certainly not all the ways practitioners have opted to study teaching-learning phenomena. Indeed, some of the work that doesn't fit offers intriguing and potentially promising alternatives. Chapter Six considers specific examples.

Digressing for a moment, because we are trying to organize completed work after the fact, I don't think it's possible to create a closed classification scheme, and, more important, I would question its value. Will we understand the structure of pedagogical knowledge better if we end up quibbling about what belongs in what category? Does scholarship on teaching and learning need that degree of standardization? Not to have considered the form and structure of the work has devalued and eroded its stature. For that reason we need to categorize, characterize, and in other ways analyze it; but as we do, questions about what kind and how much structure should be part of our thinking.

Finally, there is a goal this classification system won't likely accomplish. I'll wager that it isn't likely to change many minds about the value of pedagogical scholarship. In fact, I'm sort of worried that, despite pleas and admonitions to look at this work with an open mind, this overview will underscore lingering concerns about it. Let me be specific.

The research scholarship category looks so appropriate. This is scholarship as we've been taught to define it. This is the work that we all know and love. This is pedagogical scholarship easily credible. But then there's this wisdom-of-practice, experience-based work, where people just write about what happened to them or what they think other people ought to do. Is this even a legitimate way of knowing? How can this work ever be considered "scholarly"? An open-minded perspective asks those questions as honest queries, not foregone conclusions. That perspective will enable us to consider a variety of different ways to think about experience-based work.

There is something else beyond concerns about the experience-based scholarship; it involves how these two major categories relate to each other. They couldn't be at farther ends of a continuum if they tried. Juxtaposed as major categories, they give this literature a kind of schizophrenic feel. Is scholarship in any discipline this divergent? How can these two categories ever be formed into an integrated and coherent knowledge base? The characteristics that emerge when we look at the work on teaching and learning as a collective entity do not settle the quality issue. If anything, they raise old concerns and add new questions.

To sum up, then: out of this broad view of pedagogical work does not emerge a neat and ordered arrangement of approaches, methods, forms, or protocols. Previously published work on teaching and learning looks more like a house cobbled together by many different occupants, all working without blueprints and very little money. That it stands at all is something of a wonder. But the neighborhood has changed, thanks to greater interest in teaching generally and in the scholarship of teaching specifically. Folks are moving in and calling this place their scholarly home. But what about this house of previously completed work? Is it beyond repair? A fixer-upper? Any chance this historic dwelling could be restored and transformed into a modern home? We need to venture inside and take a much closer look.

4

The Lens of Experience:
Wisdom of Practice

A significant portion of previously published pedagogical scholarship is experience-based. That is, authors look at, write about, and draw lessons from their practice. Is this a legitimate, valid way of knowing? Can generalizations be drawn from experience—do the lessons learned in one classroom apply to others? What kind of knowledge base can be constructed from it? Is this work "scholarly"? Will it advance the profession?

Most people want to start with the validity question, and prevailing views of legitimate knowledge domains and forms of scholarship don't allow many to answer it affirmatively. Most of us know something about the origin of these prevailing views—how American universities started modeling themselves after those in Germany, and how the model has come to solidify around the discovery of new knowledge by empirical means. For decades now this dominant epistemology has guided research work at colleges and universities. Few would argue with the model's success: it has made American universities the envy of the world and advanced our knowledge and understanding across a wide family of disciplines.

However, recent years have brought a growing recognition that there are other ways of knowing—different but still legitimate knowledge forms. Among any number of scholars who have pushed for these broader conceptions of knowledge, Schön (1995) has articulately written about one kind: the knowledge that is experience-based and resides in professional practices like teaching. It is what he calls "knowledge in action" and of it he writes, "Often we cannot say what we know. When we try to describe it, we find ourselves at a loss or we produce descriptions that are obviously inappropriate. Our knowing is ordinarily tacit, implicit in our patterns of action and in our feel for the stuff with which we are dealing" (p. 29).

I first encountered tacit teaching knowledge early in my faculty development career. I convened a panel of outstanding teachers, all of whom had won teaching awards. I had been in their classrooms and knew firsthand that what they did there was exemplary. In front of a large group of their colleagues, I began to question them as to what made their teaching excellent. The first fellow said his ability to teach was a "gift" from God. Another said she just "did what came naturally" and didn't think that was exemplary. A third attributed his success to content: "Geology is the most exciting subject in the world. If I had to teach something like math or English, I would be a very boring teacher." After recovering from the embarrassment of offering a workshop where experts had this level of insight, I realized that the truth of the matter was simply this: these teachers did not know or could not articulate what made their instruction outstanding.

Extrapolating experience-based knowledge from practice involves reflection and analysis that makes explicit what is understood implicitly and seemingly accomplished naturally. The level of critical analysis required to articulate tacit understanding generates important insights for the person involved. It results in increased awareness and makes instructional practice much more amenable to control and direction. But does this knowledge transcend the individual and the context in which it was generated? Is it relevant and meaningful to others? Is it valid? Is knowledge that reports these individual experiences and insights "scholarly"? What kind of knowledge base can be constructed from it?

Along with Schön (1995) and others, I believe in the legitimacy and relevance of experience-based knowledge. Schön writes, "We should think about practice as a setting not only for the application of knowledge but for its generation. We should ask not only how practitioners can better apply the results of academic research, but what kinds of knowing are already embedded in competent practice" (p. 29). I think we justifiably use the "wisdom of practice" moniker to reflect the propriety and value of this kind work. But issues of legitimacy are best resolved concretely, by looking at and analyzing examples and by addressing questions like those at the end of the previous paragraph.

As introduced in Chapter Three, there are four main approaches in previously published analyses that report experiences: personal accounts of change, in which faculty report experiences associated with instructional change; recommended-practices reports, in which faculty offer advice or make suggestions about some or several aspects of practice or content; recommended-content reports, which are exactly the same as recommended-practices reports, except the suggestions and advice pertain to disciplinary content; and personal narratives, in which faculty share individual opinions, viewpoints, ideas, concerns, or positions.

Each of these experience-based approaches will be considered in this chapter in terms of the same five areas:

- A description, in fuller and more complete detail: What is it?

- A critical assessment: What are the quality concerns in the work that takes this approach?

- Some exemplars: What does this work look like at its best?

- Standards: How might work that takes this approach be judged?

- Contribution: What has this work contributed to the pedagogical knowledge base? What have we learned from it? And what does this say about its potential as credible scholarship and viable literature?

A fuller discussion of each of these five areas of analysis (which will also be used in the review of research scholarship in Chapter Five) appears in Chapter Three.

Personal Accounts of Change

Description

In this form of pedagogical scholarship, faculty report experiences associated with a change in instructional practice. These reports often begin with how the faculty member came to make this particular change—they decided to tackle a problem with students, content, or course structure; they learned about a new idea at a workshop, heard about it from a colleague, or, less frequently, they read about it. More central in this work is the change itself—it's described in detail, along with the logistics involved in its implementation. Increasingly, in response to journal requirements, there is some analysis of how well the change worked. More often than in the past, faculty authors use objective assessment criteria to support their conclusions about effectiveness, although use of these criteria is still not widespread.

Contrasting these common features, personal accounts of change differ in equally important ways. One of these is the extent of change. Change occurs across a continuum anchored at one end by changes that involve a single technique, such as using student-generated exam questions (see Green, 1997, in the personal accounts of change exemplar section, which follows shortly). Moving along the continuum, there are accounts that describe the infusion of a set of related techniques, such as adding a variety of active learning and cooperative learning strategies in a formerly mostly lecture course (see the Paulson, 1999, exemplar). As the amount of change increases, the move is toward the other end of this continuum, in which change is so significant and widespread that the teacher ends up with a whole new approach and often a new philosophy of education (see Black, 1993). Sometimes the new thinking about approach or philosophy results in the creation of something entirely new, with virtually everything changed, as in the development of a whole new a course (see Deiter, 2003) or curriculum (see Ege, Coppola, and Lawton, 1997).

Personal accounts of change also differ in where the change originates—its source. At one extreme there are changes that represent an entirely new technique, something heretofore unreported in the literature, an author's original idea. This happens rarely in the literature. A bit more often one finds particularly creative or uncommon uses of well-known techniques, strategies, policies, or approaches (for example, see the Woods, 1996, exemplar on participation or the Takata, 1994, design of essay exams). At the other extreme, and equally as rare, is work that reports a straight replication of a technique, strategy, or approach.

In between and much more frequent is work that adapts or applies what others have used. I think a helpful distinction can be made between these two. When the work reports an adaptation, the focus is generally more narrow. A particular strategy or policy (one the faculty member already uses or, more often, the new idea that is about to be incorporated) is adapted, that is, changed so that it better "fits" the configurations of a particular kind of content, the instructional setting, the goals of the instructor, the learning needs of students, or some combination of these. The best example here is the well-known classroom assessment technique called the "minute paper," in which students use the last few minutes of a class to quickly identify content that they do and don't understand and about which they'd like to learn more. Many adaptations of this basic technique have been reported: the questions students respond to are different, the data are collected and reviewed via various mechanisms, and faculty use the results to accomplish a range of objectives.

When the work reports an application, a collection of techniques (such as active learning, cooperative learning, or writing across the curriculum) are applied in a particular disciplinary context, most often a course. For example, Mourtos (1997) recounts experiences incorporating a collection of cooperative learning strategies in engineering courses. In this case individual strategies are still adapted, but multiple cooperative learning approaches are being used in a set of courses.

Interestingly, the fact that complex, adaptive processes are used is virtually ignored. Authors focus on what they did in a particular case—here's how we have used logs in engineering courses (see the Maharaj and Banta (2000) exemplar). That this particular design of log assignments uniquely "fits" engineering content—that this basic writing-across-the-curriculum strategy has been creatively adapted so that it gives students professionally appropriate writing experiences—is not the focus of this report. I suspect if asked to explain the processes involved in coming to these adaptations, most authors would be unable to do so. Knowing how to adapt a technique, strategy, policy, or even a teaching behavior so that it fits the content, context, and instructor is another example of the kind of tacit, implicit knowledge that Schön (1995) says is embedded in competent practice.

In sum, then, personal accounts of change focus on the details associated with implementing change. The amount of change may be small or large: a single technique or a whole new curriculum. How it gets changed may involve creation of a new technique, but more often it is the adaptation or application of already existing techniques. When using this approach, faculty typically identify what they changed and then describe in detail the logistics associated with implementing the change. They almost never explain what prompted those particular adaptations. The work focuses on *what* was changed—not *why*.

Critical Assessment

Some of the most often heard and serious critique of wisdom-of-practice scholarship has been aimed directly at these personal accounts of change. There are two principle objections: the lack of assessment, made worse by the compromised objectivity of the investigator; and inadequate referencing. We need to consider both.

Here's the first problem: if a faculty member selects a particular change and then spends a lot of time and energy implementing that new technique, policy, or approach, especially one that ostensibly improves instruction, he or she has a vested interest in its success. Rather than compensating for this potential bias with rigorous, objective outcome measures, many faculty ignore their involvement and blithely claim success. Linkon (2000) discusses the implications of this flaw: "Faculty have published a lot of teaching stories, wherein the teacher tells about what she taught, how she taught it, what happened, and how the students liked it. These are wonderful stories, but they don't necessarily get us to a deeper understanding of what's going on for students" (p. 64).

How widespread is this flaw? Chin (2002) reports these findings based on analysis of articles in *Teaching Sociology*: "Most papers published in *Teaching Sociology* still do not provide rigorous evaluation data: only 12 percent of the papers published between 1984 to 1999 used systematic comparison [such as a pre and post test, or experimental and control groups] as their evaluation design. Most (51 percent) used casual data [informal impressions], and some used a single system of comparison (18 percent) [teacher evaluations or attitude surveys, for example], or no evaluation data (19 percent)" (p. 59). In an assessment of articles in the *Journal of Geoscience Education*, Perkins (2004, p. 113) revealed that 21 percent of the articles "failed to mention anything about how the project affected student/participant learning," 51 percent "included comments or assertions about learning but gave no evidence in support," and 10 percent "included a complete and well thought out assessment."

Another kind of analysis was published in the *Journal of Management Education*. Shaw, Fisher, and Southey (1999) summarize what they found: "We have examined evaluations of OB [Organizational Behavior] course innovations presented in the *Journal of Management Education* since 1990. [A table summarizes them in the article.] With a few exceptions, evidence for the effectiveness of new OB teaching methods has been . . . impressionistic and anecdotal. When quantitative data are collected, they are usually in the form of course evaluations obtained from students at the end of the semester. . . . Criteria other than student reactions are seldom obtained, and innovative methods are rarely explicitly compared to more standard methods" (p. 510).

Based on my years of reading the literature, I believe this problem is equally prevalent in other fields. Although changes are occurring in this area and will be discussed shortly, a majority of the work that describes personal accounts of change does not, in my judgment, use rigorous enough assessment mechanisms, nor does it recognize and adequately compensate for bias that results from the faculty member's vested interest in the success of the change.

How serious is the flaw? Jenkins (1997), a former pedagogical periodical editor, is frank about the problem as he sees it in the *Journal of Geography in Higher Education:* "The current editorial guidelines state that it is 'important that educational developments be evaluated, and if possible you should report your attempts to do so.' I cannot imagine a mainstream geography journal stating, in its editorial guidelines, something like: 'In describing the geography study you have undertaken, if possible you should try to evaluate or test that what you describe is a valid or reliable statement.' In short, geographers writing in *JGHE* about their teaching are not (yet) required to apply the same standards that they would when researching and writing on the discipline per se" (p. 11).

The conclusion is unavoidable: this is a serious flaw, one that impugns the work's credibility and viability. The failure to recognize and deal with faculty bias routinely a part of these personal accounts of change implicates the conclusions. It is made more serious because faculty often end these articles with an enthusiastic endorsement of the change.

For each of these quality issues it also makes sense to consider whether it is a fixable flaw or an inherent defect. In this case we definitely have a fixable flaw. For starters, ways of objectively assessing instructional changes exist and are used in the exemplars that follow. These are but a few examples from a much larger pool, many coming to us from work on classroom research (Cross and Steadman, 1996). Finally, the pedagogical periodicals themselves have recognized the problem, and most now have guidelines requiring that these accounts of personal change include objective measures of outcomes. An editorial note in *Journalism and Mass Communication Educator* (Cohen, 2002) eloquently explains the rationale: "A useful scholarship *about* teaching and learning must contribute more than a teacher's anecdotal successes. If articles are going to foster a serious and defensible view of teaching as scholarship-based; if the journal is going to provide a scholarly foundation for faculty reflection about teaching; if *Educator* is to provide a footing for peer review of work of colleagues, then the journal must provide not anecdotal tips, but work that embraces disciplined and, as Ernie Boyer said a decade ago, inclusive scholarship that recognizes that 'knowledge is acquired through research, through synthesis, through practice, and through teaching'" (pp. 2–3). These guidelines are being implemented. I see objective assessment measures being used much more regularly now than they were twenty years ago when I first started reading this literature. Perkins (2004) statistically quantifies improvement that has occurred in the *Journal of Geoscience Education* over the past five years and includes a list of articles with exemplary assessment components.

The second problem with personal accounts of change pertains to the absence of references. Those who have written about this flaw describe it very concretely: the content is inadequately referenced. To illustrate, Calder, Cutler, and Kelly (2002) looked at twenty-six articles published between May 1996 and January 2000 in the main section of *The History Teacher* and found that "nineteen contained either no footnotes or only footnotes to standard historical sources. Only nine of the twenty-six articles referred to anything resembling serious research into teaching and learning" (pp. 50–51). A citation analysis of articles published in the *Journal of Engineering Education* (JEE) in 1993 and 1994 found that the median times a paper was cited subsequently was one (Wankat, 2004). The author does make an interesting point: "Most papers in JEE will be rarely cited in JEE. This is humbling, but not surprising since most scientific journal articles are cited zero or once" (p. 17). How widespread is this flaw? Few other systematic analyses document the extensiveness of the problem, but I would certainly list it as a common characteristic of all pedagogical literature.

How serious is this flaw? In this case, that question is interesting because of the larger query it raises: What role does referencing play when the scholarship is experience-based? Do pedagogical scholars need to summon outside sources when the lessons reported derive from their own experience? This question will emerge again when we consider recommended-practices reports, in which faculty authors offer advice based on experience.

Once again, the problem of published work without references is being addressed by the journals themselves. Editorial guidelines now include directives about references. For example, a list of evaluation criteria for articles submitted to *Teaching Sociology* includes this statement: "How thoroughly and accurately does the author ground the paper in the literature? Are there articles in *Teaching Sociology* that the author should cite? Does the paper tie in the larger literature on pedagogy?" "Instructions to Authors" in *Cell Biology Education* states: "All submissions will be evaluated for references to related educational literature." The *Journal of Chemical Education* reviewer guidelines includes this instruction: "A publishable manuscript should include a thoroughly researched bibliography." A significant increase in the amount of referencing now appears in all kinds of pedagogical scholarship, but the references are mostly to related pedagogical work within the discipline—not to relevant research in education or other fields.

The omission of references indicates a much more serious problem: pedagogical scholarship does not build on previous knowledge. As a result, some work rests on weak and unsubstantiated premises. In other cases it replicates what is already well established. Because this scholarship does not build on or integrate previous knowledge, no organized, coherent base for teaching and learning has emerged from this literature, despite many years of scholarship. In the case of this second flaw we have another widespread and serious defect that is being addressed on the obvious level but not yet on the more serious one.

A critical assessment of personal accounts of change reveals two quality concerns. The experiences with change are not uniformly assessed with rigorous methods—troublesome because in all this literature there is an implicit (if not explicit) endorsement of the change. Second, the work is not always well referenced. Both problems are being addressed with noticeable improvements in recent years. However, not yet considered are the issues of what experience-based work contributes to the knowledge base for teaching, or how that knowledge should be used in experience-based scholarship.

Exemplars

The rationale used to assemble this collection of exemplars and those in subsequent ones appears in Chapter Three.

Green, D. H. "Student-Generated Exams: Testing and Learning." *Journal of Marketing Education*, 1997, 19 (2), 43–53.

> Reports on a process that incorporates student-generated questions on exams used in an undergraduate retailing course. Exemplary in its justification of the technique based on a literature review and assessment of advantages and disadvantages from both the students' and instructor's perspectives.

Hiller, T. H., and Hietapelto, A. B. "Contract Grading: Encouraging Commitment to the Learning Process Through Voice in the Evaluation Process." *Journal of Management Education*, 2001, *25* (6), 660–684.

> Tracks the evolution of a contract grading scheme across a four-year period with 473 students in twenty-two classes and at three different universities. Exemplary in its description of the adaptations made and in its assessments of limitations and challenges as part of contract grading. Includes excerpts from syllabi illustrating different ways contracts were used.

Maharaj, S., and Banta, L. "Using Log Assignments to Foster Learning: Writing Across the Curriculum." *Journal of Engineering Education*, 2000, *89* (1), 73–77.

> Details the design of log assignments used in a sophomore-level engineering statics course. Exemplary in illustrating how a generic writing-across-the-curriculum strategy can be adapted so that it "fits" content being taught and student learning needs.

Paulson, D. R. "Active Learning and Cooperative Learning in the Organic Chemistry Lecture Class." *Journal of Chemical Education*, 1999, *76* (8), 1,136–1,140.

> Describes experiences incorporating a variety of active and cooperative learning strategies in an organic chemistry course. Illustrates how a collection of strategies can be applied in a particular course. Exemplary for the simple yet rigorous ways the impact of these new strategies was assessed.

Varner, D., and Peck, S. R. "Learning from Learning Journals: The Benefits and Challenges of Using Learning Journal Assignments." *Journal of Management Education*, 2003, *27* (1), 52–77.

> Focuses on the use of learning journals in MBA courses, where they are used in lieu of exams. Includes excellent discussions

of the theoretical grounding for journals, the objectives they are used to accomplish, and the challenges addressed during the authors' seven years of experience using them. Appendices provide samples of instructional materials developed in the process.

Woods, D. R. "Participation Is More Than Attendance." *Journal of Engineering Education*, 1996, 85 (3), 177–181.

Describes a method that involved students in the creation of an instrument used to assess involvement in class discussion and in the peer assessment of participation. Exemplary in its discussion of how faculty teaching in other contexts could use the approach.

Standards

These exemplary personal accounts of change differ significantly from other work using this approach in five ways; those differences could be used as assessment standards. Work using this approach should accomplish the following:

- Recognize the knowledge base that justifies the change

- Critically analyze the change in depth

- Contain evidence that adaptation occurred

- Draw appropriately bounded implications

- Use relevant and rigorous assessment methods

Each of these merits further discussion.

Recognize the knowledge base that justifies the change. Little justifies the implementation of a new or changed technique, strategy, or approach if no evidence supports that it makes a difference in learning outcomes. Work that stands out in this category of personal accounts of change reports and summarizes relevant theoretical, empirical, and experiential evidence that justifies the change. The citing of that evidence is not comprehensive—these are not reviews of research pieces—but the inclusion of relevant support extends beyond the discipline.

Critically analyze the change in depth. Exemplary personal accounts of change are more thoughtful and analytical than other articles that use this approach. The wisdom inherently a part of effective practice is not useful knowledge unless it is made explicit. These exemplars model rich and robust ways of thinking about teaching and learning at the same time that they present viable models of change.

Part of the depth results from the amount of detail and analysis included. The report on curricular change involved in the comprehensive revision of the basic organic chemistry course at the University of Michigan (Ege, Coppola, and Lawton, 1997) offers a complete description of how the curriculum was changed, an in-depth, well-documented analysis of the thinking behind the change, and an objective assessment of its impact on student learning.

As illustrated by these exemplars, reporting about the change is fair and balanced. There is recognition that any instructional technique, policy, or approach produces a mixed bag of results. Challenges associated with implementation, as well as means and methods used to address those difficulties, are reported honestly. The language is descriptive, not unnecessarily evaluative. It is personal and unpretentious.

Contain evidence that adaptation occurred. Even though authors may not justify why they changed a technique, strategy, or approach as they did, evidence of those adjustments is included and the changes make sense given the content, context, goals, and learning needs. For example, having students use a simple finger signal code that conceals their answer in a class of fifty fits the large class environment (Paulson, 1999, exemplar). Having students negotiate and obligate themselves to a contract mirrors what many business students will do after college (Hiller and Hietapelto, 2001, exemplar). In exemplary accounts of change, new techniques are not included because they are trendy or respond to some generic need to change; they are instructional practices molded and shaped so that they meet the unique learning needs of a particular educational situation.

Draw appropriately bounded implications. At issue here are the conclusions drawn from the personal account of change, the matter of validity. If there are no lessons learned with relevance to others, there seems little benefit in disseminating these reports of change. But if the experience being reported is limited (one instructor reporting on a change implemented in one course for one semester), or if the instructional context is highly unique (a mortuary science lab), then the author must draw limited lessons for others. The preference here is not necessarily for extensive experience in common contexts but for a recognition that experience and context are always relevant, and that implications, recommendations, or advice for others must be bounded by them. "Validity is only an issue when the researcher overgeneralizes the implications of his or her results" (C. Walker, personal communication, April 2005).

Use relevant and rigorous assessment methods. In the exemplary work here, whatever has been changed has also been assessed via systematic and objective methods. These exemplars illustrate a variety of different assessment techniques—all of which go significantly beyond an instructor's opinion as to the effectiveness of the change. That is not to disadvantage the instructor's opinion entirely, but to say that it should never stand as the only estimation of success.

Contribution

At this juncture we need to assess what personal accounts of change have contributed to our understanding of teaching and learning. First off, from them we have learned how relevant and flexible some instructional techniques and strategies are. Widespread use of certain techniques and strategies (cooperative learning, for example) across a range of disciplines by teachers with different styles and with varied students establishes their validity. They have been used successfully in a wide range of instructional settings, which means that they can be recommended to others. And they are flexible; they have been adapted so that they fit different contexts and accomplish multiple learning objectives.

There is a caveat, however. The variable settings in which the technique or strategies have been used make it difficult to generalize what has been learned from that one specific context to others. What one instructor may have "discovered" about effective cooperative learning strategies adds evidence supportive of its overall effectiveness, but that discovery does not identify the key to success or antidote to failure for teachers everywhere.

Second, from these personal accounts of change we have learned what works—not theoretically, not abstractly, not hypothetically, not in a lab, but literally, in the dynamic milieu of actual classrooms as reported firsthand by the persons who used them. Repeated use by practitioners generates a solid knowledge base of practical information—not new discoveries, but an overall affirmation of viability and a plethora of practical details.

Finally, these personal accounts of change demonstrate the power of learning from the experiences of others. From fellow teachers, often colleagues in the same discipline, faculty can read firsthand accounts of something that works or solves a problem. This is content that connects to and with its audience. Moreover, most of this literature contains the level of detail necessary for implementation. It's how-to-do-it literature in the best sense.

Personal accounts of change are a common form of the wisdom-of-practice scholarship. Over the years, many stories of "How I changed my teaching" have been published. In their least effective form, the teacher describes the change and extols the outcome. At their best, the particular change is justified with evidence from the experience or research of others. It is implemented with adaptations that fit the unique circumstances that surround its use, and its effects are assessed rigorously and objectively. It is work with potential to increase the pedagogical knowledge base and to improve practice. Although not widely seen as scholarly and not always done with intellectual richness, it has potential and can be done with rigor.

Recommended-Practices Reports

Description

This advice-giving practitioner scholarship makes recommendations. It aims to tell—mostly individual faculty but sometimes institutions or disciplines—what they should do about particular aspects of instruction. The advice offered in this literature covers so many instructional topics one is tempted to assert that advice has been offered about every aspect of instruction. A lot of the advice is directive; faculty are told what to do. Some is presented more formally as recommendations or suggestions. A bit is proposed tentatively, offered as possibilities.

The advice varies in terms of the bases on which it is being offered and the qualifications of the source offering it. Typically, the advice rests on classroom experience or empirical results, sometimes on both. However, the amount of experience or research behind the advice varies considerably. Sometimes it rests on the experience of one teacher in one classroom. Other times it is based on collective experience accumulated across disciplines. Those collective experiences are sometimes reported by the group involved and sometimes offered by someone who organizes and integrates collective experience within a discipline or for a particular instructional method. The same is true for research-based advice. Very occasionally, it is offered on the basis of one study. More often, it draws on a collection of related studies or even larger bodies of work from different fields and on different subjects (as in the advice Eison, 1990, offers new faculty or that Svinicki, 1998, presents on grading in the exemplar section for recommended-practice reports).

Some of the most impressive work in the recommended practices category illustrates Boyer's (1990) scholarships of integration and application. In the case of integration, a collection of scholarly work, usually research based and usually on the same topic, is pulled together, distilled, and summarized. Generally, reviews of research are prepared by researchers doing the work. But in the case of pedagogical scholarship, sometimes these reviews are constructed by practitioners, as in the case of Korobkin (1988), who reviews the research on humor, Hobson and Talbot (2001), who present a succinct and useful summary of the extensive research on student evaluation, or Prince (2004), who has done an impressive distillation of findings on active learning.

More often in recommended-practices reports one finds examples of the scholarship of application, where research or experience may be summarized but the focus is application—what faculty should do based on what is known. The Eison (1990) and Svinicki (1998) exemplars later in this section illustrate this point. When an integration is well done and the advice is offered by practitioners who know classroom realities firsthand, this pedagogical scholarship has great utility.

There is one unique form of application within this recommended-practices category. It involves application of disciplinary theory or research to pedagogy. For example, Billson (1986) effectively applies principles of small-group dynamics derived from research in sociology to classrooms. Keeley, Shemberg, Cowell, and Zinnbauer (1995) use psychotherapy literature to explain student resistance to critical thinking. In the pedagogical scholarship of the management field, classrooms are regularly compared with organizations and assumed to function like them. As these examples illustrate, the application of field-specific knowledge can produce scholarship of interest and value not only in that field but to other fields as well.

The credentials of those offering the advice in this literature are also diverse. Nothing prevents an individual faculty member with limited experience and almost no knowledge of the literature from making recommendations, provided they can get the piece published, and some have. At the other end is a small group of what could be considered pedagogical scholars. Sometimes these are faculty members whose multiple pedagogical publications in many sources have established their credentials. Sometimes these more credentialed authors are faculty developers, professionals (some of whom started out as faculty members) who head units charged to work with faculty on pedagogical agendas. Most of these folks are experiential experts—they know what does and doesn't work in college classrooms. A few are also equally versed in the empirical literature—they know (and in some cases have contributed to) the research base that stands behind instructional practice.

In sum, this literature is most prominently characterized by its advice-giving feature. The advice may be based on limited or extensive experience, or a little or a lot of empirical evidence, or some combination of the two. Some examples of the scholarships of integration and application can be found in this category. The qualifications of those offering the advice vary significantly, and the advice may be presented tentatively, definitively, or somewhere in between.

Critical Assessment

What are the quality issues relevant to these recommended-practices reports? First off, I could not find any published objections to pedagogical literature that offers advice. I was surprised, because two aspects of this work seem more troubling to me than either of the objections raised to the personal accounts of change. The first relates to the qualifications of the person offering the advice—the problem being that basically anybody can offer pedagogical advice. The second, not unrelated to the first, involves the justification for the advice being offered. The problem here is that advice can be offered based on a very limited amount of classroom experience and no or a very superficial understanding of what has been established by previous work.

There is an irony not to miss here. Faculty are an enormously credential-conscious group. Terminal degrees are now almost the law of the land in higher education. Most departments set rigid requirements specifying the qualifications necessary to teach a particular course, but when it comes to advice on how to teach, virtually anybody can offer it. Would an inexperienced, unknown scholar in a discipline be allowed to review, summarize, draw implications, and recommend applications?

As for the follow-up questions: Are author qualifications a widespread problem in these recommended-practices reports? Yes and no. Yes, because there is no evidence anywhere of concern about author qualifications. No, because articles that offer wrong or really bad advice are not all that common. However, there are plenty of articles in which the advice offered is incomplete, only partly right, and generally not as good as it could be, and in almost all of these cases author credentials could be pointed to as part of the problem.

Do we have an inherent defect here or a fixable flaw? It's probably not an inherent defect, but it's not an easily fixable flaw either. Journals are not really in a position to require or check author credentials with a criterion such as "three previously published and well-reviewed articles before we consider your submission." The more viable solution relates not to the qualifications of the author but to the foundation on which the advice rests.

Before settling on the solution, we need to explore this second problem: advice offered based on limited experience and that makes little or no mention of relevant literature. This problem relates to the first and it is especially serious when a combination occurs—a novice author offers advice based on limited experience and without knowledge of the literature. Is this worst case scenario widespread? No, this kind of work is not prevalent in the recommended-practices literature, but neither are examples in which recognized pedagogical experts offer advice based on extensive experience and grounded in theoretical and empirical knowledge. In other words, the room for improvement here is considerable.

Part of what makes this flaw fixable is that author credentials, amount of experience, and inclusion of established knowledge can compensate for each other. For example, advice based on limited experience teaching a particular kind of course but offered by someone with established pedagogical expertise who draws widely from the literature can contain first-rate advice (the Frederick, 1995, exemplar illustrates this). Or authors who may not have published a lot of pedagogical scholarship but who nest their advice in relevant theoretical or empirical literature can provide excellent recommendations (see the Sharp, Harb, and Terry, 1997, exemplar).

Moreover, the push by publishers to increase the amount of referencing also moves this in the fixable flaw direction. However, that push would be much more effective if it wasn't just about longer reference lists but also addressed validity as it relates to advice-giving literature and considered how this scholarship should build on and further expand the practitioner knowledge base for teaching.

Like personal accounts of change, scholarship that involves experience and recommendations raises a number of important questions—all virtually unexplored up to this point in the pedagogical literature. What role should references play when the advice is experience-based? Should faculty reference the related experiences of others in their discipline? In other disciplines? Should they reference relevant empirical findings? This last question points again to the relationship between educational research and applied practitioner scholarship on teaching and learning. How do they interface? How should they inform each other, and how does the presence of each appear in the work of the other?

Summing the quality issues a bit bluntly: we have yet to establish the ground rules for offering advice. We have not said whether these reports must reference other experience, and if so, by whom and how much. We have not said whether these reports must build on other kinds of knowledge, such as the theoretical and empirical findings of relevant fields such as education and educational psychology. And we have ignored issues of qualifications—failing to recognize that the right to offer advice starts but does not end with classroom experience.

Exemplars

The rationale used to assemble this and subsequent collections of exemplars appears in Chapter Three.

Eison, J. "Confidence in the Classroom: Ten Maxims for New Teachers." *College Teaching,* 1990, *38* (1), 21–24.

> In fewer than four pages, this article offers sensible, research-based advice for new faculty. Exemplary for the especially clear way both experiential and empirical knowledge about teaching are condensed, integrated, and presented constructively.

Frederick, P. "Walking on Eggs: Mastering the Dreaded Diversity Discussion." *College Teaching,* 1995, *43* (3), 83–92.

> Based on experiences teaching American studies and history courses, the author offers nine specific and adaptable strategies that respond to the "challenges of implementing . . . diversity discussions with students" (p. 83). Illustrates how individual experience buttressed with an array of literature can be the basis for sanguine, helpful advice.

Herreid, C. F. "Case Studies in Science—A Novel Method of Science Education." *Journal of College Science Teaching,* 1994, *23* (4) 221–229.

> Takes an instructional method not commonly used in science and builds a case for its application there. Supports information on various kinds of cases with lots of examples adapted for science programs.

Korobkin, D. "Humor in the Classroom: Considerations and Strategies." *College Teaching,* 1988, *36* (4), 154–158.

> Considers a wide collection of research on the role of humor in classrooms and learning. Identifies ways of using humor with

the potential to enhance learning and the kinds of humor to avoid. Exemplary for the way implications are drawn from research.

McKinney, K., Saxe, D., and Cobb, L. "Are We Really Doing All We Can for Our Undergraduates? Professional Socialization via Out-of-Class Experiences." *Teaching Sociology*, January 1998, *26*, 1–13.

Takes the field of sociology to task for its failure to realize the learning potential of out-of-class experiences. Builds a strong case for out-of-class-experiences with a concise summary of the literature. Concludes with a viable set of recommendations.

Sharp, J. E., Harb, J. N., and Terry, R. E. "Combining Kolb Learning Styles and Writing to Learn in Engineering Classes." *Journal of Engineering Education*, 1997, 86 (2), 93–101.

Using Kolb's four learning styles, generates multiple writing tasks and assignments for engineering students. Another exemplar that impressively adapts and applies generic strategies to the content configurations of this problem-solving discipline.

Svinicki, M. D. "Helping Students Understand Grades." *College Teaching*, 1998, 46 (3), 101–105.

Distills the enormously complex work on measurement theory into four pragmatic principles that faculty can use to create fair and sensible grading systems. Illustrates each principle and concludes with advice on communicating constructively with students about grades.

Standards

If we look at exemplary recommended-practices reports, what separates them from less-distinguished work in the category? Consider three characteristics of the exemplars that could be used to assess recommended-practices reports: relates to a meaningful aspect of instruction, offers "good" advice, and communicates constructively.

Relates to a meaningful aspect of instruction. Not all aspects of instruction are equally important. The advice offered in these exemplars relates to those parts of instruction that matter and are relevant. In some cases this has to do with its timeliness. Advice on diversity discussions (as in the Frederick, 1995, exemplar) or advice on Internet topics (such as the recommendations offered by Hammett, 1999, on helping students evaluate Web sites) is meaningful because these areas present faculty with new instructional challenges. Or the advice is relevant because it addresses a problem (the need to include writing in technical courses in the Sharp, Harb, and Terry, 1997, exemplar; the need to improve science teaching generally in the Herreid, 1994, exemplar, or the difficulties explored by van Gelder, 2005, associated with teaching students to think critically). In some cases, the advice may address an unrecognized problem (the McKinney, Saxe, and Cobb, 1998, exemplar shows how sociology fails to realize the potential of out-of-class experiences; Parilla and Hesser, 1998, in an equally comprehensive analysis, address how internships are not always effective learning experiences). Finally, the advice found in these exemplars is meaningful because it relates to aspects of instruction over which faculty have some control and can change. What is being recommended can be implemented.

Offers "good" advice. "Good" advice is advice that is correct, complete, concrete, and fits. *Correct* advice is right—what it recommends is supported experientially and empirically. Experts agree with what's being proposed; empirical evidence justifies the recommendations, as the exemplars illustrate. If implications are drawn from research (as they are in the Korobkin, 1988, exemplar), they flow from and can be linked to the findings. If the experts don't agree and the evidence contains mixed results, then the advice offered reflects that less-than-perfect knowledge. Good advice is *complete* advice. It isn't advice that takes into account half of what is known or identifies some of the maxims that affect the confidence of new faculty (see the Eison, 1990, exemplar). Next, good instructional advice is *concrete*. It proposes specific actions or concrete principles, with clear indications for one course of action over another. Yet this clarity is not at the cost of complexity; it does not trivialize complex instructional details. Finally, good advice *fits* the audience and situation. When the advice is offered to large audiences or about multiple teaching contexts (as is the advice Eison, 1990, offers new faculty or the recommendations Svinicki, 1998, makes about grading), it focuses on those aspects of the instructional experience that are shared, that transcend disciplinary boundaries, but at the same time it recognizes the uniqueness of every instructional situation.

Communicates constructively. Advice and recommendations offered to others have little value if they are not heeded. How the message is communicated certainly influences how it will be received. The trick is not only to offer good advice on meaningful aspects of instruction but to offer it in a way that motivates faculty to take action. The tone in all these exemplars is constructive, positive, and encouraging. In my early efforts to implement learner-centered strategies that students often resisted, I read and re-read Felder and Brent (1996) because it not only offered very helpful advice, it made me believe that I could handle the student resistance.

Contribution

Finally left to consider is what these recommended-practices reports have contributed to our understanding of teaching and learning and what might be learned from them that pertains to credible scholarship and viable literature. For starters, this kind of literature meets a need most faculty keenly feel. We are not trained teachers, and experience in the classroom often confirms our ineptitude. We'd like to know how to do it better or at least a bit more effectively. I think this explains our openness to the advice, even that offered in passing by colleagues whose pedagogical credentials we do not question.

Second, from exemplars in this literature we learn that to distill and translate complicated research into practical principles is not a watering down process that dilutes the intellectual currency of the original work. Rather, when done with integrity, it is about paring off what is not necessary to understand the essence and taking out lessons that can be applied to practice. When done well, this is intellectually rigorous work.

This literature contains models that use the scholarships of integration and application to identify what is believed theoretically and has been established empirically and experientially. A few of these exemplars, like McKeachie's *Teaching Tips* (2002), demonstrate the value of having repositories of collected wisdom. *Teaching Tips*, first published in 1938, is the most widely used book on college teaching and is now in its eleventh edition, which eloquently testifies to the value faculty (especially new ones) find in solid, well-documented advice. Other less luminary but still excellent books model how all that is known about a particular strategy can be assembled and organized. Millis and Cottell (1998) do this for the college-level use of cooperative learning strategies.

Of all the forms of practitioner pedagogical scholarship, recommended-practices reports have the greatest potential for organizing, integrating, and otherwise making coherent the practitioner knowledge base for teaching. Those portions of the practitioner knowledge base that have been assembled have been done in work that uses this approach. Recommended-practices reports are also the only form of pedagogical scholarship that reaches out to connect the world of the classroom teacher to that of the educational researcher. What prevents this work from realizing more of this promising potential is the failure to realize the need for it, followed by the failure to recognize its merit.

Finally, of all the forms of practitioner pedagogical scholarship, recommended-practices reports come the closest to setting standards for the profession. They say what should and should not be done, given what is known. To the multiple calls that are made time and again in this literature for more active learning and more student engagement can be credited the move among practitioners away from straight didactic instruction. Most teachers still talk too much but most now realize that they should talk less. They understand that student passivity is a problem that prevents learning. In sum, as a literature with the power to improve practice and establish the profession, and as a credible form of scholarship, recommended-practices reports have taught us much. They hold great promise.

Recommended-Content Reports

Recommended-content reports are exactly the same as recommended-practices reports, only rather than offering advice about practice, these reports make recommendations about content. The suggestions offered in these reports include advice on what content should be covered in particular courses, sequences of courses, or degree programs. Content recommendations identify concepts, skills, or professional perspectives students should acquire in a course or curriculum. Advice about content is sometimes very specific and focused, proposing ways of explaining, illustrating, and demonstrating the material students are being asked to learn. In some fields this includes problem sets or laboratory exercises.

In some pedagogical periodicals, this is the almost exclusive focus of the pedagogical scholarship. They offer all sorts of advice on what should be taught, with very little consideration of pedagogical how-tos. A good bit of this scholarship exemplifies Shulman's notion (1987) of content knowledge embedded within the discipline, and it makes several important contributions. The focus on curricular and course content adds coherence to degree programs offered at different institutions. Work that explores ways of explaining course content (such as with examples, case studies, or applications) helps students learn concepts.

In Chapter Two we raised a question about periodicals that only contain work that uses this approach. Are they pedagogical if they only or mostly treat content issues? This focus reflects and reinforces the already strong content-orientation of most faculty. It carries an implicit message: Content is the most important instructional variable—what you teach always supersedes how you teach. It is not helpful to think of content and method hierarchically; content and method serve each other. But the balance between them is worth revisiting because nothing has so successfully stood in the way of instructional improvement and enhanced learning as the content orientation of faculty. The need to cover ever more content prevents many faculty from using instructional methods documented to have a positive effect on student learning.

As a form of pedagogical scholarship, these recommended-content reports are just as much in need of review and analysis as any of the other kinds of scholarship being considered in this book. There is one problem, though. When scholarship is embedded in the discipline and focused on content, understanding it depends on a knowledge of the field. Examples of this work are not meaningful to people outside the field, and I do not think they can be assessed by outsiders. For these reasons I have opted to identify and describe them as yet another approach to pedagogical scholarship but not to offer an analysis of them in this volume.

Personal Narratives

Description

Personal narratives do not focus on a particular change, although reports of change are sometimes part of this work, nor is this advice-giving literature, although recommendations are sometimes implied. Rather, the focus of this work is personal. That is, it rests on insights from within the author. Articles in this category report individual opinions, views, ideas, concerns, and positions. The insights shared are sometimes the result of personal experience, sometimes informed by the views of others or written in response to them, and sometimes supported by empirical evidence. But the perspective is personal: this is what I think or believe; this is how I've grown or changed; this is what I've learned; this is what concerns me; and, less frequently, this is what I wonder or where I've failed.

In addition to its personal perspective, this work has an emotional dimension that is acknowledged to varying degrees. Most explicit is work that deals directly with the emotional aspects of teaching—that soft underside that a few faculty pretend doesn't exist, that many more accept but hide from, and that only a few live with comfortably. It includes those reasons that stand behind our commitments to teaching and those powerful connections that can occur between teachers and students. It also examines inherent emotional vulnerabilities: how teaching expresses personhood and how teachers serve as role models, whether or not they want to. A few personal narratives go to the dark side, where they explore the emotional toll of teaching well in unsupportive environments, issues of burnout and declining effectiveness, of power and control, and an occasional confrontation with failure.

Other personal narratives are position pieces in which the emotional dimension is less explicit. Authors advocate for or argue against a particular policy, practice, position, or philosophy. Glew (2003) uses a decade of experience to raise questions about the efficacy of problem-based learning. On a personal note, when I get too carried away making points in class, I try to remember the pointed distinction Pestel (1988) makes between preaching, training, and teaching. Even though the language is more objective and the arguments largely rational, this work bespeaks emotional involvement—care and concern motivate the expression of an opinion or the assembling of arguments to make a case.

Of the categories of wisdom-of-practice scholarship, personal narratives are the most eclectic in terms of both topic and format. Again, the topics covered are varied; some are creative, unique and unexpected, such as Gallagher's description (2000) of what he learned from his first and not very impressive student ratings,

Galbraith's critique (1987) of his teaching career, "How I Could Have Done Much Better," and Olson and Einwohner's comparative analysis (2001) of the impact of institutional environment on their growth and development as new college teachers. Some of the topics addressed are timeless. I can't count the number of times I've read a piece by Hill (1980) that compares teachers with mountain guides. I keep returning to it because she so motivates me to lead students up those high and difficult trails.

Formats are also dissimilar to other kinds of pedagogical scholarship and within the category itself. This work includes various statements of teaching philosophy—from highly idiosyncratic teaching manifestos (such as Friedman's "Fifty-Six Laws of Good Teaching," 1990) to more deliberate attempts to explore the confluence of teaching philosophy and instructional practice (such as the insightful analyses of early teaching experiences). The work also includes personal accounts of growth, change, and evolution across a career (the Tompkins, 1996, exemplar), sometimes occurring as a consequence of a significant experience (the Starling, 1987, and Husted, 2001, exemplars) or personal explorations that lead down to the bedrock, where instructional motivations are stripped of pretense (the Walck, 1997, exemplar). Finally, another collection of formats is used to express opinions. Sometimes these are written in response to another article (such as the Bailey, 2000, exemplar), or they may respond to a particular policy or practice, or they may be written to challenge a common view (the Gregory, 1987, exemplar or Spence's sharp critique of teaching, 2001).

I have a folder, now tattered, that contains my favorite pieces on teaching—the ones that have most influenced my instructional practice and teaching philosophy. I was surprised to find that eight of the twelve pieces belong in this personal narrative category. Personal narratives may well be the most interesting kind of pedagogical scholarship to read. I think that's because in these articles one teacher connects with another and part of the bond is emotional. I respond to my collection of favorites viscerally. Yes, they challenge my mind, but they also touch my heart. They make me aspire to greatness in the classroom.

Critical Assessment

Credibility issues are a problem with all experience-based forms of pedagogical scholarship, but they are most serious with personal narratives. First, this work lacks credibility because it most starkly contrasts with long-standing beliefs about how knowledge is formed and advanced. I can't think of a field in which personal, experience-based perspectives are part of the equation. Who cares what you believe or think about teaching? You are welcome to your views and perspectives, but what makes them any more valid than what I think or believe? Legitimate knowledge bases rest on something more substantial than individual viewpoints.

In this case there is no hiding from the fact that this problem with personal narratives is both a widespread and inherent defect. This objection is levied against one of the defining features of the work—its personal perspective. Fix this aspect of personal narratives and fundamentally change them. This leaves two alternatives: an outright rejection of personal narratives as a form of scholarship, or a challenge to current ways of defining pedagogical scholarship.

Disciplinary forms of scholarship powerfully shape our understanding of and expectations for scholarly work. Their long-standing preference for empirical inquiry explains why experience-based scholarship so disquiets. But what if we change the paradigm and say that disciplinary expectations need not always apply and that scholarship need not always discover something new? This opens the door to seeing personal narratives as models that illustrate productive, intellectually rich ways of thinking about and analyzing practice, models that help us understand what we do and why we do it, and models that show the value of making intuitive knowledge explicit. As the exemplars about to be listed are perused, put these questions to them: Do these articles contain wisdom and insights that relate to your practice? Did you learn anything from them? Are they pieces of work that could profitably be recommended to or discussed with colleagues? If the answers are affirmative, then what prevents them from being considered scholarly?

The very personal nature of this work is only its first credibility problem. The second one relates to its inherently emotional dimension. Although the academic community is more accepting of qualitative research and knowledge that is intuitive and emotionally based, objective rationality is still for many the preferred and more legitimate way of knowing. In this case as well we are dealing with a defining characteristic of personal narratives. Take away their emotional foundation and the work is robbed of what makes it compelling and authentic. Once again we have a widespread and inherent problem with this form of experience-based pedagogical scholarship.

However, the way out is a bit easier in this case. As already noted, some acceptance for work constructed with something other than objective rationality already exists; even more compelling is that, although many ignore it, few will deny that teaching has emotional dimensions. We have all learned (and research into the ingredients of effective instruction verifies) that as essential as content knowledge is, it is never enough alone. In further illustration of the point, consider the work of Palmer (1998), one of the most influential pedagogical scholars in the last couple of decades. More effectively than anyone in recent memory, Palmer has reconnected faculty with this affective side of teaching. One of my colleagues described his book, *The Courage to Teach*, as the long, cool drink a thirsty, tired hiker craves.

Nonetheless, even though most of us do recognize the emotional dimensions associated with teaching, few of us have considered their role in the professional growth and development of teachers, and virtually none of us has considered the terms and conditions under which work that enlightens these understandings might be scholarly. In all likelihood, legitimizing personal narratives as scholarly work will be a long time coming. In their personal perspective and emotional dimension we have identified widespread, and by current definitions of scholarship, inherent defects. They are not aspects of the work that can be "fixed." They go to the heart of its character.

Exemplars

Bailey, J. "Students as Clients in a Professional/Client Relationship." *Journal of Management Education,* 2000, 24 (3), 353–365.

> Writes in response to a previously published article critical of the student-as-customer metaphor. This piece proposes a new comparison—the student as client. Exemplary for the way it builds on previous work and constructively argues the viability of the client metaphor.

Gregory, M. "If Education Is a Feast, Why Do We Restrict the Menu? A Critique of Pedagogical Metaphors." *College Teaching,* 1987, 35 (3), 101–106.

> A position piece that argues against learning-as-storage and three corollary metaphors. Exemplary for its level of thoughtful critique. The arguments are carefully crafted; the insights are rich and provocative.

Husted, B. L. "Hope, for the Dry Side." *College English,* 2001, 64 (2), 243–249.

> A poignant exploration that delves into the role of teachers in changing attitudes about race and discrimination. Exemplary in the way personal experience is used to explore a set of much larger issues. An account that moves, intrigues, depresses, and inspires.

Starling, R. "Professor as Student: The View from the Other Side." *College Teaching,* 1987, 35 (1), 3–7.

> A sometimes humorous report of the author's experiences taking three courses not in his content area with a group of students. A powerful model illustrating what can be learned through reflective analysis of experience.

Tompkins, J. "Pedagogy of the Distressed." *College English*, 1990, *52* (6), 653–660.

> A narrative of personal growth that tracks a significant change in teaching philosophy. Exemplary for its level of insight and analysis. Buttressed throughout with personal examples and experiences. Extremely well written.

Walck, C. L. "A Teaching Life." *Journal of Management Education*, 1997, *21* (4), 473–482.

> Uses the life of a writer (as described by Annie Dillard) as a template for analyzing the life of a teacher, specifically her vision of the teaching life. Exemplary for its honest exploration of teaching's disappointments but acknowledges its ever-present promise.

Standards

What distinguishes exemplary personal narratives? Consider four characteristics that could become criteria used to assess this kind of practitioner pedagogical scholarship: in-depth, critical self-reflection; transcendence of personal relevance and application; originality of insights; and excellence of writing.

In-depth, critical self-reflection. This criterion reacts to the shallow, superficial analysis so frequently characteristic of the way faculty think about teaching generally and their instructional practice specifically. We are not used to exploring deeply, critically, analytically, or reflectively how we design courses, who we are when we teach, the political ramifications of what we do in the classroom, or how we assess teaching in light of the learning that results. The exemplars illustrate a different degree of thoughtful analysis—they take readers to new levels of insight and understanding. As these exemplars illustrate, work that uses this approach well requires careful reading and reflection and often merits re-reading. Exemplary personal narratives stimulate, provoke, and otherwise effectively exercise the minds and hearts of readers.

Transcendence of personal relevance and application. It al-most goes without saying that authors learn a great deal as they pre-pare this kind of narrative. Whether the insights come before or during the writing, these pieces take their authors to a place of fuller understanding and deeper insight. But publication of work like this is only justified if the content has relevance beyond the individual. Again, look to the exemplars for illustrations: the difficulty of open-ing student minds, of helping them question what they never ques-tioned that Husted (2001) explores so eloquently is a quest familiar to many teachers. The regular disappointment of class sessions where it just doesn't happen that Walck (1997) captures so articu-lately resonates with faculty, especially those at mid-career who sometimes find it hard to believe that good teaching still makes a difference. Exemplary personal narratives contain content from which others can learn—often touching intimate aspects of the teaching experience.

Originality of insights. There is also no justification for the public dissemination of individual perspectives if those viewpoints are widely known and held. Exemplary personal narratives offer new insights, perspectives, or understanding. It is true that little new now exists under the pedagogical sun, so to require total originality is unrealistic, but exemplary personal narratives do uncover new ideas, or they get at old issues from a different perspective, or they take an alternative approach to analysis, or they put old ideas together in new ways, or they uniquely integrate old and new ideas. There are all sorts of options, but they end with the same result: readers leave this literature thinking about new ideas or rethinking old ones.

Excellence of writing. Scholarship of any kind should be clear, well organized, and readable, but the quality of the writing is excep-tional in exemplary personal narratives. It is what draws readers in and probably keeps them going, given the lack of value tradition-ally placed on personal perspectives. Much of this work gets at how people feel and experience teaching. This necessitates the language of emotion, which in professional contexts makes most academics very uncomfortable. This means the language must not be off-putting; at the same time it must accurately describe feelings and uncover implicit understandings. Words are the analytic tool of this form of scholarship. That makes the choice of each word important.

Contribution

As we move toward the end of this review and analysis of experience-based pedagogical scholarship, it is becoming increasingly clear that previously published work on teaching and learning includes kinds of knowledge not typically a part of the empirically derived knowledge bases characteristic of many disciplines. When the issue is contribution, given the uniqueness of personal narratives, it is appropriate to ask whether this approach adds to our understanding of teaching and learning and whether it has anything to teach us relevant to making pedagogical scholarship more credible and the literature more viable.

I would make the case for personal narratives this way: Even though they advance knowledge in ways mostly unlike discipline-based research, some of them do so using methods that are systematic and rigorous. Drevdahl, Stackman, Purdy, and Louie (2002) explain why these methods make a difference: "Reflective self-study research will receive little regard in the greater academic community if teacher-researchers do not meet the epistemological and methodological challenges of conducting this form of inquiry" (p. 418). These authors, writing in the *Journal of Nursing Education*, propose a viable framework that could be applied to reflective inquiry in many disciplines besides nursing. Despite promising possibilities, however, the legitimacy of applying the "findings" of personal narratives to the knowledge base for teaching is nascent at best in people's thinking.

On the other hand, some of what personal narratives teach is easier to accept. Teaching well over the long haul requires a significant amount of emotional energy, despite our reluctance to reckon with this requirement. Most of us know firsthand that it makes us tired, and we all have colleagues who have coped by copping out. Teachers need motivation and inspiration. Personal narratives can renew and revitalize tired teachers. This work fills an empty place.

Finally, good personal narratives model more thoughtful, analytical approaches to practice. This work shows faculty that there are deeper, richer ways of thinking about teaching, and the methods that authors employ to get at the details of their individual practice are methods faculty can apply to their own teaching. Most faculty find these intellectually richer ways of thinking about teaching and learning appealing. They like reading that makes them think.

Of the four approaches commonly used in experience-based pedagogical scholarship, personal narratives most challenge conventional notions of scholarship. This is work that combines personal perspectives and emotional content to explore a wide range of pedagogical topics. In addition to content not customarily thought of as scholarly, the work uses different forms and formats. Despite these uncommon characteristics, this work connects with the needs of teachers. Exemplary personal narratives contain content that stays with readers—they stimulate, provoke, and, most impressive of all, they change what happens in classrooms.

Conclusion

Published reports based on experience are the oldest form of pedagogical scholarship; they continue prominently in this literature. Most use one or some combination of four approaches: personal accounts of change, recommended-practices reports, recommended-content reports, and personal narratives.

This chapter opened with a series of questions about the wisdom-of-practice work, beginning with the question of whether this is a legitimate, valid way of knowing. The chapter attempts to make the case that it is. Most often in academe, the validity of a particular kind of inquiry is determined in the strictest sense, the correctness of generalizing from one observation to all potential observations. However, the term can be conceived of more broadly, and those larger conceptions apply when the results of experience-based analyses are being used to solve pedagogical problems and create a literature on which informed practice might rest. The classroom experience of one thoughtful pedagogue can advance our understanding of classroom dynamics—not in the specific sense of teachers everywhere trying to replicate what that one observer experienced, but in the sense of those insights motivating the observation, adaptation, and application of those specifics in another context. At another level, we already know and accept experiential understanding—it explains why teachers first and most often turn to other teachers for pedagogical information. Does this not mandate making room in the scholarship and literature of college teaching for that wisdom that grows out of practice?

5

The Lens of Objectivity: Research Scholarship

From the vantage point of many looking at this work, pedagogical research scholarship and wisdom derived from practice could not be more different. The rigorous objectivity and rational analyses of research strikingly contrast with work that rests on experience. In fact, the relatively recent emergence of practitioner research scholarship may well be a reaction against work that is subjective, tells stories about teaching, and draws wisdom from firsthand experiences.

In the beginning, pedagogical literature contained almost nothing that would be considered research today. Experience-based reports dominated the literature. But as research gained preeminence within the academy, expectations for pedagogical literature followed suit, albeit belatedly. Today the assumed superiority of research-based pedagogical scholarship stands virtually unchallenged. Part of its easy acceptance derives from how comfortably it fits with expectations for what counts as scholarly.

The review of pedagogical research presented in this chapter, another to be read and considered with an open mind, challenges that inherent superiority. As before, the review is anchored to a set of overarching questions, the most salient among them being the following:

- What is good pedagogical research? Work that discovers, that interprets, or that explores? Work that is quantitative, qualitative, or descriptive?

- Can practitioners operating out of disciplines other than education do quality pedagogical research?

- What are the implications of studying teaching and learning with perspectives and methods borrowed from the disciplines?

- What is the likelihood of research scholarship adding to the knowledge base and improving instructional practice?

Finally, the most provocative question:

- Is pedagogical research inherently better than experience-based work? Is it more scholarly, more intellectually rigorous, and more likely to affect practice and gain respect for the profession?

The number of research methods used by pedagogical scholars has increased right along with the amount of research work being completed. Most of the research methods seen in previously published work are borrowed from the disciplines—both those fields that study teaching and learning and those that study unrelated content. As introduced in Chapter Three, research scholarship uses three main approaches: quantitative investigations, modeled on traditional social science, using experimental designs as well as comparative and correlational ones; qualitative studies, which also use a variety of borrowed approaches, such as introspective analysis, participant observation, and ethnography; and descriptive research, which employs survey and interview techniques to establish what is. Descriptive research sometimes analyzes the collected data quantitatively and other times relies on qualitative assessments.

In this case, as in Chapter Three, these are the main approaches seen in previously published work, but not all pedagogical research scholarship strictly conforms to these categories. Many hybrid examples exist in which faculty study a new treatment by using quantitative measures of learning (like the familiar Watson Glaser test of critical thinking, for example) at the same time that they assess its impact using descriptive techniques. Some of these studies even combine research and experienced-based scholarship, although this happens rarely. Some research scholarship doesn't fit into any of these categories. These unique approaches are described in Chapter Six. As also was the case previously, there is some overlap among these three categories as well as with the four experience-based approaches described in Chapter Four. The caution stated there bears repeating: none of this work was ever completed with a typology of approaches in mind.

Each of these three main approaches will be discussed separately and analyzed in the same way the four experience-based approaches were in Chapter Four. The categories of analysis, highlighted here, were introduced and explained fully in Chapter Three. Consideration begins with a detailed description, followed by a critical assessment in which quality issues are identified and explored. Then a listing of exemplars is included, followed by a discussion of those standards that distinguish exemplary work. Finally, an assessment of its contribution to our understanding of teaching and learning is offered.

Quantitative Investigations

Description

Using the tools of social science research, this practitioner pedagogical scholarship "studies" or investigates research questions. The work is experimental when it uses designs that involve treatment and control groups and some manipulation of variables across them. Among other empirical approaches seen in the work are comparative studies that examine the differences between groups on a variable of interest and correlational studies where associations between two or more variables are explored. This review focuses mainly on experimental research. Practitioners use comparative and correlational approaches more often as part of survey research, which is considered in the section on descriptive research.

This work is further differentiated from educational research by the relationship of the researcher to the study. In most cases faculty are "studying" some aspect of instructional practice relevant to them. Often the subjects are their students and the treatments involve teaching strategies, classroom policies, or approaches to assessment they use. Because interest in these topics grows out of experience, investigators frequently ask very practical and applied research questions. For example, consider the question studied in the Balch (1998) exemplar: Does the use of practice exams make a difference in final exam scores? Or the question Kunkel (2004) asks: Is the inclusion of presentation software in lecture courses affected by course type (descriptive survey course versus theory, application course)?

Because the questions are specific and the data very context-dependent, findings are typically not broadly applicable. The same could be said of many educational research findings, but in that case the research questions are usually part of a collection of related and integrated studies, so that individual results become part of a stream of convergent studies. When research questions derive from individual practice, they tend to produce atheoretical, isolated studies. The topics they explore may be related or connected to work occurring elsewhere, but here and in other types of pedagogical research scholarship those connections are not often made. In sum, then, quantitative investigations use experimental methods to explore pragmatic questions derived from the investigator's practice.

Critical Assessment

Quantitative investigations, as well as the two other kinds of research scholarship, are more often celebrated than critiqued. Journal editors and teaching advocates laud their increased presence in the literature and see research scholarship as the key to a brighter future for pedagogical scholarship. But looks can be deceiving, and in the case of many quantitative investigations, I believe they are. There are as many widespread and serious problems with this kind of pedagogical scholarship as there are with the experience-based approaches discussed in Chapter Four, and these problems look less fixable to me.

Let's begin with how quantitative research methods are used by practitioner pedagogical scholars. Because many faculty doing pedagogical research are not trained social scientists, these methods are unfamiliar, which opens the door to a less-than-impressive use of them. Sometimes the problem starts with a poorly designed study that ends up being a quasi-research investigation rather than a bona fide experimental inquiry. Sometimes the methods of analyses chosen are not appropriate given the experimental design. In still other cases it is the level of the research that is troublesome. The study is elementary quantitative research, nowhere close to the robust, cutting-edge analysis being done in the fields that developed these methods. Taken together, these problems have produced a lot of "studies" of questionable quality.

It is true that poor research design and execution are not inherent defects. Faculty could be trained in the use of these methodologies. But improvement ends up being a question of feasibility. Faculty teach, they advise, they perform service, and they do research in their fields. One analysis of quantitative research on teaching methods (Becker, 2004) proposes an eleven-point set of criteria to assess the work. Most of the practitioner research Becker reviews falls short of the criteria and illustrates omission or misuse of various aspects of good quantitative methodology. Training faculty in their use and expecting a sophisticated application just does not seem like a doable proposition, given the many and varied job tasks already expected of them.

The first problem, then, with quantitative investigations pertains to how well quantitative methodologies are used and the feasibility of fixing that flaw. The second problem involves the tendency to impose the paradigms, protocols, and conventions of the discipline onto these studies of educational topics. Said more bluntly, quantitative research on teaching and learning in any given discipline looks a lot like the research of that field, and this is true whether the designs are experimental or descriptive. I first noticed this in the early 1990s when I was preparing an article (Weimer, 1993) on these disciplinary publications. The pedagogical periodical mirrored the research journals of the discipline—so that if research is preceded by an abstract, for example, pedagogical analyses are so preceded. The influence of disciplinary conventions can be seen to varying degrees in all aspects of pedagogical scholarship, but they are most evident in quantitative investigations. How research questions are framed, how data are analyzed, results reported, and what conclusions are drawn often mirror how that discipline studies phenomena.

This imposition of disciplinary research methods is not always bad. Sometimes they fit the nature of teaching and learning phenomena, as we shall see in our analysis of qualitative pedagogical research. But other times they don't fit. Even more troubling is an underlying and erroneous assumption on which their approbation rests: teaching and learning as phenomena to be studied function the same way as whatever it is the discipline studies. Teachers don't act as economic factors do; students don't behave with the predictability of solutions mixed in a lab. Teaching and learning need to be studied with methods and approaches that take into account their fundamental features, which may or may not be shared with what the discipline studies.

Is this an inherent defect or do we have a fixable flaw? It's an inherent defect if we continue to assume that teaching and learning can be studied with whatever methodologies are known and convenient. It's a fixable flaw if we begin to specify much more clearly how these teaching and learning phenomena should be studied empirically. Before that can happen, however, we must see the imposition of methods as potentially problematic; at this point I see no recognition of that fact.

We are still not done with the problems. Whether it be the methods of quantitative research or those of a discipline, many of the methods used in previously published quantitative investigations were not designed to study education in action. Classrooms are dynamic milieus with far too many variables to control for effectively. Even if it's the same course taught by the same teacher, every class of students is different, and the content cannot be replicated exactly unless it's delivered by a machine. Then there's a whole range of feasibility questions, such as being able to assign students randomly to different treatments, controlling for class size, and a host of other background variables with the potential to bias the sample.

Even the quantitative methods of educational research are seldom used in actual classrooms. Treatments are studied in controlled environments and for brief periods of time. What this means is that, even with training and clearer guidance as to appropriate methods, practitioner quantitative investigations would still produce questionable results. Comparing quantitative research done in psychology with experimentation that faculty can do in the classroom, Nummendal, Bension, and Chew (2002) write, "Investigations conducted in the classroom environment seldom permit the methodological rigor necessary to actually rule out alternative explanations and to determine what works" (p. 169). Here we have a defect that is definitely inherent. Unless faculty want to start studying the research questions of the education field (which tend to be disembodied from practice, but that's a different problem), there is no way to fix this fundamental feature of many of the methods and approaches being used by practitioners in their quantitative investigations.

The problems with quantitative investigations, especially those using experimental designs, are major and made even more serious by the uncritical acceptance given this work. Relevant quality questions include the following: How many of these quantitative investigations have produced reliable findings? How many of the reported results are consistent with other, well-established findings? Should what practitioners have discovered be applied by others? Despite these problems, however, quality empirical work has been done and the amount of it has increased during the last decade. This is a viable, albeit difficult, approach to pedagogical scholarship.

Exemplars

Bacon, D. R., Stewart, K. A., and Stewart-Belle, S. "Exploring Predictors of Student Team Project Performance." *Journal of Marketing Education*, 1998, *20* (1), 63–71.

> The study's major findings are as follows: "that team performance is predicted by the average of the individual abilities on the team, that a slight level of nationality diversity is helpful to a team, that gender diversity is unrelated to team performance, and that larger teams are not more productive" (p. 69).

Balch, W. R. "Practice Versus Review Exams and Final Exam Performance." *Teaching of Psychology*, 1998, *25* (3), 181–184.

> Undertaken in an introductory psychology course to ascertain whether taking a practice exam or seeing a scored test more positively affected scores on the final exam. Results show that students who took and then scored a practice exam received significantly higher scores on the final.

Kennedy, E. J., Lawton, L., and Plumlee, E. L. "Blissful Ignorance: The Problem of Unrecognized Incompetence and Academic Performance." *Journal of Marketing Education*, 2002, *24* (3), 245–252.

> Looks at the ability of students to estimate grades on exams immediately after taking those exams. Results: Poorer students significantly overestimated their performance, although they improve over time; better students underestimated theirs.

Mottet, T. P., Beebe, S. A., Raffeld, P. C., and Medlock, A. L. "The Effects of Student Verbal and Nonverbal Responsiveness of Teacher

Self-Efficacy and Job Satisfaction." *Communication Education*, 2004, 53 (2), 150–163.

> Considers how students influence teachers and their teaching. Found that 26 percent of the variance in teacher self-efficacy (perception of ability to affect student performance) and 53 percent of the variance in job satisfaction were attributable to student verbal and nonverbal responsiveness.

Standards

Because so much of this work models social science quantitative research, some standards used to evaluate quantitative investigations in the social sciences can be used to judge this form of pedagogical scholarship (see the list in Becker, 2004, for example, or countless other more general sources, such as Black, 1993). However, some additional standards are also relevant. The applied, pragmatic nature of pedagogical inquiries differentiates them from disciplinary social science and educational research. This means some standards can be borrowed, but others could be extrapolated from exemplary pedagogical quantitative inquiries. Consider the following two existing standards and two possibilities extrapolated from the exemplars.

A good research design. This standard pertains to how the inquiry is structured: the size and number of the groups, how they are formed, the nature of the treatment, which variables are identified as relevant, and how they are controlled or manipulated. In this case, the principles of experimental design for social science and educational research do apply and can be borrowed.

Appropriate use of research methods. Use of methods overlaps with and is tied to research design, but is separated out to call attention to the fact that methods must fit both the kind of research question being asked and the overall study design. In the quantitative domain, this standard very often pertains to the use of statistical analysis: Are the right tests being run? Are enough tests being run? Is the analysis of results valid given the data sets produced? The methods used in this research may come from social science research generally or educational research specifically, or they may be imported from the discipline, provided they fit what is being studied and how the results need to be analyzed.

It should go without saying that study designs and research methods need to be assessed by people expert in their use. What separates good quantitative investigations from mediocre ones involves a variety of technical issues that it is neither necessary nor appropriate to digress to explain, given the purpose of this book. Countless reputable social science sources on quantitative research exist. The relevant point here is a different one: if quantitative investigations are being completed in fields where quantitative social science methods are not used, then the question of who is qualified to assess the work must be addressed—not just for quantitative inquiries but for qualitative studies and descriptive research as well. Just because it looks and sounds like research doesn't make it good research.

Viable research question. This criterion can be stated simply: Is the study of interest and relevance to others? This standard reflects the applied nature of pedagogical scholarship. In contrast, when research is discovery-based, relevance to practice is not a central issue. Research questions grow out of new findings; results spawn the next set of questions. But when discipline-based faculty do pedagogical research, the primary motivation is to improve practice, not to push back the frontiers of knowledge. Quantitative inquiries in pedagogical scholarship distinguish themselves when the questions asked have relevance to others. All faculty who use groups struggle with how to form them, and the Bacon, Stewart, and Stewart-Belle (1998) exemplar tests several relevant criteria. Many faculty have observed and been perplexed by the apparent inability of weaker students to gauge how well they're doing. The Kennedy, Lawton, and Plumlee (2002) exemplar begins to specify the terms and conditions under which that characteristic operates. All faculty who use groups worry that their use decreases the amount of content knowledge students acquire in the course. Lewis and Lewis (2005) traded one lecture session per week for a peer-led, guided inquiry approach in which students worked through course material in group activities. Through their experimental design, the authors were able to show that in this case less exposure to lecture did not result in less learning.

Exemplary quantitative inquiries are further distinguished if there is at least some degree of connection to and with previous work on the topic. With pedagogical quantitative investigations, previous studies are not the source of research questions, but a literature review (at the very least within the discipline) should identify other related queries and connect those findings to the research question(s) of this inquiry. The exemplars provide excellent illustrations of work that makes these connections in ways that prevent them from standing as isolated inquiries.

Accurately address issues of implication and application. This standard pertains to the generalizability of the results. Are there implications for others in these findings? Does the design of the study and analysis of the data justify these larger conclusions? Preference goes to work that is generalizable and to work in which the researchers do more than report results. They should accurately spell out implications. The Bacon, Stewart, and Stewart-Belle (1998) exemplar is particularly noteworthy in its recognition of this connection to and with the practice of others.

Contribution

What, then, have these quantitative investigations contributed to our knowledge of teaching and learning? What lessons do they suggest for the future? Robust quantitative investigations do add to what we know about teaching and learning. They produce valid results with implications for others, although the generalizability of isolated studies is certainly less than when collections of results are integrated and related. In addition, the amount of quality quantitative work done so far is small, limited in part by the feasibility of discipline-based faculty learning to use these methods well. Finally, the methods themselves are limited by their applicability to dynamic classroom venues, where so many variables are beyond the researcher's ability to control.

In spite of these caveats, this work does have lessons to teach about the role and power of applied research. Faculty researchers who derive questions from practice ask meaningful and relevant questions. They ask what they want to know. Because so many aspects of teaching and learning transcend content, others find the questions relevant and meaningful.

Two benefits accrue from asking these very pragmatic questions. First, if a faculty member conducts a systematic inquiry that produces answers about a particular aspect of his or her instruction, chances are that aspect of instruction will be modified as a result of the findings. For example Sappington, Kinsey, and Munsayac (2002) found out that one way of using unannounced quizzes on the reading was more effective than another. Do you think they subsequently used quizzes in the less effective way? When faculty ask and answer a question that relates to how they teach or how their students learn, there is almost a moral obligation to implement the results.

The second benefit comes to others who use quizzes. Because their approach likely involves different reading material, in a course with a different design, with other students, and a teacher with a different style, the Sappington, Kinsey, and Munsayac results may not apply. But the way those researchers framed the question probably does, as well as the method they used to ascertain the results. Others can replicate what they did. In this case, it is not the products of research that improve the practice of others, but the process. True, other kinds of research and some experience-based work provide models interested faculty can replicate, but the very applied nature of quantitative research questions makes them especially amenable to replication.

Even though pedagogical research scholarship has received enthusiastic endorsement, this analysis of quantitative investigations has revealed a number of quality issues. Despite these impediments, some quality work has been done, making this a legitimate approach to pedagogical scholarship. However, the potential contribution of this approach is limited by quality issues as of yet mostly unrecognized.

Qualitative Studies

Description

Like quantitative inquiries, pedagogical scholarship that uses a qualitative studies approach borrows methods developed and used in disciplinary research. Although discipline-based qualitative research is not a new phenomenon, use and acceptance have both grown in recent years. For many in higher education, this is still a new and unfamiliar kind of research. We'd best begin with a definition: "Qualitative research is multi-method in focus, involving an interpretive, naturalistic approach to its subject matter. This means that qualitative researchers study things in their natural settings, attempting to make sense of or interpret phenomena in terms of the meanings people bring to them" (Denzin and Lincoln, 1994, p. 2). A less formal depiction might aid understanding. Denzin and Lincoln (2000, p. 1,063) colloquially characterize the objective of qualitative research as "to study human experience from the ground up."

As Denzin and Lincoln (2000) point out in the second edition of their large handbook on qualitative research, definitions have evolved and continue to change as the field grows. Some of the distinctive characteristics emerge when the methods of qualitative research are juxtaposed to those of quantitative research. "Qualitative researchers use ethnographic prose, historical narratives, first-person accounts, still photographs, fictionalized 'facts,' and biographical and autobiographical material, among others. Quantitative researchers use mathematical models, statistical tables, and graphs, and usually write about their research in impersonal, third-person prose" (Denzin and Lincoln, 2000, p. 10). The nature of qualitative "findings" further differentiate these from quantitative analyses. These are not studies whose data support obvious conclusions. "Qualitative interpretations are constructed" (Denzin and Lincoln, 1994, p. 15).

In pedagogical scholarship, this is the smallest and most recently emerged category of the seven identified for review in this analysis. As a body of work it closely mirrors qualitative research being done within the disciplines. This means a variety of approaches and methods are being used to study a range of pedagogical topics. Obviously, qualitative methods are regularly used by educational researchers, but our focus here continues as it has been, on scholarship produced by faculty practitioners who are studying aspects of teaching and learning relevant to them, in this case using qualitative approaches. It does appear that many doing this work have been trained in the use of these methods. Most pedagogical qualitative studies are appearing in the pedagogical periodicals of fields associated with these approaches.

In this typology, qualitative studies are at times difficult to differentiate from some kinds of experience-based personal narratives. In fact, there is significant blurring and overlap between these two approaches. We characterized personal narratives as reflective, internally sourced, and frequently connected with emotional aspects of teaching. When authors make deeply introspective analyses of their teaching, as appears in the Husted (2001) and Walck (1997) personal narrative exemplars, what they are doing looks very much like qualitative research. What distinguishes these kind of reflective, analytical personal narratives from qualitative research is imposition of a qualitative research methodology. Those doing qualitative research "study" their teaching or students' learning by systematically using some methodology (such as the conversation analysis in the Haller, Gallagher, Weldon, and Felder (2000) exemplar, narrative and text analysis in the Stenberg and Lee (2002) exemplar, and hermeneutics in the Young and Diekelmann (2002) exemplar to interpret and understand a particular set of events.

In reality, however, the distinctions are still blurred, because before the recent advent of qualitative research some pedagogical scholars did look at their teaching in systematic, methodical ways. They used structures and took approaches that resemble some of the qualitative research methods, but these were not used intentionally or they were used very casually, and they were never acknowledged as research methods. This could still be said of some personal narratives being published today.

So, when the scholarship is introspective, when it looks deeply at some aspect of individual practice, there is fuzziness and morphing between these two categories. Given my insistence that this seven-approach typology not be used to file and label every piece of work, I don't think the overlap should unnecessarily distress us. Many of the approaches used in the personal narratives category are not qualitative research, and most qualitative research done on teaching and learning topics fits uncomfortably in the personal narratives category. Nonetheless, some work hangs partly between these two categories, making the boundaries between them difficult to differentiate.

Critical Assessment

Like other kinds of scholarship, qualitative pedagogical studies done by practitioners have not been reviewed and assessed as a body of work. Because this form of scholarship has only recently gained acceptance in social science and humanities disciplines, its acceptance as pedagogical scholarship is equally nascent. Said more bluntly, just because objections have not been raised does not mean that everyone views qualitative studies as credible scholarship. Those who resist these approaches characterize them as "unscientific," "exploratory," and "subjective." Those doing the scholarship have been called "journalists" or "soft scientists" (Denzin and Lincoln, 2000, p. 7). However, arguing the legitimacy of qualitative methods would sidetrack us from this book's focus. For the most part, in the social science and humanities disciplines this work is now accepted. Many are doing it, and as the body of work grows, so do the conventions and protocols regarding the use of its various approaches and methods.

Interestingly, many of the methodological concerns that emerged in the critique of quantitative methods do not apply here. Overall, the quality of qualitative studies that have been published in pedagogical periodicals is excellent. Two facts may be credited for this situation. First, as intimated, most of this work is being published in fields in which faculty are familiar with these methods; in the two exemplars that hail from other fields, author teams had access to qualitative researcher expertise. Moreover, unlike many quantitative approaches and methods, these ways of analyzing pedagogical phenomena fit. They are designed for naturalistic settings like the classroom. It is expected that researchers will be involved with the objects of study.

In sum, unlike all the other kinds of scholarship explored so far, there are no real quality issues with this small category of scholarship in the pedagogical literature. The problems are more attitudinal than executional—although that may change as faculty in other fields opt for these approaches.

Exemplars

Haller, C. R., Gallagher, V. J., Weldon, T. L., and Felder, R. M. "Dynamics of Peer Education in Cooperative Learning Workgroups." *Journal of Engineering Education*, 2000, 89 (3), 285–293.

> Uses conversation analysis to understand how students in a chemical engineering course taught and learned from each other in a cooperative learning group. Group members engaged in two types of teaching-learning interactions: they assumed the distinct roles of teacher and students, or they worked together with no clear role differentiation. A strong implications section extrapolates guidelines for instructors.

Stenberg, S., and Lee, A. "Developing Pedagogies: Learning the Teaching of English." *College English,* 2002, *64* (3), 326–347.

> Challenges how teachers are trained and how teaching skills develop and proposes pedagogical inquiry as an alternative approach. Authors demonstrate by analyzing their interactions— a director of writing (author Lee) and a first-time teacher (author Stenberg)—over events such as syllabus construction and classroom observations.

Young, P., and Diekelmann, N. "Learning to Lecture: Exploring the Skills, Strategies, and Practices of New Teachers in Nursing Education." *Journal of Nursing Education,* 2002, *41* (9), 205–212.

> Seventeen new teachers tell a story about an early teaching experience. Transcripts of audio tapes are analyzed hermeneutically to identify the relational themes and patterns interpreted from the new teachers' experiences.

Standards

Because qualitative studies in pedagogical scholarship so closely mirror qualitative research done in the disciplines, as with quantitative inquiries, there is no reason not to apply established standards used to assess qualitative research. These standards depend on the approach taken (such as case study, personal experience, introspection, interview, or artifacts), the method of analysis used (such as semiotics, narrative, ethnomethodology, phenomenology, hermeneutics, cultural studies, or participant observation), and the triangulation of approach and method used to interpret the data.

Many sources (like Denzin and Lincoln, 1994, 2000) further delineate the technical details associated with standards for qualitative research. To these standards borrowed from qualitative research generally, we might once again add that within the pedagogical domain these inquiries should be of value to other practitioners. They should explore aspects of teaching and learning relevant to others and produce findings of interest and with implications to others who teach.

Contribution

These new ways of exploring teaching and learning do open new areas of understanding. Because they focus on naturalistic settings, they confirm the value of knowledge embedded in practice and provide powerful mechanisms for making implicit understandings explicit. They challenge traditional definitions of knowledge and allow views of teaching that uncover issues of power and politics.

However, all that stands in the way of faculty developing expertise in quantitative methods pertains to the acquisition of know-how with qualitative methods. Moreover, as the exemplars illustrate, these methodologies are labor-intensive. The analyses are deep and detailed. Once again, it just doesn't seem likely that faculty from other fields will reach a point where they can use these approaches with sophistication. If they are used incorrectly or poorly, that compromises their effectiveness as research tools, credible scholarship, and viable literature.

These studies also provide models of how practice can be analyzed. Even though the interpretation of study details may not apply directly, the value derives from how these methods stimulate others to think, analyze, consider, and examine more closely aspects of their own instruction as well as those of colleagues within their departments and across their discipline. A qualitative exploration of the relationship between the amount of content and the development of thinking skills in nursing curricula (Ironside, 2004) illustrates just how provocative this work can be.

Here too, there is a caveat that may well limit the future contribution of this approach. As was the case with quantitative inquiries, this research does not make for easy or interesting reading. In general, the analyses are overly long, with aspects under study explored in excruciating detail. The idea that group conversation can be examined to discover how students teach and learn from each other (Haller, Gallagher, Weldon, and Felder (2000) exemplar) is fascinating, but making one's way through the details of that analysis would cure insomnia of even the most seriously wakeful. For faculty who don't regularly read pedagogical literature, if you wished to recommend something that might motivate more and further reading, I don't think it would be a qualitative study.

In sum of this approach: qualitative pedagogical scholarship completed by practitioners is currently a small and emerging category of work. So far, it mostly appears in fields or involves researchers familiar with these methodologies. Qualitative research has won acceptance as legitimate scholarship grudgingly—which certainly implicates its acceptance within the pedagogical domain. Its greatest potential lies in the models of self-reflection it provides and the power of its research methodologies to uncover details and aspects of instruction long assumed and otherwise taken for granted.

Descriptive Research

Description

As the name implies, this is research that describes. It seeks to establish what is. Descriptive studies have been used for that purpose with a wide range of instructional topics. This is the largest and most well developed kind of practitioner pedagogical research. The exemplars illustrate the range of instructional topics and approaches used in these previously published descriptive analyses: Allen, Fuller, and Luckett (1998) surveyed students for their views of a problem, cheating; Auster and MacRone (1994) queried students about an instructional practice, participation; Bacon, Stewart, and Silver (1999) solicited from students descriptions of best and worst experiences; Deeter-Schmelz, Kennedy, and Ramsey (2002) generated a model of student team effectiveness and surveyed students to test the model; Miller and Gentile (1998) used faculty and student responses to create a comparative analysis of course goals; and Wagenaar (2002) surveyed faculty within a field to ascertain the impact of a policy, learning outcomes assessment. Throughout this discussion other excellent descriptive studies will be highlighted.

The research tool used most regularly to establish these pedagogical baselines is the survey. Within the pedagogical realm, the most convenient samples available to descriptive researchers are faculty and students. In some cases, both are surveyed and the results compared. An example of that occurs in the Miller and Gentile (1998) exemplar, in which faculty teaching introductory psychology courses were surveyed regarding the content and goals of the course and then students were surveyed about the extent to which their introductory psych courses realized those faculty-identified goals. For another example, see Sojka, Gupta, and Deeter-Schmelz (2002), who compared student and faculty perceptions of student evaluations of teaching and found significant perceptual differences.

Faculty and student samples are assembled from various groupings. Some samples are local—the researcher's students or those at his or her institution and the researcher's colleagues, also at the local institution. Sometimes student samples are collected from different institutions or a cohort of them is systematically assembled from a set of different types of institutions. In other cases, the cohorts are grouped by or across disciplines, majors at a particular institution or several of them, and faculty within a department or across the whole field. In a few cases, samples of students from across higher education are surveyed, as are cohorts of faculty from different institutions and disciplines.

It is not always students and faculty who are surveyed in this work. Griggs, Jackson, Marek, and Christopher (1998) surveyed introductory psychology course texts and then used a content analysis approach to document and describe the extent to which those texts covered a variety of critical thinking topics.

Different kinds of survey instruments are used as well. Sometimes the descriptive data are acquired in face-to-face interviews. In the Auster and MacRone (1994) exemplar, students in a research

methods class interviewed other students, asking them a set of prepared questions. McCabe and Powell (2004) used interview questions to explore faculty perceptions of grade inflation. Interestingly,
they found that faculty thought grade inflation happened in other
classes but not their own. Most frequently, the instruments use
closed questions, although data from some open-ended queries appears in the literature (Buttner, 2004, for example), and some descriptive instruments combine both, as did the instrument in Buttner,
although that study analyzed open-ended query responses only.

Data generated from closed-question surveys are analyzed using
a variety of statistical methods, including some tests used to analyze
data generated by quantitative investigations. Similarly, responses
to open-ended queries have been analyzed with qualitative research
methods, which blurs distinctions between all three kinds of research approaches and makes this typology of value only as a general description of how practitioners have studied teaching and
learning. Many individual studies combine the approaches or exist
in the borders between them.

Critical Assessment

Overall, few serious problems exist within this category of pedagogical scholarship, and it bears asking why pedagogical researchers
have used this approach more successfully. I would attribute its quality to four factors. First, these methods of inquiry fit the phenomena being studied. Students and teachers have beliefs, attitudes, and
experiences that can be collected and assessed with descriptive measures. Second, a sufficient number of subjects are conveniently available; pedagogical researchers have students, colleagues, and easy
access to more of both. Third, the methods of analysis used in
descriptive research are well established, and packaged statistical
programs make for comparatively easy data analysis. Finally, I would
credit the quality to the classroom assessment work of Angelo and
Cross (1993), who successfully and appropriately persuaded many
faculty that they need to collect and analyze data related to the

impact of their instructional policies and practices if they wish to understand how their students are learning. Collecting survey data is the easiest way to obtain this feedback, and publishing findings resulting from these inquiries is a next logical step.

Even though overall the quality of descriptive research is better than that of experimental work, not all the studies are excellent and without error. Examples of published work in which there are problems with instrument design, sample construction, and data analysis do exist. When these errors are egregious, they do so seriously compromise the outcomes as to render results bogus. But even in those cases, the flaws could be fixed and the study rerun; the instrument's reliability could be strengthened, the sample size could be increased and made more representative, or more appropriate statistical tests could be run. The barriers here are neither inherent nor insurmountable.

However, the simplistic level of research is something of a problem. What practitioners are doing well here, for the most part, qualifies as basic descriptive analysis. Some studies that use sophisticated research designs or complex statistical analyses have been published, but their scarcity brings us back to the issue of faculty trained to do disciplinary research and the difficulty of developing a second area of research expertise.

Exemplars

Unlike with previous research categories, where I had to search for exemplars, my folder of exemplary descriptive research overflows. Other excellent examples are noted and described throughout the chapter.

Allen, J., Fuller, D., and Luckett, M. "Academic Integrity: Behaviors, Rates, and Attitudes of Business Students Toward Cheating." *Journal of Marketing Education*, 1998, 20 (1), 41–52.

> Uses a sample of 1,063 students enrolled in an undergraduate marketing course to explore a variety of cheating issues,

including a comparison of self-reports of cheating behavior with simulated behavior described via scenarios. That comparison suggests that self-reports of cheating may underestimate actual rates of cheating. Exemplary for creative design and readable discussion section.

Auster, C. J., and MacRone, M. "The Classroom as a Negotiated Social Setting: An Empirical Study of the Effects of Faculty Members' Behavior on Students' Participation." *Teaching Sociology*, October 1994, *22*, 289–300.

Asks a random sample of 132 students to think of a class in which they participated most and one in which they participated least. For each class, students assess the frequency of certain faculty behaviors. Based on the findings, researchers recommend that to increase student participation, faculty should call on students by name when they volunteer, provide positive reinforcement and encouragement, ask analytical as opposed to factual questions, and solicit student opinions even when they don't volunteer.

Bacon, D. R., Stewart, K. A., and Silver, W. S. "Lessons from the Best and Worst Student Team Experiences: How a Teacher Can Make a Difference." *Journal of Management Education*, 1999, *23* (5), 467–488.

Sets out "to provide teachers with actionable, empirically supported recommendations for effectively creating and administering student teams" (p. 468).

Uses the responses of 116 MBA students about their best and worst experiences in student teams to test seven hypotheses identifying teacher-controlled factors that contribute to effective group experiences. Results confirm some of the hypotheses but not all of them. Example: completion of basic management courses was not a factor in best team experiences.

Deeter-Schmelz, D. R., Kennedy, K. N., and Ramsey, R. P. "Enriching Our Understanding of Team Effectiveness." *Journal of Marketing Education*, 2002, *24* (2), 114–124.

> Uses the literature to develop an input-process-output model of team effectiveness, which is tested using survey data from eighty-five teams from marketing classes. Results document the positive and direct role of cohesion as an input variable. Exemplary in its inclusion of a variety of exercises that can be used to develop cohesion within student teams.

Miller, B., and Gentile, B. F. "Introductory Course Content and Goals." *Teaching of Psychology*, 1998, *25* (2), 89–96.

> Conducted a nationwide survey of faculty to establish content included in the introductory psychology course and to identify goals instructors most want to accomplish in those courses, then surveyed students at four different colleges about goals and experiences in their introductory psychology courses. Results document significant differences between faculty and student expectations for the course.

Wagenaar, T. C. "Outcomes Assessment in Sociology: Prevalence and Impact." *Teaching Sociology*, October 2002, *30*, 403–413.

> Surveyed several hundred faculty sociologists regarding the use and impact of different assessment strategies. Results: "As for degree of impact . . . only about one-fifth of the respondents indicated a substantial impact from outcomes assessment on the curriculum and on teaching" (p. 410).

Standards

As with the other categories of research pedagogical scholarship, it makes sense to combine already established standards with additional standards derived from the exemplars.

Good descriptive research design and analysis. Because these pedagogical studies borrow methods from well-established descriptive research protocols, they recognize that there is no need to re-invent the wheel. The standards of descriptive research that allow identification of excellent work prescribe creation of appropriate samples (regarding size and representativeness), construction of survey instruments (regarding validity and inter-rater reliability), and statistical analysis of results (regarding appropriate tests and justifiable conclusions). Again, the technical details involved are well addressed by literature on descriptive methods; we need not digress to repeat. However, the point made earlier about expertise being essential to evaluate this work bears repeating. Descriptive studies are not good automatically or inherently.

Tied to relevant theory and connected to related research. All of these exemplars are well connected to the literature—that is, to previously published and relevant pedagogical research, to relevant theory and research within the discipline, or to work in education and other disciplines. The Deeter-Schmelz, Kennedy, and Ramsey (2002) exemplar illustrates how, in addition to justifying the research queries, literature can be used to generate models, and descriptive studies can then be undertaken to test whether those models accurately capture the interaction between specified variables.

Obviously, this standard can be met to varying degrees, and we need to hold realistic expectations for the literature reviews of practitioners. Descriptive studies most often fail to meet this standard when they are isolated, context-specific inquiries, as when a faculty member is curious about an instructional policy or practice and constructs a survey to ascertain its impact. These kinds of inquiries produce data of interest to the instructor but their validity, even in that isolated context, and certainly their applicability to others are greatly enhanced when the work draws on relevant theory and previously published studies.

Addresses important topics. As we have noted elsewhere, not all instructional topics are equally important, especially when it comes to public dissemination of the work. When the work addresses important topics, it focuses on aspects of instruction that transcend content and context. In some cases, this value to others is immediately apparent. What instructor would not benefit from knowing specific, concrete behaviors with documented positive impacts on student participation (Auster and MacRone, 1994, exemplar), or what to do about those variables shown to affect group performance (Bacon, Stewart, and Silver, 1999, exemplar)?

Propose appropriate implications. Applicability is an inherent strength of descriptive pedagogical research. These data have implications for others, and the exemplars illustrate how those can be spelled out clearly for others. Based on their findings about best and worst team experiences, Bacon, Stewart, and Silver (1999) make six recommendations that pertain to aspects of group experience that faculty can control. Allen, Fuller, and Luckett (1998) conclude their study of academic integrity among business students with a detailed, specific, and very helpful discussion section that prominently features implications. Deeter-Schmelz, Kennedy, and Ramsey (2002) support their finding that cohesion and teamwork affect group performance by including five exercises that can be used in student groups to develop cohesion and build teamwork.

Several of the exemplars explore professional issues relevant to many academic fields, even though the study itself collected data that pertain to particular disciplines—for example, psychology and sociology in the case of the Miller and Gentile (1998) exemplar as well as the Wagenaar (2002) one. The findings from these two descriptive studies are very valuable to those fields. But there is a second, equally relevant area of validity. These discipline-based exemplars identify important areas of inquiry and demonstrate viable approaches to research. In this case, it is not the findings per se that have relevance, but how they motivate reflective analysis in other fields and how they model easily replicable methods.

Contribution

What does descriptive research contribute to the practitioner knowledge base? Does it add to what we know about teaching and learning? It does indeed, and the case is best made with examples—

more, beyond the exemplars. Equally impressive is the potential this work has to improve practice. More examples illustrate both the depth of this scholarship and its power to motivate change.

The improvement potential of descriptive work exists on several different levels—the individual faculty member doing the research, other individual faculty who learn about the findings, whole disciplines that may be challenged to consider standards, as well as the entire profession of college teaching. For individual faculty, descriptive work accomplishes change for the same reason quantitative and qualitative work do: faculty ask and answer questions directly relevant to their practice. Why would they not act on what they discovered?

Improvement for other faculty happens in several different ways. The first is the most straightforward; two examples will illustrate. Houston and Bettencourt (1999) conducted a descriptive study of what professors and students perceived as being fair. Their research generated the data needed to construct an impressive list of specific, doable actions that create an environment of fairness in a course. For any instructor who cares about treating students fairly and with integrity, the list offers an easy way to improve individual practice. Ackerman and Gross (2005) surveyed students about procrastination. From their results they were able to identify characteristics of assignments and other learning tasks that encourage students to procrastinate. What instructor would not be interested in knowing how to design learning activities so as to prevent procrastination?

Second, descriptive work can improve practice because it gives faculty benchmarks against which individual practice can be measured and assessed. Consider extra credit, for example. Some faculty give it; more are opposed to it; students frequently ask for it. Most faculty have opinions on the practice, but not much more than opinions. Two straightforward descriptive studies (Norcross, Dooley, and Stevenson, 1993; Norcross, Horrocks, and Stevenson, 1989) add a wealth of detail to what most faculty know about the use of and attitudes toward extra credit. Between 12 and 22 percent of courses in these two samples offered students extra credit options. For faculty, the most frequently cited argument against the practice was that it encouraged lax and irresponsible student attitudes; those who offered extra credit did so most often because it gave students the chance to explore a topic in more depth; and students most valued extra credit because it gave them a second chance. When presented with six situations in which giving extra credit might be a possibility, between 60 and 70 percent of the faculty in the 1993 study rejected extra credit in all situations. Data support the conclusion that the instructor's general attitude toward extra credit, rather than the circumstances of the individual case, largely determined whether it was provided.

These findings do not establish whether instructors should or should not give extra credit, but descriptive research like this gives faculty some perspective on how what they believe and do in the classroom compares with what others believe and do. They make fewer instructional decisions in a vacuum. Collectively, this kind of research can build the knowledge base for many aspects of instructional practice; that foundation makes it easier to develop the standards needed to bring college teaching to a professional level.

Third, some descriptive work improves the practice of other faculty members, not because the findings are directly applicable, but because the questions asked are powerful and relevant. What VanderStoep, Fagerlin, and Feenstra (2000) discovered that students remembered about the course of the first author has limited applicability to other courses, but I can personally attest to the power of the question they asked students:

> As part of my research on college students' memory for course concepts, and also as a way to improve my teaching . . . I am interested in what students remember from this course. Let your mind wander freely as you do this assignment. Think back on the semester as a whole, and report to me the first ten things that come to your mind as you answer the question: *What do you remember from*

this course? Don't "edit" your thinking as you report your memories; don't worry about your memories being "correct." Simply review the course in your mind and report to me what you remember. (pp. 89–90)

As students in this study did, my students do not most often identify aspects of course content; they listed activities in which they participated with their classmates. For my money, that's telling feedback with large implications for my practice.

Finally, individual practice can be improved because the study challenges assumptions. Mooney (1998) studied the impact of guest speakers on student decisions to enroll in another sociology course, on interest in the major, and on perceived value of the field. She found that guest speakers accomplished none of these goals. For faculty, the findings don't mandate discontinuing use of guest speakers, but their assumptions about effects have evidence for support.

Beyond improving individual practice, some previously published descriptive research helps whole fields. The analysis of critical thinking coverage in introductory psychology texts provided by Griggs, Jackson, Marek, and Christopher (1998) illustrates how this occurs. How useful and time saving for faculty to have this information when selecting a text and how important for a field to have knowledge of the extent to which its beginning texts focus on critical thinking. Wouldn't other fields benefit from having this information about texts used in their introductory courses? The same point could be made about the relevance of the Miller and Gentile (1998) and the Wagenaar (2002) exemplars. These studies are models, excellent research designs ready for replication, and revelatory in what they could establish about the state of practice in other academic disciplines.

Of the three approaches to research scholarship, we have learned the most from descriptive studies, and they hold the greatest potential as literature than can make a difference to the profession. This is research faculty can be persuaded to read. Many of the topics it explores are directly relevant to others, and results are usually presented in easily decipherable charts and tables, which expedites progress through data presentation. As the examples in this discussion illustrate, these results also have implications across disciplines and in various instructional settings.

Conclusion

This analysis of pedagogical research scholarship began with a series of questions; it can end with answers suggested by the chapter's contents. What is good pedagogical research? Work that discovers, that interprets, or that explores? Work that is quantitative, qualitative or descriptive? The exemplars enable us to answer, all of the above. However, this review does challenge the easy acceptance given research scholarship. Like experience-based work, the quality of previously published research scholarship on teaching and learning exists along a continuum. In this case, the prospect of practitioners doing quality work using quantitative and qualitative approaches is limited.

Are perspectives and methodologies borrowed from disciplines other than education the best way to study teaching and learning? They are conveniently available and well known to faculty in those fields, but their effectiveness as modes of inquiry depends on whether those perspectives and methods fit the nature of the phenomenon being studied. Not all the methods being used fit. Clearer guidelines are needed to help establish which methods practitioners should use when they study teaching and learning.

Then there is the question of whether pedagogical research is inherently better, as in always more scholarly, than wisdom-of-practice work. The answer suggested here is no. The problems with each are different and not comparable, but there are just as many difficulties with research-based scholarship as there are with experience-based work. Despite these quality issues, however, some first-rate pedagogical research has been completed by practitioners.

Research continues to be the scholarly approach of choice in the academic realm, which makes it easily convincing that moving pedagogical scholarship in that direction would finally gain for it credibility and respect. But that sword cuts in both directions. Yes, excellent pedagogical research is credible scholarship, but if it's not well done, then the work will only serve to reconfirm what many have long suspected: teaching is second-class; its scholarship is not equal or viable.

6

Promising Possibilities

Up to this point, our primary focus has been on traditional forms of scholarship—mostly articles published in the pedagogical periodicals. As I explained in Chapter Two, I opted to focus the review here because this scholarship is familiar and because it is the most common form of pedagogical literature. But previously published pedagogical scholarship includes more, and the goal of this chapter is to introduce some of these other forms and structures.

The chapter starts with articles. But these use methods of analysis and formats not like those reviewed previously. Least unusual in this group are articles that combine two or more of the seven basic approaches discussed in Chapters Four and Five to create a kind of hybrid approach. Next is a group of articles that use methods of analysis unlike those reviewed so far, or that use the methods reviewed in highly unusual ways. Then there is a category of articles that don't look or read like conventional pieces of scholarship.

Innovation in previously published work on teaching and learning extends beyond articles. Certain aspects of the pedagogical periodicals themselves are unique. Beyond articles and journals, there is the scholarship contained in books, informal publications such as newsletters, and other course-related materials (especially those now available online). Promising possibilities can be found in each of these, and this chapter will highlight some with an eye toward exploring their potential as viable literature and credible scholarship.

As just described, this chapter sounds organized, and it is, but not as tightly as others. The attempt to build a structure into which innovative work can be fit risks diminishing what makes it creative and unusual. As a result, some digressing occurs in this chapter. As I'm putting the chapter together I'm thinking of a Sunday drive through a scenic countryside where some unscheduled stops and a bit of meandering are part of what makes it interesting. Next chapter, it's back on the four-lane.

Also to be considered are the criteria used to determine whether a piece of previously published pedagogical scholarship is unique in a noteworthy way. Most obviously, work qualifies when it is not like what is commonly found in the literature. But different doesn't necessarily mean better. Given the purpose of this book to showcase exemplary work, the examples selected for the chapter are good pieces of work I found interesting and compelling. But these are not the only examples, and others who look at the literature might make different choices. Regardless of the choices, the goal ought to be a collection of previously published pedagogical scholarship that pushes traditional definitions of scholarly work in the interest of stimulating still more open-minded thinking about credible scholarship and viable literature.

Article Possibilities

To review briefly, this chapter considers three types of articles: hybrids, articles that creatively combine two or more of the seven major approaches described in Chapters Four and Five; innovative approaches, articles in which the method of analysis is not one of the seven major approaches but is either something different or an especially creative use of one of the approaches; and unique formats, in which material presented is structured in some unusual way. In addition, sometimes the content of articles is unusual and creative. Examples of articles with innovative content were identified and discussed in Chapter Two in the section on article content. Atypical content and format often appear in the same article, so again we are dealing with a set of categories more fluid than fixed.

Hybrids

Hybrids combine two or more of the common approaches identified in Chapters Four and Five in their analysis of some aspect of teaching or learning. The borders that separate hybrid articles from those that use a single approach are fuzzy. Even though I tried to select exemplars that clearly illustrate a single approach, some of them still incorporate bits and pieces of the other approaches. It helps to think about these as existing along a continuum, with the single-approach exemplars at one end and the articles here on the opposite end. Work that falls at points on the continuum between these two also exists, but the intent here is to identify examples that so thoroughly combine the approaches as to sometimes end up with what might be considered a new approach.

Most hybrids are located in the research category; an article by Miller and Groccia (1997) illustrates one of the more common approaches. The objective of this study, say the authors, "was to compare the impact of a cooperative learning format with that of a traditional lecture-oriented format in the teaching of introductory biology" (p. 266). To assess the effects of these two formats, Miller and Groccia looked at outcomes across five learning-related dimensions and collected data using a combination of descriptive and empirical approaches. They surveyed students (using a standardized instrument, the College Student Experiences Questionnaire, and a local student ratings instrument), and tested students (using a standardized instrument, the Watson-Glaser Critical Thinking Appraisal and instructor-created course content exams). As for what they found: "The results of this study affirm the viability of using a cooperative learning approach instead of the traditional passive lecture format" (p. 266). Some hybrids combine qualitative and quantitative approaches, as Jacobs-Lawson and Hershey (2002) did in their analysis, which documents that concept maps can be used effectively to evaluate students' knowledge.

A bit more unusual, Shindler (2004) combined descriptive analysis with a personal narrative. He used survey data to assess his students' experiences with two collaborative exam formats. In the discussion section, in a very personal and highly engaging way, he explores the implications of the findings for his own instructional practice and philosophy of education. Here's a research article that's interesting reading! As for what he found: "The results of the study suggest that the collaborative assessment conditions compared favorably on all four dimensions of soundness [validity, reliability, efficiency, and effect on learner]" (p. 273).

Other Approaches

The seven approaches identified, illustrated, and analyzed in Chapters Four and Five are not the only approaches taken in the pedagogical literature. They, along with the hybrid category, do account for most of what appears in the literature, but some published material analyzes aspects of teaching and learning in entirely different ways. Here are some examples that illustrate.

To analyze the impact of infusing technology on course ratings in a veterinary immunology course, Allen, Wedman, and Folk (2001) used a kind of case-study approach. They started with some statistical analysis that enabled them to control for factors known to influence ratings and to establish significance, and then explored, mostly via critical reflection, how the addition of increasing amounts of technology in the course changed the ratings. As for what happened: the ratings dipped on almost every scale for the first three years. Then they recovered and in some cases surpassed the baseline values.

Ashbaugh, Johnstone, and Warfield (2002) use an uncommon experimental design to assess the impact of professionally relevant writing experiences on accounting students. Terenzini and others (2001) pushed the descriptive approach with a creatively designed survey instrument that uses student self-reports of learning gains to compare courses using active and collaborative learning with those in which those instructional methods were not used. This study is noteworthy for a second reason: it was conducted by a group of higher education researchers but was published in the *Journal of Engineering Education*. Educational researchers almost never report results in these practitioner publications.

Digressing briefly, it is appropriate to point out again that for many considering pedagogical scholarship, some of the approaches themselves are pretty innovative. Personal narratives would probably top most people's list. But even within that category are unusual examples, such as Noel's reflective analysis (2004) of why an innovation implemented early in his career failed. His description is poignant and his assessment honest. Confrontations with failure appear only rarely in the pedagogical literature—who wants to go public with an admission of incompetence! But what teacher hasn't had those moments, those days, and for some of us, whole classes? Regrettably, most of us are more likely to run than learn from those encounters with failure.

If you are checking references, you will have noted that a number in this chapter are to articles that have been published in the journal *Innovative Higher Education,* a cross-disciplinary pedagogical periodical that very much lives up to its name. Its contents (which are mostly, though not exclusively, devoted to pedagogical topics) are not unusually innovative, but the methods of analyses and structures used to report results very often are. For authors and editors interested in a journal that publishes innovative alternatives, this one merits review.

Unusual Formats

Some previously published pedagogical literature pushes the envelope in terms of article format. I remember the first time I encountered a pedagogical piece structured in an entirely unexpected way. The "article" appears in an early issue of the *New Directions for*

Teaching and Learning series and is actually a series of letters exchanged between two faculty members (Elbow, 1980). They used the letters to explore aspects of their relationship related to their efforts to team-teach a course. I was impressed by how much they learned about collegial collaboration and how much the exchange enlarged my thinking about how colleagues could relate to one another. The letter format added spontaneity and a personal feel to the exchange, which made for good reading, at the same time as it allowed ideas to be explored and elaborated back and forth. Less directly about teaching but also about the anatomy of a collegial relationship and formatted rather unconventionally, a chapter by Cary and Spelman (1997) provides another example of using scholarship to explore personally relevant issues significant to others.

In some cases, the uniqueness of a particular article format is enhanced by its presence among more traditionally structured articles. The journal *Academic Medicine,* written for medical educators, has this formal, science-journal feel. But accompanying its long, mostly empirical articles is a regular feature called "Medicine and the Arts," which contains short and surprisingly affective reflections. For example, the May 2004 issue (Carr, 2004) begins with a one-page excerpt from a book. It describes a young man, recently returned from WWI, broken by the experience, who receives a commission to restore a very old painting hidden on a local church ceiling. It was moving, but after reading it I wondered what in the world it had to do with medical education. It is followed by a one-page commentary (Connelly, 2004) that uses the short excerpt to explore a wide range of issues related to the personal commitment professionalism requires of health care providers, but actually it is relevant to all educators who must help students understand what it means to be professional.

The articles highlighted so far in this chapter illustrate what happens to a literature when boundaries and expectations do not constrain its development. In most of our disciplines, well-established protocols constrain creativity. If an article defies established conventions, the chances of it being published diminish. Although expectations for pedagogical scholarship are increasingly being defined, overall they have not been a limiting force in its development. This lack of constraint has not always positively affected the quality of this literature, as we have already seen and will discuss more subsequently. Conversely, not having to conform to expectations has produced some promising possibilities for scholarly work on teaching and learning.

Promising Possibilities Beyond Articles

Beyond articles are some unique features of these journals themselves. Then there are books, and beyond them, the pedagogical literature broadens to include other kinds of publications, such as newsletters. Technology has pushed the limits of this literature still further, making possible the development of online course materials and resources as well as other Web-enabled teaching supports. Books and articles are easily equated with scholarship—newsletters, course materials, and teaching resources are not. As ways to enhance scholarly work on teaching and learning are explored, the question now up for discussion is whether those conceptions should change.

Special Features of Journals

As already mentioned, even a cursory look at this family of pedagogical periodicals reveals enormous diversity. The features they share in common are matched by those that differentiate them, and this includes the variety of special features and sections regularly a part of these publications. Some of these are noteworthy not just for their uncommonness, but because of what they contribute to those in the journal's field and the examples they provide journals in other fields. To illustrate, every other issue of *Issues in Accounting Education* includes a topical "Educational Research" section, and many of the articles that appear there exemplify the scholarship of application. Very impressive is one on self-regulated learning by

Smith (2001). Here's how she describes what her review does in fact accomplish: "This paper introduces the concept of self-regulated learning and its related attributes and processes that are being studied as a means to promote self-motivated, independent, lifelong learning. Research . . . from outside the field of accounting has found that the classroom environment can support the development of self-regulated learning and stimulate involvement in one's own learning. This paper discusses the major findings of this research and provides guidance to accounting educators for classroom applications, and to accounting education researchers for studying the effectiveness of approaches to promoting self-regulated learning environment in the accounting curriculum" (p. 663).

Other innovative examples include a section of student essays that regularly appears in the *Journal of Natural Resources and Life Science Education*. The *Academy of Management Learning and Education* publishes lengthy interviews with noted educators in the field. These ably edited conversations help to document the history of pedagogy in the field at the same time that they provide a permanent record of the pedagogical thinking of some of its key educators.

Over the past several years a number of these journals have devoted special sections and individual articles to the subject of the scholarship of teaching (for an example, see the June 2002 issue of *PS*, a journal in political science). In its January 2003 issue, *Communication Education* inaugurated a special section within the journal, the Scholarship of Teaching and Learning in Communication (SOTL/Com). It is described this way in the journal's statement of editorial policy: "SOTL/Com recognizes that teaching communication is a form of scholarship, just as is the scholarship of discovery or of critical analysis. Submissions for SOTL/Com will explore questions about student learning in relationship to a particular teaching practice or innovation. Typically these questions will be posed by teachers about their own teaching." Darling (2003), who edits the section, describes its content as "work that encourages an empirical examination of teaching in relation to student learning"

(p. 47). Journal editor Rubin (2003) writes that "SOTL is *different* than the traditional scholarship of discovery . . . different, but definitely *not* deficient" (p. ix).

Innovative Books

Beyond a brief mention in Chapter Two, I have not written at all about the many, many books that are a part of the previously published literature on teaching and learning. Faculty practitioners have authored books regularly across the years. The category could be divided into two major parts: generic books, mostly about how to teach, but now some on learning; and books on teaching a particular kind of content, written for an audience within a discipline. In the generic category, McKeachie's venerable *Tips for Teachers* (2002), which has been in print continuously since 1938 and is currently available in its eleventh edition, is the best known. Still, it is but one of a very large collection. Discipline-based books are fewer but still common. Sometimes they are edited anthologies, such as *Mastering Management Education: Innovations in Teaching Effectiveness* (Vance, 1993). Sometimes they are written for new faculty and address multiple aspects of successfully beginning a career, such as *The New Professor's Handbook: A Guide to Teaching and Research in Engineering and Science* (Davidson and Ambrose, 1994). Sometimes they contain advice on pedagogy and content, addressing both how and what to teach, as in *Five Easy Lessons: Strategies for Successful Physics Teaching* (Knight, 2002).

The vast majority of books on teaching use the recommended-practices approach described in Chapter Four. Faculty practitioners, who are often experienced teachers and sometimes award-winning or recognized expert teachers, write advice for colleagues on how to teach. The bulk of the advice is experience-based. The McKeachie book is one of the few that blends experiential and empirical advice— perhaps that explains its longevity. Also noteworthy here is the lack of distinction between generic books and those based in the discipline in terms of the pedagogical advice they contain. Discipline-based books do not offer advice responsive to unique content considerations. Rather, the same recommendations are repeated across many different disciplines.

Beyond generic books on teaching, a smaller but still diverse category of special topics books exists. In this case, practitioners (and sometimes non-faculty experts) have written books on particular aspects of instruction. Among my favorites are Strommer and Erickson's book (1991) on teaching freshmen, Jacobs and Chase's great resource (1992) on testing, and two excellent books on active learning (Meyers and Jones, 1993; Bean, 1996). Again, some topical books are anthologies, like Christensen, Garvin, and Sweet's exceptional collection of chapters (1991) on discussion leadership, and Cooper, Robinson, and Ball's recent collection (2003) on small-group instruction. Once in a great while you will find a topical book written by a researcher who seeks to explore implications research with practitioners. Karabenick's well-edited anthology (1998) on the help-seeking behavior of students illustrates the value of books that attempt to bring research to practice.

This general discussion of pedagogical books could be considered a digression, but it seems necessary to provide context for those books that are unusual and unique. Some of the innovative books I'd like to propose as viable and valuable alternatives exist within the disciplinary domain, and some are general. Some are written by faculty practitioners, some are not. A look at books not authored by practitioners exceeds the boundaries set for this book, but given the chapter's aim to expose innovative alternatives, and given what more books like some of these might contribute to the viability of pedagogical literature, they too seem worth a brief digression.

Starting with innovative alternatives authored by faculty practitioners and positioned within disciplines, consider two examples. Andre and Frost (1997) edited a collection of nineteen personal essays written by management and business faculty, who explore the synergies they experience between teaching and research. It's a book that illustrates how research and teaching work together in the careers of some faculty. Even though the book exists within a field, it offers insights relevant to all faculty interested in better connecting their research and teaching lives. Also positioned within a discipline but a very different model, Puente, Matthews, and Brewer (1992) assembled a collection titled, *Teaching of Psychology in America: A History*. Those outside of psychology will not find the history particularly interesting, but how valuable for a field to have a record of its pedagogical roots.

Among the more generic but still practitioner-authored books, Tompkins (1996) has written a creative personal narrative that describes lessons learned in school that she spent the rest of her life in the classroom trying to unlearn. Her book is autobiographical, a memoir, but it raises questions about the educational system and challenges the way many faculty think about teaching. Equally personal is a wonderful collection of essays by midcareer faculty women compiled by Freeman and Schmidt (2000), *Wise Women: Reflections of Teachers at Midlife*. The essays are not just about teaching, although all touch on it; they also explore many midcareer issues, such as burnout, changing priorities, and moribund academic cultures. Some of the essays are depressing, others inspiring, but all place teaching in the large, rich, complicated context in which it occurs. This is not just a book for women. A book by bell hooks (1994), *Teaching to Transgress*, bridges the gap between innovative books written by practitioners and those written by others. In this case, hooks does teach, but her reputation is based on much more than what she has accomplished in the classroom. This book, too, is personal, but it is more philosophical. It is not at all about how to teach (in fact none of the innovative books mentioned so far are), but about why we teach and what assumptions justify teaching as we do.

Among those of us who work with faculty on teaching and learning agendas, the Jossey-Bass *New Directions for Teaching and Learning* series, published since the early 1980s, has provided much excellent information on emerging issues related to instruction. It is a unique model. The series has an overall editor(s), Marilla Svinicki and Eugene Rice at the moment, as well as individual issue editors. Issue editors have included faculty practitioners, faculty developers, educational researchers, and a range of other experts. Each issue is devoted to a current topic; the issue editor assembles a collection of individually authored chapters in which various aspects of the topic are explored in depth. Quality ranges depending on the issue, but overall the series has covered all the important instructional topics and many others besides. Unfortunately, material from the series is rarely referenced in any of the discipline-based publications, but the same could be said of almost any of the generic books on teaching and learning.

I'll conclude this section by proposing consideration of a couple of books authored not by a practitioner but by an educational scholar. I'm referring to Kohn's two books (which I find myself regularly referencing and recommending), one on the negative role of competition, with education being a key example (1986), the other on the demotivating effects of grades and other rewards for learning (1993). Both books reference, distill, and otherwise summon much research to make a case against widely held assumptions about learning, and they do so in a particularly engaging manner. Both changed my mind and my practice. They may not motivate others to change, but they are books with content that begs to be discussed and that changes the caliber of faculty exchanges. We do need books on how to teach—probably not as many as we have—but those are not books that inspire substantive intellectual discourse. At some point, to be viable a literature must rise above the pedantic. Models of literature that do this for teaching and learning are few and far between.

Newsletters

A considerable amount of previously published pedagogical material has been made available to faculty through newsletters. Many of these are local, in-house publications, frequently produced and distributed by a college or university's teaching center. In addition to promoting those local activities, resources, and services that support instruction, most of these in-house newsletters do contain material on teaching and learning, some of it written by faculty at the institution, the rest coming from a variety of sources.

In addition, there are several national newsletters, offered by subscription to individual faculty or to their institutions. Some of these address all aspects of teaching and learning (*The National Forum on Teaching and Learning* and the *Teaching Professor*), some are directed to particular audiences (*The Adjunct Professor*), and others are topical (*Online Classroom* and *Assessment Update*).

In yet another brief digression, I would like to explore the potential of newsletters as credible pedagogical scholarship. My eighteen-year editorship of the *Teaching Professor*, a national newsletter published ten times a year by Magna Publications, has afforded me considerable time to contemplate the interesting ways newsletters challenge conventional definitions of scholarship.

Traditionally, something as informal as a newsletter article is not considered a scholarly publication. Yet the *Teaching Professor's* 85 percent rejection rate rivals that of any top-tier journal. Traditionally, one measure of the worth of a piece of scholarship is the amount of impact it has in the field. So, which has more—an article in a refereed journal with one thousand subscribers, many of which are libraries (which is more than a lot of the periodicals under review here), or a piece in a newsletter that circulates to fifteen thousand practitioners? Even granting that there's a bit of apples-oranges comparison here, if one of the goals of pedagogical scholarship is improved practice, a piece in the *Teaching Professor* stands a much better chance of changing what faculty do.

Articles in newsletters are short—seven hundred to nine hundred words in the *Teaching Professor*—and if an article doesn't conform to our length requirements, we condense it until it does. The assumption is that these short pieces trivialize complex issues. Perhaps my editorship compromises my objectivity on this issue, but I don't think a succinct summary inherently trivializes. It seems to me that it's the difference between standing up close to view a painting and looking at it from across the room. Up close you see more detail; across the room you can't make out the detail, but you may have a better understanding of the whole picture. A good summary of complicated issues accurately represents and positions the essential ideas so that even though the details are not apparent, their presence shapes what is seen. You can write a short article so that it trivializes complex details—you can do that in a longer piece, for that matter. I have learned, though, that a short article that captures the essence of complexity is just as difficult, if not harder, to write as those longer pieces.

For some, the fact that articles in newsletters aren't refereed compromises their potential as scholarship. Deadlines posed by a monthly publication do not make elaborate review mechanisms viable. But articles in a newsletter are refereed in an even more compelling way when publications are supported by subscription revenues alone. If readers find nothing of interest or relevance, if they try proposed techniques and discover that they don't work, they will stop subscribing. This vote-with-your-feet power is as effective as any peer-review process. Either the publication has quality content or the publication will no longer exist. Another lesson I've learned well during my editorship of the *Teaching Professor* is that classroom practitioners are a discerning lot when they pay for a publication.

I regularly write letters about articles in the *Teaching Professor* that have been authored by faculty under review for tenure and promotion. Here's a statement I use that appropriately sums these points relevant to newsletter content as scholarly work on teaching and learning: "This article clearly, concisely, and accurately presents substantive pedagogical content. It was published in the most widely read pedagogical periodical in North America. For that reason, it may affect the practice of faculty in many disciplines and at many different institutions. Given the quality of its content and potential impact, it should count favorably in the assessment of this individual faculty member."

Course Materials and Other Online Work

Some teachers devote a great deal of time to the preparation of course materials. Starting with the syllabus, now almost universally a part of courses, faculty also prepare carefully crafted course study guides, handouts that elaborate on content, and other materials that offer advice supportive of student efforts to master material. Beyond these supplementary materials, some faculty have constructed elaborate and creative assignments that very effectively promote deep and lasting learning. Others have tinkered ingeniously with testing and grading methods. Interest in teaching portfolios has motivated (in some cases required) faculty to prepare teaching philosophy statements in which beliefs about teaching and learning are reconciled with practice. And with the technology aids now available, even more faculty are creating and using online resources to support instruction.

Few of these course-related materials are contained in the body of previously published work on teaching and learning. Faculty have learned about the good ideas of their colleagues mostly by word of mouth—it is amazing how much instructional knowledge has been part of essentially an oral tradition. Good ideas have been passed around and encountered mostly by chance—that is, until recently. Technology now makes it easy to preserve and share with others some of these artifacts of teaching.

At this point, most of the pedagogical periodicals reviewed in this book have Web sites, all of which make available current and at least some, if not all, previously published content. Some of these Web sites contain additional instructional resources, including course materials of various sorts. One of the most extensive collections is offered by the *Journal of Chemical Education*. Editor Moore (2004) characterizes the journal as an iceberg. "Nine-tenths of it is invisible to the reader of the printed page. The rest is the vast quantity of material in *JCE Online* that you can only see through electronic media" (p. 1,383). What's contained in that electronic collection? Computer-editable versions of handouts that accompany published labs, additional supplementary material such as raw data, extended discussion of results, spreadsheets that accompany content articles, online versions of chemical demonstrations and animations, a test bank containing thousands of quiz and exam questions, and much more. The editor notes that in 1998 subscribers received 150 MB of content. In 2004 they received 1,400 MB.

National associations (some in conjunction with a pedagogical periodical and others independent of one), such as the National Association of Teachers of Biology (NATB), the American Association of Physics Teachers (AAPT), the National Association of Geosciences Teachers (NAGT), the Society for the Teaching of Psychology (one of the Directorates of the American Psychological Association), to name but a few examples, now have on their Web site collections of resource material for teachers, including assignments, sample syllabi, classroom exercises, test questions, and reviews of materials (such as videos and other Web sites).

There are some generic online sources now available as well. For example, George Mason University supports a "syllabus finder" site (http://chnm.gmu.edu/tools/syllabi/) that works in conjunction with Google to identify online syllabi for hundreds of courses. The University of Texas supports a site that contains an enormous collection of online course materials assembled from around the world (http://www.utexas.edu/world/lecture).

What's tremendously useful here is the way instructional resources can be shared. Faculty members now assigned to teach a course they have not previously taught need not labor to design the course or construct its syllabus in isolation. They have a range of resources just a few clicks away. What's innovative about this more permanent and visible role for course materials is the proposition by some that these artifacts of teaching might be considered "scholarly." Again, the scholarship-of-teaching movement is leading the way with a variety of projects that showcase how course materials, both as they have been thought of conventionally and as they can be supported with analysis and assessment, can be used to illustrate that teaching does involve intellectual work. An article by Hatch, Bass, Iiyoshi, and Mace (2004) highlights a number of these projects, including an online Gallery of the Scholarship of Teaching and Learning supported by the Carnegie Foundation that contains a variety of faculty-authored Web sites in which individual courses are not just described, but their impact on student learning is assessed robustly, and faculty reflections link course content and approach to educational philosophies (http://gallery.carnegiefoundation.org). The Visible Learning Project at Georgetown University offers another intriguing model demonstrating how seventy humanities and social science faculty are using a variety of Web-based tools to share investigations into their teaching (http://crossroads.georgetown.edu/vkp).

Technology enables course-related materials to be configured, disseminated, and thought of in some very different ways. The idea that they might represent scholarly work should not be ruled out before examples like the ones referenced here are perused and their contents examined.

Previously published scholarly work on teaching and learning contains articles of various sorts, including some that use different approaches and formats to create unique perspectives on aspects of teaching and learning. But previously published literature contains much more—some easily conceived of as scholarly, such as books, and some well beyond what has been traditionally considered scholarship. Considering the purposes of pedagogical literature, are some of these alternatives viable? This chapter presents them as possibilities and challenges thinking that would force work on teaching and learning to fit conventional expectations for scholarship.

7

Looking Ahead:
Learning from What's Behind

Questions have played a central role in this book so far. The goal has been to use them like flashlights—pointed beams of light shined into dark places: What kind of written resources do college teachers need? If more of the literature were like the exemplars, would faculty read it? What if pedagogical literature played a significant role in the development of teachers—would teaching be more respected and learning more valued? Is pedagogical literature a unique form of scholarship? What research tools best suit the study of teaching and learning by practitioners? What standards should be used to assess it? If done well, should it count the same as disciplinary research?

We have now reached the point where the light needs to be shined in the direction of answers. This chapter aspires to provide that illumination—to extract from the review and analysis of previously published pedagogical literature the lessons that will take us to a new, different, and better future as classroom practitioners and scholars of teaching.

I structure the summary this way: First, we consider what kind of foundation previously published literature provides. Looking back and surveying this body of literature, what characteristics and features do we find? Then we need to look ahead, now with the intention of answering the book's two central questions: What will make pedagogical scholarship credible? What kind of pedagogical literature will improve instruction and advance the profession? After that, we should be able to lay what we have alongside what we need and see how well they fit. If the fit isn't close, then we can explore what needs to change in order for us to enhance scholarly work on teaching and learning.

The task before us in this chapter is a daunting one. As we have seen, there is much pedagogical literature to review, no existent summaries to fall back on, and flashlights reveal less than floodlights. But using the light we have, we can still learn from what's behind and use answers to find our way to a brighter future.

What We Have: Characteristics of the Foundation

Taking a step back from the details, what generalizations might be made about previously published pedagogical work? How could it be described collectively? What are its defining features and characteristics? This broad view includes the exemplars, but they represent the best of previously published work—what it could be. This inclusive view is of all that has been published. Collectively, it becomes the baseline against which needs can be measured: here's what we have and here's what we need. I see five defining features of previously published scholarly work on teaching and learning. Each needs to be explained and its influence on the development of the existing literature assessed.

Applied Literature

Previously published pedagogical literature is applied in the sense that it is mostly about how to teach. Recently the focus has broadened to include material on how to promote learning. As a literature, it is functional and pragmatic. It addresses problems, answers questions, analyzes issues, and makes recommendations about a host of large and small instructional topics. This feature defines both experience- and research-based scholarship.

This applied characteristic has positively influenced the literature in a couple of ways. For example, the literature is relevant. It addresses issues of interest and concern to those responsible for classroom instruction. In addition to being about topics that matter, this literature is written by teachers directly to other teachers. Many of the accounts derive from firsthand experiences.

The literature capitalizes on the positive features of collegiality. There is a spirit of sharing, a sense of one colleague reaching out to help another. Even though previously published pedagogical scholarship is conventionally copyrighted, intellectual property seems like an irrelevant issue. This is material to borrow, use, adapt, and pass on, not to guard, protect, or horde. I like the justification O'Leary (2002) gives for sharing with colleagues: "After all, we all work for the same firm and our goal is to serve a common client" (p. 92). It's a strength when a piece of literature is directly relevant and freely shared.

This pragmatic feature has negative aspects as well. As literature, previously published pedagogical scholarship is largely atheoretical. Any given article (especially the experience-based ones, but even a lot of research pieces) exists in the moment, for the here-and-now. More often it's about *how* you do something, not *why* you do it. Theoretical bases for strategies, approaches, even for research questions, as well as links to other research, are not acknowledged, and one strongly suspects they have not informed the current line of inquiry. This is not literature that connects well to past research or seeks to direct future inquiries. Work this disconnected has diminished credibility and utility—it may rest on flawed premises.

This isolated, atheoretical framework means that previously published pedagogical scholarship does not exist as a systematic, coherent knowledge base. It does not function as a foundation providing support for what's being proposed or studied. Routinely oblivious to this omission, authors focus on the need to know *an* answer or to solve *a* problem. In an article about engineering education, Clough and Kauffman (1999) make the case for a theory and research framework for teaching. They explain its importance: "Such a framework promotes coherent pedagogical decision-making that reflects the best available knowledge base for effective teaching and reform in engineering education" (p. 527). Obviously, this point pertains to pedagogical decision making in every discipline.

Experience and Research Coexist

Wisdom from practice and knowledge generated from systematic inquiry cohabitate in previously published pedagogical literature. That they exist together, side by side, in the same literature makes this body of work pretty unusual, albeit, as noted earlier, a bit schizophrenic in feel. In the beginning, experience-based work dominated the literature; now research-based knowledge is preferred and the amount of experience-based work is declining, although it is certainly not disappearing. Their coexistence has largely been without impact, despite their potential to uniquely define and positively affect the literature.

Their long, uncontested, joint presence tacitly confirms the value of each. But the real strength of this association lies more in what their presence makes possible: a viable connection between research and practice. In most of our disciplines the gap between research and practice remains wide, impoverishing both endeavors. In the pedagogical literature they stand side by side—still not connected—but close enough to explore jointly how their separate but related findings might be integrated and applied.

What could have happened, however, has not occurred. Despite the fact that these two different ways of knowing have explored many of the same issues and shared a common literature, they have existed without acknowledging each other. The ways in which they may have influenced or been influenced by each other have never been articulated. So this very unique feature of the literature has resulted in naught, and now their uncontested coexistence is jeopardized by the push for work that is more research-based.

Diverse Literature

Previously published pedagogical literature is diverse in content, touching on a stunningly wide array of instructional issues and topics. It is diverse in approach: multiple methods have been used to study pedagogical phenomena. It is diverse in structure and format: articles and other kinds of literature are organized and presented in various ways. This diversity exists within the pedagogical literature of a single discipline as well as across the range of them.

Diversity that celebrates difference almost always has positive effects, and it certainly has in this case. Pedagogical literature offers a plethora of interesting models and creative alternatives (see Chapter Six for specific examples). This allows the literature to meet a variety of needs—it has something for everyone. As we contemplate a different future for pedagogical scholarship, this literature provides a deep well of options and a plethora of possibilities.

When diversity equates with disparity it generally has negative effects; that is true of this literature in the sense that the quality is widely diverse and consistently uneven. Because pedagogical literature has not been taken seriously, its growth has been wild in an unruly, untamed, anything-goes sense. Think of a climbing rose that's grown wild in an abandoned back yard. It's gone everywhere, grabbing hold where it could, blooming like mad, even though unnoticed. There is exuberance, beauty, and resilience about this kind of growth, but a neglected rose carries a lot of dead wood and disease. It's not all the rose that it could be, or might have been, had a gardener been present.

Holistic Treatment

In addition to covering a diverse range of topics associated with teaching, this literature addresses all aspects of teaching, including those unrelated to content or method. Most notably, it does not shy away from the affective domain. The fact that teaching has emotional dimensions and requires a great deal of personal investment is regularly dealt with in this literature. The rational, objective, fact-driven culture of academe infrequently and uncomfortably deals with emotion. It is mostly ruled out of discovery-based scholarship, but it is a prevalent feature of this applied literature.

Coverage of the affective dimensions of teaching does not happen at the expense of work that focuses on the intellectual parts of teaching—the know-how needs that result from not having been trained to teach and the information needs that derive from changing students, curricula, and instructional environments. The few who read this literature find material that motivates, informs, challenges, guides, inspires, argues, advocates, and persuades. This is a full-service literature.

This holistic feature has positively influenced the literature. Faculty have legitimate information needs, but if that were all the literature contained, it would inadequately support their instructional endeavors. Most faculty teach for reasons other than intellectual ones. They are motivated by lofty ideals, such as the commitment to learning, the love of a content area, and the role of education in a democratic society. Their efforts in the classroom are sustained and challenged by experiences imbued with emotion—the student who finally gets it, another whose behavior disrupts the learning environment, the class that spontaneously claps when the course ends, another that regularly circumvents the teacher's authority. That a literature acknowledges and explores these emotional forces is definitely to its credit.

If there's a weakness, it resides not in the literature, but in the mindset of those who read it. Work that plies these waters moves upstream, against a strong current of conventional thinking about what scholarship is. Faculty can be uplifted, motivated, encouraged, chastised, or moved to tears by work that touches these real and legitimate parts of teaching, but most do not see the work as scholarly or think that it takes mental rigor to create.

Disciplinary Differentiation

The identity of previously published work on teaching and learning is more generic than disciplinary. A large amount of the work occurs within disciplinary contexts, but even given that fact, shared features significantly outnumber those that are discipline-specific. These shared features include topics—across the board, this body of literature deals with issues that transcend pedagogical context, such as student passivity, motivation, preparedness, and academic integrity, and such as teacher authority, organization, presentation and style. It deals with strategies, such as group work, problem-based learning, writing-across-the-curriculum, classroom assessment; and with instructional approaches, such as learner-centered teaching and distance education. The work in separate disciplines also shares the methodological approaches identified and explored in Chapters Four and Five. I was a bit surprised at how consistently these same approaches have been used in one field after another. That's not to say they've been used equally by all fields, but you will find examples of most in every field. I would go so far as to say that if five articles on a topic such as group work were selected from five different fields and the field-specific references were deleted, it would be impossible to identify the field of origin.

All disciplines have pedagogical literature on how to teach content, as in what content, how to explain and illustrate key aspects of content, and how to test mastery of it. This feature is shared, but obviously the content is not. But beyond this discipline-specific content and differences in pedagogical and learning skills considered important by a field, what this literature shares in common is much more significant than what differentiates it by discipline. Pedagogical literature can be considered prolific parents of a large family. Their offspring have families of their own. But when everyone gets together, it's pretty obvious they share the same family tree.

The effects of this shared identity have been decidedly mixed. Beginning with the positive, the strength of pedagogical literature having evolved on its own without strong disciplinary connections is that its features (those we are currently in the process of exploring) reflect the nature of the phenomenon, not the priorities of the discipline. As noted before, teaching and learning phenomena are discrete entities, separate and independent of disciplinary content though inextricably linked to it.

For example, previously published pedagogical scholarship does not look like scholarly work done in most of the disciplines, even though its format and structure may mirror the protocols and conventions of the field. It is more applied, more pragmatic, not all empirical, and mostly not discovery-based. As such, it is disenfranchised and devalued when discipline-based research standards are used to assess it.

Balancing this positive effect are problems that have resulted from pedagogical literature being defined generically. They start with the fact that when scholarship is disconnected from a discipline, it exists in some amorphous place where it belongs to no one. That has been the reality for this scholarship—no organization, no institution, no collection of individuals has claimed ownership for it, so it has developed willy-nilly on its own. Existence in this disassociated place explains why it has had so little impact on practice and even less on the careers of those who have produced it.

Moreover, despite the shared features of this literature, there are still aspects of teaching disciplinary content that are unique or that require an adaptation of generic teaching skills. Those unique characteristics and special adaptations cannot be proposed by outsiders, which explains why faculty prefer to talk about teaching physics (name a discipline) with someone else who teaches physics. When pedagogical literature is not owned by the discipline, it is less likely to address those aspects of teaching that are unique; as the review in Chapter Four revealed, it deals less often and less explicitly with the process of adaptation.

Even though faculty assume that teaching physics (name a discipline) is unique, most cannot say how or why. On a related note, to most of us involved with pedagogical scholarship, Shulman's notions (1987) of pedagogical content knowledge make sense; despite those ideas being well known and widely referenced, however, few disciplines have identified or otherwise described what that knowledge is in their field. Why is that? Could it be that prevailing generic understandings of teaching and learning prevent faculty from seeing what is unique about teaching a particular kind of content?

Finally, disciplines continue to be the places of faculty identity and bastions of power within the academy. This previously published scholarship demonstrates what happens to a literature that does not belong to them or is not well positioned within them. It has ended up not being taken seriously, not having credibility, and not having counted for much of anything.

These, then, are the major defining features of previously published pedagogical literature. As we look to the future, this is the foundation that past work provides. Do these features make a solid foundation? Is it the one that we need? Can we build a new and better scholarship on it?

What We Need

The what-do-we-need question has been answered from the beginning of the book: we need for work done by practitioners on teaching and learning to be credible scholarship and viable literature. Asked here, the question is a bit more nuanced. What we need to make the scholarship credible and literature viable is considered theoretically, hypothetically, independent of what currently exists. With that identified, we can put what we have alongside what we need and more easily see where we are.

We cannot consider what we need independent of current conditions. Given present-day realities, it once again becomes apparent that some of what would make the scholarship credible and the literature viable has nothing to do with characteristics of the literature itself, but could be achieved by changing the context—populating higher-education environments with academic leaders knowledgeable and supportive of pedagogical scholarship, or mandating professional growth and development for teachers, for example. However, those kinds of changes are not the primary concern of this book. The focus here is on the literature itself and what would make scholarly work on teaching and learning done by practitioners credible and viable.

Credible Pedagogical Scholarship

The credibility of any scholarship is a function of its quality, and quality is measured by agreed-upon standards. For pedagogical scholarship, the difficulty lies in determining *what* and *whose* standards should apply (Kreber, 2001a). In Chapters Four and Five I illustrated what they might look like if drawn from examples of quality work that currently exists. Given how criteria are used to assess scholarship within the academic community, the standards must be specific and functional so that those reviewing the work, particularly promotion and tenure committees, can apply them to individual pieces and collections of work belonging to an individual faculty member.

New standards require new thinking—thinking that sees intellectual richness in approaches other than those used to discover new knowledge. Stenberg (2005) addresses this need in her description of work that emerges out of practice: "In praxis-oriented work . . . the teacher-scholar is reflective about his or her specific, embodied location and the contexts he or she works within. Additionally, praxis-oriented work is developmental, not conclusive. The goal is not to come to final answers, but to participate in dialogue that has the potential to change the teacher, the students and the field. Finally, praxis-oriented scholarship need not look like scholarship that is already valued in the discipline; indeed, it can change the way we understand scholarship" (p. 52).

The benefit of differentiating pedagogical scholarship from what is done in the disciplines is that it allows the crafting of a kind of scholarship that fits the needs of practitioners and the nature of the phenomena without gutting the intellectual currency of the work. Is that a realistic possibility? I think so and would return attention to the exemplars. Are they shoddy pieces of scholarly work? Most definitely their intellectual robustness is different from scholarship in most disciplines, but I would firmly contend that *different* in the case of these exemplars does not mean *diminished*.

Alongside the question of what standards, there is also the question of *whose* standards? Those of the discipline, those of discovery-based scholarship, or those of educational research and its related specialties? Or perhaps what is needed are new standards that reflect the unique features and different goals of pedagogical scholarship. I think new standards make the most sense, but gaining acceptance for them will be yet another struggle. I'm reminded of an observation offered by Diamond (2002), whose work with the disciplines on creating statements that broadened definitions of scholarship has been instrumental in creating this window of opportunity for pedagogical scholarship: "When fundamental values and long-standing traditions are affected, as they will be, the process will not be easy; we can expect extensive debate and a great deal of heat" (p. 76).

That's the reality of the environment in which scholarly work on teaching and learning needs to become credible scholarship. To move in that direction we need high standards that reflect the unique features and functions of the work. It also means openly considering new standards, because many of those used to assess other kinds of scholarship do not apply.

Viable Literature

The need here is to identify those characteristics or features of the literature itself that would enhance its viability. Let's consider four possibilities. First, and probably most important, the literature will gain viability to the extent that its content has a real and positive impact on instruction. It must make classroom policies, practices, and behaviors more effective. It must promote the development of teachers as critical, reflective practitioners with a rich and deep understanding of classroom dynamics. It must also be about learning, identifying the instructional implications of what is known about learning and exploring those instructional strategies that promote more and better learning. Finally, it must advocate for teaching and learning within disciplines and professional associations, at institutions and within departments, as well as across the broad range of policymaking environs where decisions affecting the quality of teaching and learning experiences are made. If faculty and academic leaders encountered literature that made a difference, perceptions about it would change. The literature would be looked at differently, turned to regularly, and recommended routinely (she writes hopefully, without unfounded optimism).

The content of the literature, then, is an essential part of its viability, as is its coherence as an integrated knowledge base. A viable literature is one that organizes and integrates individual inquiries and isolated studies into a coherent knowledge base. A literature that is not so organized has diminished credibility and utility.

The need for a coherent knowledge base brings us to an area where current realities complicate the situation. Several different knowledge bases already exist in the teaching-learning area. There is the applied knowledge base that contains what has been discovered (experientially and empirically) by practitioners about how to teach and how to promote learning. We haven't yet sorted out how knowledge in this base that transcends disciplines relates to knowledge that is discipline-specific. It would be unnecessarily duplicative to have a practitioner knowledge base for each discipline when so many aspects of teaching and learning are shared across disciplines. It would be equally erroneous to fail to recognize that some of what has been discovered and would improve practice falls into this domain of pedagogical content knowledge.

Even more vexing is the question of how this practitioner knowledge base relates to what has been discovered and documented by educational research, a whole field of knowledge we have not covered in this book, for reasons outlined in Chapter Two. But our focus on practitioner pedagogical scholarship does not deny the existence of another whole knowledge base for teaching, some of which confirms practitioner findings and recommendations and some of which is at odds with them. Although the relationship may start with these areas of agreement and disagreement, it is in fact much more complicated and interesting than this. How do these two knowledge bases relate conceptually? What premises and assumptions ground them? Could they move beyond acknowledging each other to a place where they might actually get involved in each other's questions and answers? Answers to those questions could bridge the persistent and counterproductive disconnect between educational research and practice. At this point, however, closing that gap seems several light years away. Long before that, there is the fundamental need to recognize that a literature's viability is a function of how clearly and definitively its knowledge base has been articulated.

Third, a viable literature plays a role in setting and maintaining professional standards. A literature that accomplishes this goal is much less possible without an articulated knowledge base out of which the standards can be derived, which inextricably links these two features of a viable literature. Although neither the practitioner knowledge base explored in this book nor the better organized educational research base have been used to set standards for college teaching, what is known does justify establishing benchmarks and identifying at least some preferred, if not best, practices. Of course, the state of our knowledge, coupled with disciplinary differences and dynamic teaching venues, does not justify standards in the absolute, imputable sense of laws. The objective is not a conformity of practice that denies teachers choice or regulates the vagrancies of individual teaching style. But some instructional strategies, methods, and approaches are more effective than others; some promote learning that is deeper and more self-regulated; some more effectively connect with today's college students. A literature is viable if it is ethically responsible to the profession and helps ensure the integrity of practice in the field.

In light of the reality of modest or missing commitments to the literature on the part of the profession and individual teachers, the viability of pedagogical literature will be enhanced by one last, pragmatic feature: pedagogical literature for the college teaching profession needs to be written well and readable. The particulars involved here begin with language that is accessible. Extensive jargon and specialized language have made the research of many fields, including education, impenetrable to outsiders. Use of specialized language may be justified when the research aims to advance knowledge, but when a literature is applied and seeks to improve practice, it needs clear and unpretentious language.

Academic writing is off-putting for another reason. It is prose that values objectivity and precision above readability. Again, this may be justified when the goal is a totally accurate representation of procedures and findings, but when the aim is better practice, what must be valued is writing that connects with readers, writing that is not only clear and accurate but that also motivates and empowers. We're after writing that folks in the trade call "a good read"—writing that is inherently interesting and ends up becoming part of the reason people keep reading.

To get faculty reading the pedagogical literature, we also need to think about formats other than articles in journals and books. I've already admitted my biases about newsletters, but I think their success shows that faculty will read pedagogical literature if it's delivered in convenient, easily digestible forms. The problem with these abbreviated literary forms is that they can be written so that they trivialize complex instructional issues. No one should think that they've learned all they need to know about the role of participation in student learning after having read a four-inch column that highlights three effective techniques. Nonetheless, a viable literature needs to use structures that expedite access, especially in the absence of norms that obligate faculty to keep current. Newsletters are by no means the only alternative format that ought to be considered, especially given what technology and widespread Internet access make possible.

I'm not claiming here that a well-written and conveniently formatted literature will be read just because of these features. But they are even more imperative given how little pedagogical literature faculty currently read. I am suggesting that making the literature viable involves content with impact, a coherent and articulated knowledge base, literature that plays a role in setting standards, and readable, alternatively formatted material.

A Synergistic Relationship

Credible scholarship and viable literature are linked: advancement will be reciprocally felt. But the relationship is stronger than a simple linear connection—it's more a synergistic coupling with magnified effects. An example will illustrate: Imagine making pedagogical scholarship a viable option for more faculty. Before exploring the synergistic effects, let's start with what's needed to make doing scholarly work on teaching and learning an option for more teachers.

For starters, faculty need to be able to do pedagogical scholarship to different degrees. Full-time engagement in pedagogical scholarship should not be the only option. Work on pedagogical problems should also be possible for faculty with heavy teaching loads—the very teachers who most need to regularly stand back and think about what they are doing and why. Doing this type of scholarship should be an option for faculty who wish to commingle pedagogical scholarship with discipline-based work, or who do pedagogical scholarship at some times during their careers but not others. The problem here is creating a scholarship that can be accessible to those who are unable or not interested in doing it full-time. Often, discipline-based research is very difficult for "part timers" to complete—they don't have the equipment, it's hard to keep up with the latest developments, and they lack institutional support or the time to engage in cutting-edge research.

Given that pedagogical scholarship can be characterized more broadly than discovery-based research and defined on its own terms, it is possible to envision a future where faculty could participate to varying degrees. That would be possible if we set realistic requirements for things like literature reviews. We expect that personal accounts of change, descriptive studies, or any of the other approaches used in the analysis of pedagogical issues include documentation, references that establish what others have discovered or what is already known, but we do not expect all-inclusive lit reviews. We also set reasonable expectations for methods, which means we recognize that investigators involved with their subjects have difficulty doing quantitative research. We acknowledge how challenging it is to control variables in actual classroom settings, and we allow alternative kinds of research (more to come on these). In much the same vein, we recognize the difficulty (indeed improbability) of discipline-based faculty mastering the intricacies of cutting-edge educational research methods. We legitimize those methods that can be learned by faculty in fields unrelated to education. Obviously, the concern here is that we're cutting corners that compromise quality, but that depends on the goals of this kind of scholarship and the standards used to assess it.

That's a look at some of what might be required to make doing pedagogical scholarship a viable option for more faculty. How might having more faculty doing scholarly work on teaching and learning synergistically advance the credibility of the scholarship and viability of the literature? If more faculty did this kind of scholarship, that would improve the quality of the work overall and that would enhance its credibility. It would also make the work more commonplace, and that would force promotion and tenure committees to confront many of the assessment issues raised in this book. If more faculty did pedagogical scholarship, that would improve the literature—increasing its power to affect practice, further establishing the knowledge base, and making it easier to establish benchmarks and best practices. More faculty doing pedagogical scholarship would mean more faculty reading the literature, more faculty discovering its relevance, power, and viability as an information source. More faculty seeing value in the literature would likely mean more faculty seeing the value of pedagogical scholarship. Synergistic relationships grow back and forth by leaps and bounds. As we shall see in Chapters Eight and Nine, this particular synergism also jumps from credible scholarship and viable literature to improved practice for the individual doing the work and a better climate for teaching and learning at the institution.

What Needs to Change

With the features of previously published pedagogical literature identified and a proposal as to what's needed in hand, what remains is to assess how well what we have matches what we need. Does previously published pedagogical literature meet the four needs just explored? It does, but only on a few accounts. Within the body of previously published work are models (some showcased in previous chapters) that demonstrate what viable literature and credible scholarship might look like. They are well-written, interesting, and relevant. Their content has the power to improve practice. They draw on and appropriately reference what is known. They illustrate a level of pedagogical scholarship that merits reward and recognition.

However, much of the published literature is not of this caliber. In addition, the history of what has happened to faculty who have written previously published material roundly attests to the fact that pedagogical scholarship has not been a professionally viable option for most faculty. So, even though we can point to examples of good pedagogical scholarship, continuing on as we have will not make the scholarship credible or the literature viable. It may accomplish bits of both, but the future is much brighter if both goals are fully realized.

Before turning our backs on what has been done, however, we ought to consider changes with power to move the literature we have in these desired directions. What needs to change if the foundation established by previously published work is to support a future where pedagogical scholarship is credible and the literature viable? Consider five changes that could better align pedagogical literature with the established needs.

How We Think About Research

As noted previously, many believe that if pedagogical scholarship were more like research, it would be better (for an example of this thinking, see a series of editorials by Prados, 1996; 1999; 2001). For some, this means if pedagogical scholarship were more like discovery-based research and uncovered new knowledge, it would be better. Other times, the objective is to make pedagogical scholarship more like educational research or more like research in the discipline. Most of the time, though, the thinking is not terribly specific—it's more a general sense that pedagogical scholarship needs to look and feel like research.

Earlier in the book, we explored problems associated with this approach. Discipline-based faculty practitioners are not well positioned to do discovery-based research because they are involved with their subjects and because actual classrooms contain far too many variables to control effectively. Moreover, because they are not trained in this type of research, practitioners find it difficult to use the sophisticated research tools now being employed to make new discoveries about teaching and learning. Sometimes they substitute discipline-based methodologies, which may or may not fit the instructional phenomena being studied. Taken together, these problems raise an interesting query: Why push pedagogical scholarship in the direction of research when there are already whole fields doing the kind of research that enlarges the frontiers of knowledge? What benefit is gained by having practitioners doing the same work?

I think the push in these directions is motivated by the need to make pedagogical scholarship more robust and the fact that the credibility of research is rarely questioned. But if the push produces poor-quality research, then, as noted at the end of Chapter Five, the move will backfire. It will reconfirm what many in the academy already believe: when faculty study teaching and learning, they do second-class scholarly work.

Also pointed out previously, scholarship that reports research results is less effective at improving practice; it is not easy to read, and the implications of its findings are not always clear or applicable. It's hard to imagine more research literature leading to more pedagogical reading by faculty for many of the same reasons that textbooks do not motivate most students to read more academic material. Finally, given the difficulty of discipline-based pedagogical scholars doing this work well, a move in this direction will make pedagogical scholarship an option for fewer and fewer faculty.

At this point in the discussion, I need to make clear that I am not proposing that we abandon the research forms of pedagogical scholarship. As the exemplars illustrate, quality research work has been done by discipline-based pedagogical scholars. Some research approaches have been used more successfully by practitioner-scholars than others, but all kinds of research should continue to be an option. What needs to change are the assumptions that this is the best kind of pedagogical scholarship and that making more pedagogical scholarship research-based will establish its credibility.

Besides not seeing research scholarship as always more preferable, we also need to consider defining it more broadly. In addition to the standard forms of research scholarship (such as those illustrated in Chapter Five), there are other options, beginning with classroom research. Building on the amazing success of classroom assessment (Angelo and Cross, 1993), Cross and Steadman (1996) proposed what seemed to be the natural next step. Whereas "classroom assessment describes *what* is happening, classroom research tries to find out *why*" (p. 7). Defined as "ongoing and cumulative inquiry by classroom teachers into the nature of teaching and learning in their own classrooms" (p. 2), classroom research is differentiated from educational research in a couple of important ways. First, this is not research that results in generalizations applicable across the board. It produces results that are context-specific. Second, classroom research is predicated on the assumption that those most involved and most affected by the research cannot be excluded from it.

Despite the fact that this next step makes such good sense, few faculty have taken it, even among the very enthusiastic implementers of classroom assessment. The terms *classroom research* and *classroom assessment* became confused and have ended up being used interchangeably, with classroom assessment almost always being the referent. Even though faculty have not been captivated by classroom research, however, it is a model worth revisiting, especially for its developmental potential. It's a great place for faculty to get started thinking about systematic analysis of classroom dynamics. More on this in Chapter Eight.

Furthermore, many connections exist between the ideas of classroom research and action research, a large term that now includes practitioner research, participatory action research, and collaborative inquiry, as well as a variety of other iterations. Action research has been defined as "a participatory, democratic process concerned with developing practical knowing. . . . It seeks to bring together action and reflection, theory and practice, in participation with others, in the pursuit of practical solutions to issues of pressing concern" (Reason and Bradbury, 2001, p. 3). (In addition to this comprehensive handbook, I'd recommend two other how-to resources that provide details on doing action research: Stringer, 1996; and Bray, Lee, Smith, and Yorks, 2000.) Among its key components, action research involves participants and researchers in the generation of knowledge and draws heavily on experiential knowledge. Anderson and Herr (1999) discuss its role in basic education, what it can contribute, and how its validity can be assessed. In the higher education context, Bensimon, Polkinghorne, Bauman, and Vallejo (2004) contrast traditional research with a practitioner-as-researcher model and then provide details about a project in which the approach was used. Action research (much like other emancipatory pedagogies) often has a political agenda, and that, coupled with its unconventional methods, predicts slow acceptance within the academic community.

Stenberg (2005) proposes narratives that rely on reflexive inquiry as a "knowledge-making activity that involves the interplay of visions and practices, both of which require reflection" (p. xviii). Her book illustrates a new way teachers can learn about and from individual practice. This approach fits comfortably with personal narratives and could do much to add rigor and robustness to that kind of individual inquiry.

I am not suggesting that classroom research, action research, or other possible iterations of qualitative research, such as reflexive inquiry, singly or collectively are the new definition needed for pedagogical research. Rather, I'm offering them as examples to illustrate that alternative approaches to conventional research exist, and some of them dovetail with practitioner needs and capabilities as researchers. What would most help us at the moment is letting go of our automatic preference for pedagogical scholarship that is research-based and the narrow definitions of research that prevent us from considering other kinds of systematic inquiry.

How We Think About the Wisdom of Practice

Some of us need to start seeing experienced-based knowledge as a legitimate way of knowing. More of us need to move beyond tacit, begrudging acceptance to a place where we see that valuable knowledge can be extrapolated from practice. We need to recognize that extracting this level of insight and understanding does not happen without deep reflection and critical analysis. It requires mental rigor—the kind that makes this work scholarly. (For examples, return to Chapter Four or consult Stenberg, 2005, whose book contains sample narratives that are then analyzed in terms of developmental and scholarly potential.)

Most of us are prevented from finding our way to this place by the literature itself. You cannot read long before happening on one of those "war stories" about what happened in the classroom when the author did X. Perkins (2004) describes the problem: "Through hard work we figure out what works and what does not for *us*, in *our* classrooms. We have gut feelings and anecdotal evidence from our peers. However, we fail to carry out the painstaking investigations necessary to really figure out how our teaching affects student learning" (p. 113). For this reason, a lot of experience-based work is not scholarly and most of us know it when we read it. Schön (1995) sets this challenge: "New scholars must produce knowledge that is testably valid, according to criteria of appropriate rigor, and their claims to knowledge must lend themselves to intellectual debate within academic . . . communities of inquiry" (p. 27).

In addition to specifying the terms and conditions under which reports based on experience qualify as scholarship, we need to recognize the power of doing pedagogical scholarship, especially those kinds that are experience-based, to affect positively the perceptions and practice of the person involved. Mallard (2002) believes that realizing the developmental potential of doing scholarship requires a paradigm shift "that focuses not so much on the product of research as on the person and research process" (p. 59). Weston and McAlpine (2001) describe a continuum of growth that reflects how faculty thinking and interaction change as the skills required to do scholarly work on teaching and learning emerge. The potential of pedagogical scholarship to develop teachers underscores the value of making this work a viable option for many faculty.

The work of beginning scholars is not always exemplary, and with pedagogical scholarship the quality issue must be an ever-present concern. But we could consider alternative forms and venues for the public dissemination of experience-based work. Stuck in a top-tier, refereed-journal mode of thinking, we rarely consider other options, even those that do not challenge the dominance of journals. Listserves (local and discipline-based), electronic bulletin boards, Web-based resource collections, online writing support groups, interactive online journals (where readers respond to articles), and newsletters could all provide outlets for work. Even more provocatively, something else that might need to change is our thinking about how a viable pedagogical literature might be structured and formatted. Are journals the best option when the main goals are to improve practice and advance the profession?

Finally, besides more positive and specific thinking about experience-based scholarship and seeing its potential as a development tool for faculty, we need to begin thinking about how the knowledge it generates relates to what is being documented by research. Obviously, this need goes in both directions—we also need to think about how research knowledge connects with experience-based understandings. The classroom and action research models offer workable ways of incorporating experience into research. What is often missing when experience-based work is less than robust is the structure and systematic analysis that research inquiry provides. The fact that experience and research-based work cohabitate in the same literature makes this kind of movement toward each other, this blending of the two approaches, possible. Accomplishing that objective might very well result in a truly unique form of inquiry, yet another feature to differentiate and distinguish pedagogical scholarship from other kinds of scholarly work. Moving the research and experiential approaches closer together would also help to alleviate the schizophrenic feel that results when reading literature that uses such diverse approaches.

How We Think About the Scholarships of Integration and Application

This change is pretty simple and straightforward: basically, these kinds of scholarship need to be valued. They need to be valued in the sense of being rewarded, but more important, what they contribute needs to be recognized. A scholarship of integration would take what practitioner scholarship has documented (both experientially and empirically) and begin to put it together, to say what we know, and then to say how that relates to what else we know. Absent from the pedagogical literature because of our failure to see the need for it, scholarship that integrates is also absent in our disciplines because the push to discover has been valued more than the need to relate what we know. Braxton, Luckey, and Helland (2002) assert that the scholarship of integration "has received the least amount of scholarly attention of Boyer's four domains" (p. 45).

Scholarship that applies, that says what to do about what we know (the recommended-practices approach) appears more often. But how can practices be recommended when so little scholarship of integration has occurred? As noted in Chapter Four, the recommendations may be based on research in education, they may be based on experience, or they may rest on nothing more than the opinion of the author who offers them, which brings us right back to the necessity of scholarship that credibly distills and brings together what we know.

When the scholarships of integration and application are exemplary, they require sophisticated intellectual skills. Translation of unfamiliar jargon and research methodologies occurs. Summarizing is involved—a long study or several related ones are pared to their essence. In some cases, research findings are integrated, with theory and results combined to create a principle, guideline, or general conclusion. Sometimes what has been learned experientially is integrated with what is known empirically. Doing this work well requires intimate knowledge of the content. In most disciplines, when scholarly work is integrated, distilled, and applied, that task is assigned to well-established experts in the field. If an example might be more convincing, take a look at Prince's integration and application of the research on active learning (2004). What a needed and valuable piece of scholarship! How many fields and faculty beyond engineering would benefit from its contents?

In sum, we must come to see that this work is needed—that viability of the literature and credibility of pedagogical scholarship are diminished without it. We must recognize that when this work is done well, it is intellectually challenging. It is work that merits reward and work that establishes the reputation of a profession.

Thinking About the Relationship Between Pedagogical Scholarship and the Disciplines

Pedagogical scholarship can't belong exclusively to the disciplines, for reasons already uncovered. It will lose its identity, become inextricably entangled with the discipline's standards for scholarship, and forever be second-class. But pedagogical scholarship cannot exist as an island. It lacks the resources to be self-sustaining, and part of its identity and all of its purpose are connected to those disciplinary mainlands. Could it be an isthmus? Part of the mainland but clearly separated and differentiated from it?

The reasons practitioner pedagogical scholarship must belong to the disciplines are compelling. Promotion and tenure decisions will continue to be made there. This is the arena in which faculty work is counted, and there is no impetus to change this current reality. In addition, some aspects of teaching disciplinary content are unique. A detailed rationale for locating pedagogical scholarship within the disciplines is offered by Healey (2000) in an exceptionally well-documented piece.

Pedagogical scholarship also must belong to itself. Much research, like that conducted by Murray and Renaud (1995), has shown that teaching behaviors, at least as students see them, are remarkably consistent across the disciplines. There are many instructional issues that transcend the disciplines—they confront teachers everywhere. But it is what teachers can learn from colleagues in other disciplines that really justifies pedagogical connections outside the discipline. When faculty confront instructional issues together, when they see how teachers in other contexts with different content and different students resolve problems, they learn from them and find their way to solutions that work in their situation. Collegiality, the kind that motivates and sustains teachers, transcends disciplines.

What needs to change here is our dichotomous thinking: either pedagogical scholarship belongs to the disciplines or it is generic. In reality it needs to be both, and all of us committed to this scholarship and the literature that represents it need to advance its causes jointly. Together, we can accomplish much more than any discipline can on its own. I hope that showcasing work from many disciplines has illustrated how much we can learn from each other. Our thinking needs to start to mirror the complexity of these issues. The causes of pedagogical scholarship are not best served by moving it to the disciplines and shutting the doors to outside influences. The causes of pedagogical scholarship are not best served by ignoring the disciplines. The reality of the situation demands thinking that is creative and integrative, not simplistic and polar.

Our Vision of What Needs to Change

Since the Boyer report (1990) first launched interest in the scholarship of teaching, much effort has been expended. Most of it has focused on issues that pertain to its production—definitions, new characteristics, and avenues of dissemination. Scholarship-of-teaching work has been done in some new and very promising ways (see Hutchings, 2000, for examples). To all teaching advocates, recent interest in the creation, publication, and reward of pedagogical scholarship is a thrilling turn of events. But it is not enough.

Our vision should be larger. Pedagogical scholarship is not an end in itself. It should benefit more than just those who create it. Scholarship that is applied aims to improve practice—that's one of its defining features. So far, we haven't quite got that vision. Of what value is great pedagogical scholarship if it is never read or implemented? How do we get to instructional practice informed by the literature? How do we get to norms expecting that literature (in whatever form) will play a key role in the growth and development of teachers? How do we get to thinking that defines college teaching in professional terms? As much as we need pedagogical scholarship legitimized and counted, we need pedagogical literature seen as a vibrant repository of collected knowledge about teaching and learning. We should be focusing on developing and promoting the literature as much as we are focusing on creating and recognizing the scholarship.

Both are inextricably linked and synergistically related. Scholarship that is more credible, more recognized and rewarded, will make the literature more viable. Viable literature is better scholarship. If addressed simultaneously, both will advance further faster, with the needs of each better balanced with those of the other.

As this chapter concludes, the review of previously published pedagogical scholarship also ends. An analysis of what we have set against what we need shows that previously published pedagogical literature provides some of what we need, but not nearly enough to make scholarly work on teaching and learning credible scholarship and viable literature. However, it provides a foundation—one that certain changes will strengthen. We can build on it a different and better future. Mallard (2002) captures the essence and spirit of a new future for scholarly work on teaching and learning: "A new value in scholarship is to envision, honor, celebrate, and relate to the whole being of scholars—not only to their minds, but also to their souls, not only to their reasoning, but also to their passion, not only to their dossiers, but also to their dreams" (p. 69).

8

From Looking to Doing:
Advice for Faculty

With the review of previously published pedagogical scholarship complete, in this chapter the gears can shift; now the focus is on doing scholarly work on teaching and learning. This chapter has advice for faculty who have never done it before and advice for those who have done some but would like to do more and do it better. In this chapter I write to you directly. My goal is to get you doing pedagogical scholarship and to offer advice that will help you do it well. I begin with a litany of reasons that you should, add a few reasons not to, and then make suggestions for getting started and doing more.

The Reasons

For many years it was assumed (still is by some) that doing research directly and positively affected teaching quality. Good researchers made good teachers. Although social science research is equivocal on many educational issues, this is not one of them. For a convincing collection of data, see a forty-four study meta-analysis (Feldman, 1987), the results of which showed a .12 correlation between research productivity (as measured by number of publications) and teaching effectiveness (as measured by student ratings). The relationship is neither positive nor negative; rather, in terms of these variables, there is no relationship between research and teaching.

When the scholarship is pedagogical, it's a very different story. Here the relationship between the scholarship and the teaching is strong and synergistic, as those of us who have done it will readily verify. *Doing pedagogical scholarship does make you a better teacher.* And better teachers are those whose students learn more. For those unconvinced, consider seven interconnected reasons that show how and why pedagogical scholarship positively affects teaching. Their cumulative weight will, I hope, bury the reasons that have prevented you from doing pedagogical scholarship or kept your efforts to a minimum.

1. *You explore the questions that interest you.* Do you have questions about what's happening in your classroom? I think every teacher does, and pedagogical scholarship gives you the opportunity to explore the questions about teaching and learning that interest you. Are you concerned about what does and doesn't motivate students? Do you worry about cheating? Do you wonder if making course material available online will expedite student study efforts? You can think of these as research questions. Faculty do scholarship in areas that are of interest to them. Scholarly work on teaching and learning should be no different. You can use it to pursue answers to those questions that intrigue you. That's energizing work; we are always motivated to learn when there's a need to know. Pedagogical scholarship makes you a better teacher because exploring questions of interest makes it likely that you'll learn from the answers.

2. *You develop instructional awareness.* Most of us have not been trained to teach. We learned how in the school of hard knocks, which means we aren't always explicitly aware of the details. Say you start studying student motivation. All of a sudden you become much more aware of motivation in your classroom. You see students who are and aren't motivated. You see yourself reaching out to those who aren't, and you begin to assess the approaches you use. Doing pedagogical scholarship adds details and depth to your understanding of how you teach; in this way you become a reflective practitioner—someone who knows what they do and why they do it, and someone who begins to discover the wisdom in practice. Pedagogical scholarship makes you a better teacher because it fosters an awareness of instructional details; if you know the details you can handle them better.

3. *You think more deeply about teaching and learning.* Once again, because we lack training, but also because we work in a culture (sometimes at our institutions, generally in society) that devalues teaching, we frequently fail to see the intellectual intrigue inherently a part of teaching and learning. Instead, the daily details consume us—what active learning strategies to use with these problems, will a quiz today motivate more to read the next assignment, how much time can be devoted to examples. Or we can't take our eyes off the content. We wear blinders that keep us always looking at how much we have to cover and what will happen to us if we don't.

Please now, I'm not advocating for content-free courses or saying that details don't make a difference (that would contradict reason two). Rather, the point is that pedagogical scholarship improves teaching because it uncovers the complexity and intrigue that make work on the details intellectually rich and satisfying. Understanding the motivation to learn is a good example. We all know that a teacher cannot learn anything for a student. At some point the student's responsibility starts and the teacher's responsibility ends. But where is that point? When has a teacher done enough? Most of us have thought very little about who's responsible for what in the teaching-learning process. Once you start, all sorts of vexing issues emerge. Do teachers positively affect the motivation to learn when they require certain actions related to learning (such as attendance, participation, pop quizzes)? Or do they create an addictive dependence on extrinsic motivators that ends up inhibiting the lifelong, self-regulated learning now a recognized ingredient of professional success? Scholarly work takes thinking about teaching and learning to much more interesting places.

There's another benefit that accrues when our thinking about teaching and learning is more intellectually robust. Respect and value come with the recognition that educational phenomena are complex, not yet well understood, and still mostly unexplored. In that way teaching and learning are no different from phenomena studied in our disciplines. Pedagogical scholarship makes you a better teacher because it expands intellectual curiosity, out of which emerges respect for the craft of teaching.

4. *You improve for the right reasons.* Scholarly work on teaching and learning makes better teaching a positive and constructive endeavor. Unlike many instructional improvement initiatives, it's not premised on notions of remediation or deficiency. You're not trying to make changes so students will give you good ratings. You're not trying to make changes because your department chair hinted that your raise might be affected if you don't. You're not doing pedagogical scholarship because you need to improve. You do it recognizing that any aspect of instructional practice can be studied, better understood, and more effectively executed.

Doing pedagogical scholarship connects your motivation to a different energy source. You are looking at something specific, a particular part of your teaching or student learning, as opposed to its global, overall effectiveness. You analyze it systematically. You generate results or come up with conclusions that are concrete. They have implications. The results enable you to change specific aspects of instruction. You can see that the changes make a difference, and that motivates continued effort. Pedagogical scholarship makes you a better teacher because it makes improvement something you want to do—not something you have to do.

5. *It keeps your teaching fresh over the long haul.* We underestimate what it takes to keep teaching alive and well across a career. So much in our teaching lives stays the same. The content: of course knowledge is advancing and changing, but back in those beginning courses, the basic building blocks in most fields stay the same. The students: of course they've changed a lot over the past twenty years, but they still ask many of the same questions and give a lot of the same (not very good) answers. Our colleagues: of course some endear

themselves to us more each year, but others drain our energy and make us cynical. Administrators: of course they come and go, but their initiatives seem to recycle endlessly.

Doing pedagogical scholarship offers a way past all that stays the same. It changes your perspective. You see new things or see old ones from a different angle. Even though content, students, colleagues, and initiatives may become enervatingly familiar, how you teach—the strategies you try, the design of learning activities, the methods of evaluation, the policies set in place to create a climate conducive to learning—these can change. They can evolve, grow, or be transformed. They can be added, deleted, revised, or re-engineered. Pedagogical scholarship makes this about more than change for the sake of change. These alterations you study, analyze, and assess systematically. They are changes you can connect to what matters most: student learning.

Pedagogical scholarship makes you a better teacher because it makes teaching a journey and keeps you moving from one destination to the next.

6. *It improves conversations with colleagues.* A lot of teaching talk drags us down. It's that endless stream of complaints: students aren't what they used to be, classes are too large, administrators don't fix problems, textbooks dumb down the content, grades are inflated. Once again, I mean not to trivialize bona fide barriers that stand in the way of learning. It's just that when negative talk infects our thinking, pretty soon we're not feeling good about teaching, and when you don't feel well, performance suffers.

Talk about teaching that never rises above the trivial can also enervate. Is it better to have two or three excused absences in one course? Do students cheat less if the exam is printed in different colors? How many points should be deducted if a student is late to class? Good decisions about all these details need to be made, but teaching and learning are about so much more; pedagogical scholarship changes the agenda. There's a new idea to bounce off someone else, an honest query that can't yet be answered, a resource to share, a viewpoint on an issue to be argued, or a finding to be explored for implications. Conversations focused on instructional substance enable us to take advantage of all that our colleagues can be: inquisitive co-learners, challenging interlocutors, reflective practitioners, and intellectual soul mates. Pedagogical scholarship makes you a better teacher because it makes collegial conversations substantive and stimulating.

7. It fosters learning in new ways and from new people. If you've read the rest of this book, you can probably guess the logic behind this reason. Our disciplines become safe homes; all too often we no longer venture outside despite the fact that, in the case of pedagogy, many instructional issues, topics, and questions are not discipline-specific. What to do when students lack the motivation to learn confronts faculty in every field.

Scholarly work on teaching and learning offers a chance to collaborate with a new set of colleagues, folks whose disciplinary perspectives give them a different vantage point from which to view the pedagogical world. Cross-disciplinary associations need not be about changing your view to theirs. More often they're about the power of a different worldview to clarify the vision of our own. Pedagogical scholarship makes you a better teacher because peers can and do learn from and with each other.

Legitimately, some of the motivation to do scholarship derives from the desire to advance professionally. Increasingly, professional advancement is coming to those who do scholarly work on teaching and learning. Ultimately, we hope that this outcome is as absolutely guaranteed as it is for disciplinary research. But standing alongside that reason is this equally compelling one, which the process alone achieves: Doing pedagogical scholarship makes you a better teacher.

A Few Reasons Why Not

Do not embark on a program of pedagogical scholarship if any of the following reasons are what motivate you.

You want "right" answers to pedagogical problems. When human behavior is involved, there are few straightforward, definitive answers. A systematic study of some aspect of instructional practice gives you a still picture, a view of what was happening at a particular point in time and space. You need a video that streams across the whole course and then jumps to different courses; at this point even the most sophisticated methodologies briefly capture the interplay of a few variables. You can design inquiries that produce straightforward answers, but when you go to act on what you've learned, the situation will have changed and the answers may not apply.

One of the ways we devalue teaching (even those of us deeply committed to it) is by looking for and believing in definitive answers to instructional problems. Attendance problems could be cured if we had just the right policy. Cheating could be prevented if we could invent just the right system. Motivation could be produced by just the right balance of quizzes and extra credit. Pedagogical scholarship will not solve everything perplexing about teaching and learning. It will enlarge your understanding, move you closer to answers, and that way make you a better teacher, but if you're after once-and-for-all answers, you've got a Don Quixote quest on your hands.

You think it's easy. You can do pedagogical scholarship that is easy; some work of that caliber has even been published. But that's not good scholarship, and this book is not an invitation to devalue teaching with slipshod, second-class work. Good pedagogical scholarship, like any other scholarly work, is rigorous and challenging. It takes time and energy to complete. If you're not persuaded that this work has intellectual integrity, let me once again invite you to read the exemplars showcased in the book. They are not examples of work completed on a weekend.

You think you can get anything published. Chapter Two includes information on the rejection rates of pedagogical periodicals; they rival those of top-tier journals in most fields. Increasingly, the journals are saying if the pedagogical piece isn't equal in quality to a piece you'd submit to the top-tier research journal, don't send it in for review.

Does this mean that it's all but impossible to get pedagogical material published? No, persistence and perseverance pay off with pedagogical publications just as they do with discipline-based research. There are lots of outlets. But if you're doing pedagogical scholarship assuming whatever you send out will come back with three stars and a congratulatory kiss, you're going to be disappointed.

You want your colleagues to respect you. Pedagogical scholarship is becoming a viable and accepted form of scholarship, but there are still many faculty who, despite this growing acceptance, remain convinced that it is not as legitimate or worthy as research in the discipline. Doing pedagogical scholarship is not the easy way to gain stature and reputation in most departments. If that's your objective, do disciplinary research and lots of it.

You expect to get tenure and promoted (and live happily ever after). At many more places now, it is possible to get tenure and be promoted with pedagogical scholarship in your dossier. In some places, it will carry the day on its own (along with evidence of good teaching and performance of service). In some places, pedagogical scholarship can take the place of some expected research scholarship. In some places, the policy says pedagogical scholarship counts, but there aren't any or very many examples of where it has. Pedagogical scholarship may get you tenure and promoted, but don't make that assumption without having analyzed the evidence pretty carefully.

Getting Started: Moving Past Fears

I think fear prevents a lot of faculty from getting started. It derives from different sources and circles around a number of issues relevant to scholarly work in general. Let's see if we can identify and address some of those worries.

Finding Something That Hasn't Already Been Done

Chances are all but guaranteed that you aren't going to find something that hasn't been done already. Here's an example of how orientations to discipline-based research color our thinking about pedagogical scholarship. If the scholarship is not discovery-based (and most pedagogical scholarship isn't), finding something heretofore unstudied is not a requirement. When the research is applied (and most pedagogical scholarship is), a different set of goals drives the effort. For example, one of the goals is to further our understanding of how something works in different contexts (with your content, your students, your teaching style, and at your kind of institution). Another goal involves exploring how the modification or application of a technique, policy, or approach affects the outcomes. Many articles have appeared on the feedback mechanism called minute papers. You're right, we don't need more analyses establishing that this approach positively affects learning (for both students and teachers), but we are still benefiting from work that illustrates the effects of different iterations—how the technique can be modified, how it can be used in different settings, how it works with particular kinds of content, and how various teachers use and respond to the results. Don't worry about your work being original research. Go with what's of interest to you. I can't think of any instructional topic about which we couldn't beneficially learn more.

Tracking Down All That Other Scholarship

You can let go of this concern for a couple of reasons. First, with most instructional topics it is not humanly possible to track down all the relevant work. It has been conducted across multiple fields and has appeared in a wide range of sources, including places where you'd never think to look for pedagogical material. As noted elsewhere in the book, the various knowledge bases for teaching and learning are not well organized or well integrated.

Moreover, despite this need to better integrate pedagogical knowledge, when research is applied, lit reviews serve a different purpose. They provide an overview and sample of related work. Because an applied inquiry does not aim to make new discoveries and because the question it will answer derives from practice, not previous research, the need to summon and connect all that is known or has been discovered previously is not as compelling.

Now, as explored in Chapters Four and Five, this does not excuse pedagogical inquiries from recognition that others have been here and produced relevant findings. Whether or not it has been collected and distilled, a research and experiential knowledge base supports most instructional techniques, policies, and approaches. Good pedagogical scholarship is well documented, but even the exemplars showcased here do not include comprehensive reviews of the literature. You want to push yourself to read widely and document extensively, but don't hold yourself to an exhaustive review of the literature.

Not Knowing How to Do Education Research

Answer this fear by telling yourself that you're not doing educational research. That's what people with Ph.D.s in education and its various related fields do. As a faculty member in a discipline other than education, you're doing practitioner pedagogical scholarship. It may or may not use the methodologies of education and other social science fields. Return to the exemplars in Chapter Four for examples of quality work that don't use the methods typically associated with these fields. That doesn't mean the work is without standards, or isn't systematic, or happens without the application of mental muscle. For the most part, however, what you end up doing won't be discovery-based educational research.

Now, you may need or want to employ quantitative or qualitative methods not used in your fields and with which you are unfamiliar. Obviously, if you're going to do good work, you will have to learn how to use these methods well. But there are colleagues who can help (both from your discipline and in these fields), and most faculty excel when there's something to be learned.

Having Something Creative or Innovative to Report

First question: How do you know if you are doing anything creative or innovative? I've lost track of the number of times faculty members have described to me a very imaginative, unusual, interesting, creative approach to which I've exclaimed, "You need to write that up!" and to which they've responded, "Naw, it's really nothing." I never cease to be amazed at how even teaching's most committed practitioners devalue what they do. So, don't start out convinced that there's nothing exemplary about your practice. Best advice: go ahead, write it up, and let others determine its merit.

There's a second response to this fear. Pedagogical scholarship is about much more than innovative aspects of practice. It can just as profitably be about an instructional problem and your quest for a solution. It may be a critical reflection that explores the connection between what you believe and what you do. It may be a hypothesis to subject to testing. It may be advice summed from a careful analysis of experience. It may even be a failure from which important lessons were learned. Move beyond thinking about pedagogical scholarship as writing up some novel thing you do in the classroom—that's only one of many possibilities.

No Time to Pursue Pedagogical Scholarship

If you're still reading this book, I would guess that you do laud recent interest in the scholarship of teaching. Like the rest of us, you believe that good scholarly work on teaching merits reward and recognition. What frightens you, however, is the possibility that now, in addition to teaching well, you will be expected to do scholarship about it. I don't think you need to worry. In all the literature I reviewed to prepare this book I did not once read a call to make pedagogical scholarship mandatory. The literature consistently proposes making it an option, seeing it as something that would further value teaching, something that would promote long overdue reward and recognition.

Moreover, finding time for pedagogical scholarship may be easier once you consider how many objectives the process accomplishes. First, it's an effective professional development activity for you, with equally positive outcomes for your students. Better teaching and more learning run on parallel tracks. Second, pedagogical scholarship is increasingly becoming a viable avenue for professional advancement. These are publications that count at more institutions than ever before. And third, pedagogical scholarship offers you the satisfying opportunity of contributing to the practitioner knowledge base for teaching. Your work can help us understand important instructional issues better.

There's one last feature of pedagogical scholarship that makes doing it possible even when time is limited. You can dive in intermittently and stay in for comparatively short periods. In yet another way, it's not like cutting-edge research in a field in which, if you are absent for a year, it may well take two to catch up. Applied scholarship is about what we do—it's about analyzing all that lives and grows in a lake, not the quest to discover new lakes. Obviously, if you only dive in once every five years, you will not make the same kind of contribution as someone who lives in the lake, but you can still contribute. Many examples could be summoned to support that claim.

The Fear of Not Getting Published

You won't know whether you can succeed in getting your work published until you've tried. The best way to get past this fear is to review reasons for doing pedagogical scholarship. Those highlighted in the first part of this chapter still accrue even if your scholarly work on teaching and learning never gets published. Getting published may not even be the most important reason for doing this kind of scholarship.

You can also allay this fear by broadening your thinking about publication. Maybe your first pedagogical work doesn't appear in a top-tier journal. Maybe it's shared in a local newsletter or in a memo to departmental colleagues. Maybe it's a contribution to a Listserve, material posted on a Web site, or a presentation at a conference that showcases work on teaching and learning. From there you might move on to shorter and more informally structured articles, like those that regularly appear in some sections of the pedagogical periodicals. With all these options, it's pretty hard to imagine not finding a venue through which your work can be shared. You can start with more modest expectations, or you can first reach for the stars and then settle for something much closer to earth.

Getting Started: The Practical First Steps

The best place to begin is to start thinking concretely about doing it. Explore possibilities, identify the aspects of instruction that are of interest, making a list of them, if that works for you. Start framing your interests as questions or thinking of them as hypotheses. What don't you know and what would you need to do to generate answers? How could you test a hypothesis of interest? For good answers to these questions, review the classroom research models proposed by Cross and Steadman (1996). They show how questions arising from practice can be framed as queries amenable to systematic inquiry and include examples of scholarly work that uses these approaches.

Even if you are thinking more along the lines of one of the wisdom-of-practice approaches identified in this book, questions are a great way to define and focus the topic. What did you change? Why change that? How did you implement the change? What was the impact on student learning? How was that impact measured? Or, if you're thinking about a recommended-practices report, on what grounds do those recommendations rest? How is the advice you'd offer alike or different from that proposed by others? How broadly applicable is the advice you'd offer? I recommend questions because I think they're a great way to get minds moving.

At the same time, besides thinking generally and specifically about areas of interest and questions to pursue, start reading. I know, this smells like an author trying to sell books. All I can tell you is that my pedagogical reading came first and, despite my many vested interests in published material on teaching and learning, I know as an in-the-trenches teacher that reading has been terribly instrumental in my development as a teacher. I have learned and continue to learn a great deal from the literature on teaching and learning. That does not mean all articles are equally good; neither are all those containing research scholarship in our fields. But I find enough pedagogical literature to keep my nightstand cluttered and my reading light on late.

When preparing to do scholarly work on teaching and learning, I think you ought to be reading for three different reasons. First, you read because you need to start collecting material on those topics that are of interest. Second, you read to explore the various formats, approaches, structures, and options that have been used to analyze pedagogical issues. What kind of article do you want to write? Which of the approaches described in this book or that you identify on your own fit the questions that are forming in your mind? Remember to consider possibilities with an open mind—various approaches have been used in previously published work. Some of the best models (my opinion, of course) don't look like research completed in any discipline. Finally, I recommend reading for the most fundamental reason of all: read to learn! Read because you need to know more about a wide range of pedagogical topics. What you learn can be applied to your practice, but it may also uncover new areas of interest.

What to read first, assuming pedagogical reading has not been a regular part of your preparation to teach? I usually push folks in the direction of their discipline's or a related discipline's pedagogical periodical (see Appendix A for a list of them). In the beginning, faculty connect most easily and comfortably with those who share their content. Obviously, I'm a pretty big fan of newsletters and other succinct summaries as a way of easing in and making time for reading. There are lots of good books—but the best advice on what to read relates to the third and final suggestion for getting started.

Start talking. On almost every college campus or within your discipline, there are folks who either do or are consumers of pedagogical scholarship. Find those colleagues! Ask them to direct you to good articles, books, or periodicals. Read something they recommend and then talk with them about it. Once you start reading, use references cited in the material to lead you to other sources of interest.

Seek out colleagues with whom you can exchange ideas, even those early, not especially well-formed thoughts. Aspire to have substantive, intellectual exchanges with colleagues over teaching topics. Imagine conversations that take you to new places in your thinking. Share your early thinking and writing with those colleagues who understand and apply the principles of constructive feedback. You need criticism; you need praise; you need encouragement; and you need a colleague who can deliver all three authentically.

Getting started may well be the most difficult part of doing scholarly work on teaching and learning. Some stand on the dock a long time before finally taking the plunge. Others wade in very cautiously. But once you're wet and acclimated, I'm certain that you'll find swimming in these waters invigorating. In fact, you may end up like some of us: still in the water at the end of the day.

Advice on Doing It Better

A fundamental rule applies here: the more pedagogical scholarship you do, the better your work becomes. One learns and grows in this arena as in any other; no one is born doing it well. But sometimes folks are motivated to intervene and move this natural progression in the direction of greater improvement accomplished more quickly. For them, I'd offer these concrete suggestions, most drawn from the playbook that has worked for me.

Re-Do

Take a piece of pedagogical scholarship already completed; yes, even a piece that may have been published, and re-do it. Make it better. Add new sources. Refine the questions. Try a different method of analysis. Further mine the results for implications. If the thought of revisiting sounds way too boring, how about doing the next analysis, the exploration that logically follows the first? The goal here is to go back to a place you've been and use the knowledge gained to dig deeper. In most cases this is not boring. Finished analyses often raise as many questions as they answer, but frequently we don't follow up. If we did, we would discover an avenue to deeper and richer understandings that then reemerge in our practice and scholarship. I have discovered one liability with this approach: the new work is often so stunningly better, the inquiry that spawned it ends up being something of an embarrassment.

Have Scholarship Aspirations

I keep a file of the kind of work I want to be doing. Some of the material covers topics I've wanted to write about. Some describes policies, practices, techniques, and assignment designs I wish I had created. Mostly, the material models the depth of thinking, level of insight, and intellectual richness I'm striving to achieve. So, when I am writing something that tries to pull together and make sense of different work on the same topic, I look at how educational psychologist Pintrich (2003) orders the research on motivation. This detailed review isn't easy reading, but after spending time working through it, I get the picture. I see how the research on motivation relates, interconnects, and fits together. The article is a masterpiece—some of Pintrich's last and very best work.

For years I've held on to a piece by Thomas (1982) called "The Art of Teaching Science." For me it models the power of carefully framed questions to trigger whole new worlds of thinking. Also in my file are a couple of chapters from Smith's eclectic history of higher education, *Killing the Spirit* (1990). He's a historian who transforms boring details into fascinating stories and then uses them to make some pretty interesting points. I wish I had Kohn's ability (1986, 1993) to translate, assemble, and then use research to attack aspects of practice at odds with what has been discovered. He sees how research relates to practice more clearly than anyone else I've read. I love Elbow's way with words. I keep lots of quotes from his *Embracing Contraries* (1986) in this folder. He can pack enough ideas in two or three sentences to supply my intellectual lunch for a week.

Elsewhere in this book I've referred to my file of favorite articles on teaching. These are pieces that I connect with as a teacher. The file I'm describing here contains the kind of work I aspire to do. I connect with it as a scholar. I'm not recommending that you have two collections, or that you even keep articles, but I do believe you can improve the quality of your pedagogical scholarship by carefully considering the characteristics of pedagogical work you deem exemplary. When my motivation burns low, I use this folder to fan the embers.

Formulate Next Goals

Part of improving at anything involves the ability to set realistic goals, to identify the achievable next steps. As a pedagogical scholar, this means planning where your work is next headed. It may involve the topics you want to explore next, but it needs to include more. What's the next goal for you as a pedagogical scholar? Is there a more prestigious journal on the next rung up the ladder? Is it a featured article in a journal as opposed to a short piece in the "best practices" section? Is your next step a book? Maybe an edited anthology or coauthored manuscript first? Could it be something quite unconventional—perhaps not a traditional publication at all?

Beyond next goals for content and dissemination, think also of personal development objectives. If you've written and published three personal accounts of change, it's time to consider other approaches used in pedagogical scholarship. If you've only written for a discipline-based audience, it's time to consider writing more broadly. If you've never done scholarly work on teaching and learning with a colleague in a completely different discipline, it's an option well worth considering. The value of these goals relates less to getting more publications (and therefore recognition, a little fame, and almost no fortune) and more to the potential of pedagogical scholarship to develop your prowess as a teacher.

Join a Pedagogical Writing Support Group

The idea here is to get a small number (I'd recommend the four-to-seven range) of faculty interested in doing pedagogical scholarship to form a group to which members bring materials for review. These groups work best if members are allowed to bring pieces of work at all stages of development, from early ideas and tentative outlines to final drafts and submitted articles returned for revision. All members read each other's work. In the beginning, before the group has a track record, it may be wise to let authors identify the questions about their work they'd most like the group to answer. Later on, after a level of trust has developed, members may be free to comment where they will. Be realistic about time commitments. Try for thirty minutes per review, and don't let the conversation get stuck on one issue. Do two or three reviews per meeting, and let members volunteer when they have something to review. However, group members should not be allowed to stay in the group if they never submit work for review.

My experience facilitating one such group convinced me of their value. Most members in my group were new to pedagogical scholarship. A couple had done some work; no one had the fleet of publications I could claim. I really saw myself as facilitator of the group, but I did believe strongly that everyone in the group needed to share material. All I had at the time was an almost finished article. I shared it with the group, but did so telling myself that there wasn't likely to be much these folks could offer a veteran with an article just about ready to submit. Halfway through their review of my article, my face was flushed. By the end, I was writing as fast as I could. I remember feeling angry on the way home (I should have felt embarrassed): I was going to have to revise that piece significantly. I spent the whole weekend re-doing it and ended up with a better article.

This particular group met for a semester; at last count, three members have published something that they worked on in the group. The last time we met, a member observed that it was one of the best interactions with colleagues that she could remember having. I would have to agree.

Make a Commitment to Writing

Your pedagogical scholarship will improve if you devote time to the writing process. I firmly believe that you can use writing to learn, as in to clarify, elaborate, and enrich your thinking. I thought I had my ideas on pedagogical scholarship well in hand when I started this book. But the process of writing it has changed my thinking; my ideas have evolved. The preface I wrote more than two years ago when I started on this project must be scrapped. It describes the book I intended to write, not the book I ended up writing.

There's another commitment to writing quite unrelated to its power to promote thinking that I believe makes pedagogical scholarship better. Pedagogical writing needs to be different, as in better than most academic writing. I could pontificate at length here about what I see as a wasteland of jargon, equivocation, and obfuscation. Some wonder why our good research has so little impact on the pernicious problems of people, their societies, and our planet. I don't wonder at all: nobody can understand what we've written. Researchers don't see themselves as translators, which is fine, but then the academic culture in general doesn't value the work that seeks to make what is known accessible and relevant.

Having already made some of these points in Chapter Seven, I must move quickly to the new point. We have the chance to build on our history. Most previously published pedagogical scholarship is written so that it can be read. As it moves more in the direction of research, that claim stands in jeopardy unless we remain mindful that scholarly work on teaching and learning is being published in journals read by practitioners, people with the power to do something about what they read. Let's continue to write to each other as intellectually able colleagues, as fellow learners and committed professionals. Let's be clear, succinct, and discursive. Let's be objective, reasoned, and rational, but without forgetting teaching's affective aspects. Let's continue to define the writing associated with pedagogical scholarship uniquely, making it serve the needs of practitioners first and foremost. To sum: I'm proposing that you'll do better pedagogical scholarship if you let the writing teach you and if you write mindful of your audience and purpose.

Push the Envelope

Pushing the envelope, taking risks, putting yourself close to the edge can positively affect your pedagogical scholarship. This should not be the modus operandi for all aspects of your instructional practice and pedagogical scholarship; for most of us, that's the fast track to burnout. But to avoid getting trapped by deep ruts, we need to keep at least one wheel running out of the groove and on the edge.

The possibilities are endless, but they need to fit you, sort of. What you want to achieve here won't be accomplished by doing what's already comfortable. The goal is find those activities that take you to new and different places, places where you feel just a tad uncomfortable. I'll share a bit of what's worked for me, but not because that's what you should do. Think of these ideas as water you can use to prime your own pump.

Nothing has pushed me more than taking courses—outside my discipline—with students. I'm not talking about observing or auditing a course. I'm talking about being a student who does the homework and takes the tests. Two weeks into the chemistry course I took with twenty first-semester students I was back to instructional bedrock, forced to examine every premise on which my instructional practice rested. Teaching looks so different from the learning side of the classroom. Before I took chemistry I knew what the research said: students can learn from and with each other. After chemistry, I had experienced what the research said. When others asked how I did it, I heard myself attributing my modest success in the course not to the teacher, not to what happened in lab, not to the textbook, but to my study group.

The underlying principle here is that learning something new, something unlike what we already know, forces us to use whole new sets of mental muscles—often they are ones not regularly exercised. Maybe you don't have time to take courses (it is a time-consuming endeavor), but learn something. Whether it's how to back a trailer, play a dulcimer, or identify Oregon Pinot Noirs, I firmly believe we're better teachers and better pedagogical scholars with learning experiences fresh in our minds.

Reading is another vehicle I use to take my thinking to different places. Last summer it was a beautiful collection of favorite poems selected by teachers (Intrator and Scribner, 2003). It made teaching feel pure—like swimming in the cool, clean, clear lake I'm lucky to live on during the summer. I was refreshed, invigorated, and full of new ideas.

One of my colleagues "journals" a course. After every session, she writes freely for five to ten minutes whatever comes to or is on her mind about that class. She doesn't allow herself to read anything she's written until the course is over. I tried this and came to understand much more clearly how courses ebb and flow.

Don't look for causal relationships between activities that push the envelope and improved pedagogical scholarship—they don't exist in the linear paradigm of cause and effect. But I remain convinced that a positive effect accrues when you keep one wheel out of the groove, rolling over uneven ground, bumping in and out of holes, and slipping around corners too fast.

Handle Rejection Constructively

We chide our students because they are so vested in their performances. But we are no different. Rejection humbles us. We pour over the feedback, dispute every sentence, and take ourselves to the woodshed over every infraction, even those not mentioned by reviewers.

It's easy to admonish against unhealthy responses like these, but it's terribly difficult to prevent personal, gut-level, emotional reaction to rejection—and new scholars are especially vulnerable. However, you must work to put rejections in perspective. If you don't, rejection will erode your confidence to the point where you start doubting your potential and stop doing pedagogical scholarship.

Rejection is a part of the process, and sometimes the process is whimsical and capricious. I frequently tell students about the first paper I wrote in graduate school. I worked on it for hours and when I turned it in, I was convinced it was the best paper I'd ever written. It was returned literally covered with comments, all negative, and the devastating grade of D. After an hour's meeting in his office, during which I tried to argue more reasonably than passionately that the paper was not that bad, the professor changed the grade to a D+. Despite this less-than-impressive beginning, I did manage to finish my Ph.D. In the process of sorting out materials from my classes, I happened on this paper. I re-read it through his comments and still thought it was good. I keyed in a clean copy and sent it off, mostly out of spite, to the most prestigious place I knew. And that's the story of my first publication (Gleason, 1982).

Sometimes material is rejected because it isn't very good or doesn't fit the mission of the publication to which it was sent. Sometimes material is rejected because far more material is submitted than can be used—this necessitates saying no to good material. And sometimes material is rejected because editors and reviewers make mistakes. Take a look at the feedback. Let a colleague help you consider it calmly and dispassionately. If the feedback would make for a better paper, do the revisions. If not, promptly send it off to some-place else. Play getting published like a game; some rounds you win and some you lose.

Advocate for Scholarly Work on Teaching and Learning

Granted, becoming such an advocate will improve your individual scholarship less directly. Nonetheless, pedagogical scholarship still needs advocates—not just faculty who do it, but teachers who understand its power to improve practice and change the professional stature of college teaching.

You can advocate for pedagogical scholarship in many ways. First, be a consumer who reads and has informed opinions about the nature and purposes of this literature. Second, promote the literature. Is it available to faculty on your campus? In the library, teaching center, online? If it is available, call it to people's attention and make recommendations about what they should read. Third, you can get involved with pedagogical publications. Consider being a reviewer. Many of the pedagogical periodicals make public calls for reviewers, in print or online at the publication's Web site. Review informally—send the editor an e-mail about an article you consider good or topics you'd like to have covered. Finally, when serving on promotion and tenure committees, develop enough expertise so that you can help committees make fair and informed decisions about pedagogical scholarship. This may seem like a circuitous path to improving your scholarship, but ultimately it will get you to that destination. With more advocates, pedagogical scholarship will continue to improve; as it advances, your work will move forward with it.

It is hard to write a conclusion that effectively sums and distills the interconnecting content of this chapter. All the reasons that you should do pedagogical scholarship tumble together. They connect with the benefits students gain when their teachers examine and learn from their practice and the benefits pedagogical scholarship gains when more faculty are involved and doing high-quality work. The ultimate beneficiary is the college teaching profession, which is finally supported by a credible and viable literature. It feels like many small streams converging to make a river. Individual reasons commingle and sacrifice their identity to become a larger and more dynamic force.

9

From Looking to Doing:
Advice for Academic Leaders

Academic leaders can do much to promote the viability of pedagogical literature and the credibility of pedagogical scholarship. Like Chapter Eight, this chapter offers advice, in this case to those interested in providing the leadership and setting the conditions that enhance scholarly work on teaching and learning. Again my aim is to offer advice directly. The process begins with setting the agenda, next there are actions that will advance it, and finally there's a constellation of issues that pertain to evaluation.

The Agenda

By *agenda* I'm referring to the context or frame within which scholarly work on teaching and learning is being promoted on a campus. Because no academic leader can "force" faculty members to use or produce pedagogical scholarship, this is about creating a climate, putting in place those policies and practices that foster a natural connection between faculty and scholarly work on teaching and learning. I'm proposing that an agenda with three features will produce conditions conducive to the creation and use of pedagogical scholarship.

Breadth

My experience is consistent with that reported by Kreber (2003). Teachers laud the interest in teaching and the move to see it as scholarly work, but they don't want to be *required* to do it. At one level, this resistance results from already feeling overworked, under-paid, and at some places not appreciated. At another level, it's the sense that teaching in and of itself merits reward and recognition. Practicing pedagogues shouldn't need to do scholarship on teaching and learning to have what they accomplish in the classroom valued. Less explicitly, the resistance may be an outgrowth of some of those fears described in Chapter Eight. Not only have most faculty never done pedagogical scholarship, they are not familiar with scholarly work on teaching. It's not just a question of can they do it; it's the more basic, what is it query. Given these feelings and fears, a move in the direction of mandating that all teachers produce pedagogical scholarship will likely engender results, but it will move teachers in the opposite direction.

It might be helpful to know that most institutions have not responded to the interest in the scholarship of teaching by making pedagogical scholarship required. Rather, it has been presented as an option—a different way to accomplish current requirements for scholarly work. Because the process of producing pedagogical scholarship accrues so many benefits, as I described in Chapter Eight, I think the option can be vigorously promoted, but let that endorsement stop short of a requirement.

More benefits accrue if the agenda is defined more broadly. Make it be about more than faculty doing scholarly work on teaching. I would frame it as creating norms expecting professional development for teachers at every career stage. I would make the agenda be about teaching and learning as complex intellectual phenomena, something much more intriguing than a skill set. I would focus the agenda on pedagogical literature in general: what would make it viable, informative, inspirational, and otherwise useful to practice? The agenda could even be about conceptual change, the kind needed to make substantive and lasting alterations in teaching and learning.

As I wrote in Chapter Seven, the issue isn't just making room at the academic table for pedagogical scholarship. If we accomplish that goal, more faculty may get tenure, promoted, and otherwise recognized for doing scholarly work on teaching, and that will be wonderful. However, we actually have a much larger problem on our hands. We have many faculty not trained to teach who learn to teach and continue to teach without ever going beyond insights derived from individual experience. This explains why faculty reject practices with benefits well established by research. This explains why faculty who have taught for years could write all they know about learning in one short paragraph. The instructional practice of many faculty rests on a small, internally informed, and often unchanging knowledge base. Fortunately, there are exceptions on every campus, but overall the report card of the professoriate on knowledge of teaching and learning would not make the dean's list. We very much need a viable literature that forms the basis for informed instructional practice. So, a broadly conceived agenda for pedagogical scholarship lauds its use as much as its production.

Here again a norm expecting informed practice will not be created by requiring faculty to read pedagogical literature. A better way to that goal makes part of the agenda exploring and assessing previously published pedagogical literature as a resource for teachers. What kinds of written and electronic materials do in-the-trenches teachers need? Does work like that highlighted in this volume address current needs? What changes would make faculty more likely to access its contents? The logic involved here reckons that when faculty starting seeing what the literature can (or potentially could) contribute to their practice, they may start accessing it more regularly and the motivation to contribute will be born or will grow stronger.

Creative, Innovative, and Open

Building on the idea of a broadly framed agenda, my advice here is to opt for equally broad definitions of pedagogical scholarship. As discussed previously, there is already a strong move afoot to make disciplinary research the model for pedagogical scholarship and to embed scholarly work on teaching and learning deep within the disciplines.

There are significant problems associated with making this paradigm the only or most desired model, as discussed previously. Faculty interested in doing discovery-based pedagogical scholarship and work that explores aspects of teaching and learning unique to the discipline should be encouraged to do so. But in the long run, I think we're far better served by attempts that focus on defining pedagogical scholarship uniquely—in light of needs it fulfills and the purposes for which it is being created.

Especially when scholarly work on teaching and learning is first being considered, I think it makes sense to use inclusive rather than exclusive definitions. The previously published work highlighted in this volume verifies that scholarly work on teaching and learning has taken many forms. This analysis of what has been done marks a place to begin. Let new and creative definitions be welcome. Explorations of the inventive might launch with an analysis of work and approaches highlighted in Chapter Six. Two questions can be used to constrain what might be too unconventional and border definitions that are too inclusive: What does it take to make this kind of work scholarly (issues of quality and standards)? What does it take to make this kind of work useful to practitioners (issues of relevance and applicability)?

Positive

The pedagogical scholarship agenda should not be motivated by any sort of need to improve—even though, for the reasons outlined in Chapter Eight, scholarly work on teaching and learning holds great instructional improvement potential. As we have learned from long, lackluster efforts at instructional development, resting any instructional initiative on premises that even once smelled of remediation and deficiency all but ensures its rejection. Improvement shouldn't be a dirty word. All of us can improve, and most of us should. However, it is wise counsel not to link this agenda to any negative needs. Rather, make the interest in pedagogical scholarship about a way of valuing teaching, a way of coming to respect its difficulty and complexity, a way of discovering how much there is yet to learn, and a way of building the practitioner knowledge base for teaching and learning.

I am optimistic about the power of a broadly conceived, creative, and positive pedagogical scholarship agenda, but I'm not naïve. Faculty who have not been trained to teach, who have taught successfully without knowing much about why something works, who have not been expected to grow and develop as teachers, and who have little or no history of pedagogical reading will not rush to endorse this agenda. My optimism is fueled, however, by years of acquainting faculty with good material on teaching and learning and having them respond favorably. I do not believe that most faculty are fundamentally opposed to learning about teaching and learning. They want to teach in ways that promote learning. If a well-written piece of scholarship that explores an aspect of instruction and extrapolates implications is put before them, faculty read it, often with interest. They will talk about it with others and do something about it in the classroom—at least that has been my experience. I think an agenda on pedagogical scholarship, properly set, has the power to change norms and improve practice by making faculty more reflective practitioners. It can also further establish the practitioner knowledge base for teaching and learning and gain greater recognition for teaching as scholarly work.

Actions to Accomplish the Agenda

For years, faculty have complained that administrators pay lip service to teaching, and those of us who work with faculty know that they change their minds slowly. For that reason, what is *said* about pedagogical scholarship will not be examined as carefully as what is *done*. In my brief tenure as an administrator, I learned that faculty accusations about lip service are not always fair. Administrators do act, but sometimes they are constrained from talking about those actions. If a faculty member is denied tenure on the basis of poor teaching, an administrator can't very well discuss the case. Still, the old adage about actions speaking louder than words remains true, which necessitates thinking more about actions and less about statements.

Many actions can be taken. I'm going to suggest two different lists: one for the broadly conceived agenda I've just advocated and a second specifically for encouraging and supporting those faculty who are doing or aspire to do pedagogical scholarship. Most of these actions cost comparatively little, a benefit indeed during these times of tight budgets.

Actions That Advance Work on the Agenda

First, academic leaders can advance the broad agenda proposed by bringing pedagogical literature to faculty. We face a long history of faculty not seeking out material on teaching and learning on their own. In the beginning, expect to have to bring it to faculty. Make it available in many ways—in the library, online, and in faculty mailboxes (electronic and otherwise). What to make available? Again, there are many possibilities, including books, periodicals, Web sites, newsletters—excellent material has appeared in all these sources. If you have faculty who are consumers of the pedagogical literature, ask them for recommendations. As noted elsewhere, initially faculty connect most easily with pedagogical materials in their disciplines. The local library ought to have subscriptions to at least some of the discipline-based pedagogical periodicals, but if the faculty is small and the budget tight, opt for some cross-disciplinary or generic publications as well. Cross-disciplinary publications also serve to show faculty that they can gain valuable pedagogical insights from colleagues in other fields. (These publications are listed in Appendixes A and B.)

Putting pedagogical material in faculty hands can be tackled creatively. Many institutions now have a sizeable cohort of new faculty and are in the process of acquiring more. At one place I know, the academic dean asked current faculty to recommend one or two of their favorite books or other sources of pedagogical information. He compiled the recommendations into a list and sent it to all new faculty with an invitation to order up to $100 worth of materials. The list of recommendations has grown from three pages to ten across the past four years.

I have worked with several institutions that have initiated a pedagogical "book of the year" program. These featured books are selected by faculty. Every faculty member gets a copy, and various discussion opportunities, including regularly convened reading groups, happen during the year. Several of these places have brief author-in-residence programs that bring the author to campus to meet informally with various groups that have read or are in the process of reading the book.

Less creative approaches, like regularly circulating good articles, can be just as successful. In the Preface, I write about my early experiences making copies of articles available to faculty. Their enthusiastic response stunned me. Faculty who receive the material could be invited to join discussion groups in person or online.

I would also gently remind of the power of leading by example. I recently participated in one of the author-in-residence programs described above. Individuals and small groups who wanted to discuss my book were invited to schedule time with me. I was very surprised to see the college president on my schedule. I figured it was a courtesy call. It was not. He brought the book, had notes, dog-eared pages, questions, and disagreements. The interactions I had with faculty at that institution were the most thoughtful and thorough of any place I've gone to discuss my book.

In addition to making pedagogical literature available, academic leaders, especially those, like department heads, who work directly with faculty, need to *talk teaching*. This would seem to contradict the advice to act more and talk less, but there is a distinction. This talk is not about how teaching is valued, how it matters and counts at the institution; this is teaching talk. It's another case of leading by example as well as modeling a different kind of conversation about teaching and learning. It isn't about academic leaders having all the answers; I won't point out how high that flies. But academic leaders are in positions where they can put teaching topics on the agenda and influence the caliber of exchange that occurs about them. They can place bellwethers in the swirling current of faculty opinions. This is not talk that accuses or confronts, rather it questions, raises honest queries. "Easy graders get higher student ratings in their courses? That's what you think? Have you read any of the research on this?" "You believe that grading on the curve motivates students' best efforts? Why? How does that work? If we looked at the literature, I wonder if it would support your position."

I know how busy academic leaders are. It is not realistic to expect that they develop expertise on all things teaching and learning. But again, we are talking about the necessity of leading by example. An academic leader cannot endorse learning, growth, and change for teachers if his or her own thinking remains stuck in time and space. At some level and to some degree, academic leaders must be in this literature if they hope to advocate successfully on its behalf.

Finally, I think academic leaders advance the cause of scholarly work on teaching by promoting and supporting efforts to find answers. Traditionally, beliefs about teaching and learning have not been held to the same levels of evidence and logic required for knowledge in the disciplines. Faculty beliefs about teaching and learning find their bases in experience and opinions (theirs and those of trusted colleagues). That experiential wisdom can be elaborated and tested by more thorough and systematic analyses. I'm not necessarily talking about full-blown research projects, but something more akin to classroom research at the institutional level. Look at some of the descriptive research highlighted in Chapter Five and imagine collecting data from your students and faculty on some of those issues.

Most colleges of any size now have some sort of institutional research capacity. Are those resources ever harnessed to questions that pertain to teaching and learning? If they are, that can be used to convey a number of important messages. It is an action that demonstrates the commitment to the pedagogical scholarship agenda. Data-driven answers to important instructional questions illustrate the value of knowing more definitively, of having evidence standing behind opinions. These inquiries also model approaches to doing scholarly work on teaching and learning, and if the knowledge generated influences the development or revision of policy, that demonstrates the power of applied scholarship.

Some caveats do exist: Data collected in classrooms or from individual faculty need to be aggregated in ways that protect anonymity. Sometimes macho teaching attitudes mask fragile teaching egos. This means it doesn't matter what faculty may say, their investment in teaching is personal and emotional, and that makes them vulnerable. The goal is not to use a measure of student involvement in individual classrooms to "out" those professors whose students are not engaged. Do that once and faculty will never permit data collection again. This agenda is positive. We collect data in the interest of creating a large picture, a sense of what is happening across campus, not in individual corners. We collect data so that we aren't exchanging opinions, but have concrete evidence that documents the degree and level of student involvement. We use that data to discuss the issue generally, the terms and conditions under which student involvement occurs productively, the strategies and techniques that enable students to see the role involvement plays in their learning. Institutional research that answers relevant questions shows the value of scholarly work on teaching and the benefits of informed pedagogical practice.

Institutional research is not the only way to support the effort to find answers. At one institution I know, faculty are encouraged to identify instructional topics of interest—things like motivation, the role of technology in learning, academic integrity, or the impact of class size on learning. Near the end of the academic year, a group of faculty sit down and frame a set of questions relevant to the topic. Then the academic dean commissions a faculty-prepared paper on the topic. For $750, a faculty member who has expressed interest in preparing the paper spends time during the summer reviewing relevant theory, research, and practice and distilling important principles, findings, and practices into a twenty-page (plus bibliography) paper. The paper is then presented and discussed in a variety of venues during the fall semester. I've seen several of these papers and can attest to their excellence. This strategy is an equally effective way of getting faculty interested in doing pedagogical scholarship.

Whether it is making pedagogical literature available, talking the talk, or supporting the quest to pursue answers systematically, the point of activities like these is to illustrate to faculty that there is a different way of knowing about instructional practice. This better way involves using scholarly work on teaching and learning to understand more fully what happens when we teach and students learn—and it can be fun!

Actions That Encourage and Support Doing Pedagogical Scholarship

Here again, there is a range of options, with only a few possibilities highlighted here. Start by making sure that the regular mechanisms available to support scholarship apply to scholarly work on teaching and learning. For example, it should be possible to devote a sabbatical to pedagogical scholarship—more than just a possibility, there should be examples of folks on campus who have used their sabbaticals to pursue scholarly projects on teaching and learning. Travel funds should be available to support presenting pedagogical work at teaching conferences or attending those conferences to learn more about the kind of pedagogical scholarship other faculty are doing. Perhaps an internal grants program whose funds to support instructional projects might include graduate or undergraduate research assistants, clerical support, money to acquire materials, even course releases. Some folks see irony in rewarding teaching by releasing one from doing it, but I've never understood that. An occasional course release to overhaul a course, plan a new one, collaborate with a colleague on a learning community, prepare a resource for colleagues on motivation, or conduct a systematic pedagogical inquiry may be time away from the classroom, but it isn't time off from teaching. Moreover, course releases recognize the importance and necessity of non-classroom activities to continued freshness in the classroom.

For faculty first doing pedagogical scholarship, access to expertise is another support that can be very helpful, but generally this kind of pedagogical expertise is in short supply on most campuses. The problem is that beyond knowing the pedagogical periodical in their discipline (and even that is not known to some faculty), most are unfamiliar with pedagogical literature. This means they don't know where else something might be published or otherwise disseminated, and more serious, they do not know how to find literature on a topic of interest. A sign of an institution's commitment to the pedagogical scholarship agenda might be its willingness to support development of that expertise on campus. An interested faculty member gets a semester or course off to become familiar with some of the major sources of pedagogical literature. Or if some expertise exists on campus, perhaps in the teaching-excellence center, those experts are supported in their efforts to mentor faculty doing scholarly work on teaching and learning.

Based on experiences I wrote about in Chapter Eight, I'm convinced of the value of pedagogical writing support groups as another way to support pedagogical scholarship. Sharing successes, frustrations, and questions, as well as getting constructive feedback from a group of colleagues also working on pedagogical projects greatly empowers faculty whose pedagogical interests may not be shared by departmental colleagues. Academic leaders can support these groups with simple acts such as facilitating their convening and supplying refreshments. When I was working with one of these groups on my campus, I very much appreciated the notes from my academic dean that asked for updates and offered assurances of continued support.

Another form of support and encouragement is to showcase and celebrate success when it occurs. Many campuses have a research forum at which discipline-based research is presented to colleagues. It should be appropriate to share pedagogical scholarship there as well. Because much pedagogical scholarship is of wide interest, presentations can be made at faculty meetings or posted online. Certainly, when work is published or otherwise disseminated, success should be acknowledged. Whether it's a note, an e-mail, or a comment made in passing, faculty value acknowledgment of their accomplishments.

Evaluation, Reward, and Recognition

Like any other scholarly endeavor, to have credibility, to merit reward and recognition, scholarly work on teaching and learning must be evaluated. Unlike the informal positive feedback and endorsement of effort I have just described, the focus here is on the formal mechanisms for evaluating, rewarding, and recognizing scholarly accomplishments within the pedagogical realm.

The stakes could not be higher. As noted in Chapter One, a window of opportunity is open. Institutions that have never looked seriously at pedagogical scholarship are doing so. Those of us— academic leaders and other teaching advocates—interested in advancing the agenda for scholarly work on teaching and learning must step up to the plate and address the issue of standards directly. To have credibility within the academic community, we must be able to say what makes a piece of pedagogical scholarship excellent. On that we all agree. But establishing those standards locally so that they can be used by promotion and tenure committees and by department chairs responsible for assessing individual performance is no easy task.

Preexisting conditions that surround instructional evaluation are not positive. For years now institutions have struggled with how to evaluate teaching. Practices involving students' ratings and some sort of peer assessment are now widespread but uniformly unpopular with faculty. Often they distrust rating results and discount the value of the student input these results provide. Research further attests to the less-than-impressive impact of ratings. For most faculty, ratings are stable; they do not change. Repeated collection of ratings and dissemination of results does not improve subsequent ratings. For documentation of this, plus many other aspects of evaluating instruction that have been explored empirically, see two excellent books that sum this extensive research and propose practical implications for policymakers: Braskamp and Ory (1994), and Centra (1993).

In addition, the involvement of peers has done little to improve the process. To imagine that faculty colleagues, not themselves trained to teach, with no experience observing instruction, no criteria other than their own, on the basis of limited time in the classroom, might be able to judge the teaching observed is preposterous. Regularly reported inter-rater reliability statistics verify that observations so conducted do not produce reliable assessments (as in Centra, 1975; Cohen and McKeachie, 1980; Feldman, 1989). Tenured senior faculty, frequently short on time, stagger under the weight of a peer review process that involves substantial classroom observation. The long and short of the story is that we have yet to reckon with the amount of effort it takes to assess teaching effectiveness well.

Out of this troubling context, the standards and processes needed to assess scholarly work on teaching and learning must emerge. Granted, the most common products of pedagogical scholarship take familiar forms: articles in refereed journals, chapters in books, presentations at conferences—all of which are more easily handled than dynamic classroom venues. But the negativity of the evaluative climate, coupled with the quality issues raised elsewhere in the book (primarily Chapters Four and Five), make the task facing us a challenging one. To recap previous issues, a lot of pedagogical scholarship has been produced in an environment of evolving standards.

In the beginning there were none; when they started emerging, they were not at the same level as those held for research in the disciplines. Remember that until recently this was not scholarship that counted. The standards bar for pedagogical scholarship continues to be raised, but I've already made the point several times that quality in previous and current work is consistently uneven, which makes setting standards a confusing task.

Add to this wide variation in quality the growing expectation that exemplary pedagogical scholarship should look like discipline-based scholarship and the logical corollary that we can then assess it using those standards. As noted elsewhere, if discipline-based research standards are used to assess pedagogical scholarship, little of it will ever measure up. It is applied scholarship, much of it not discovery-based. It serves different purposes. At this point, promotion and tenure committees, department and division heads have thought little about the goals of pedagogical literature and often have no previous experience evaluating it. Little knowledge and no experience increase the motivation to select familiar standards over new ones.

A serious and rigorous assessment of pedagogical scholarship must begin in this not-very-positive climate in which standards, the need for them, the lack of them, as well as the propriety of those selected for use are central issues. The question is how to provide leadership in light of these realities.

Working with Those Who Evaluate Pedagogical Scholarship

As discussed in Chapter Four, one of the important outputs of the scholarship-of-teaching movement has been the creation of standards that can be applied to scholarly work on teaching and learning (Diamond and Adam, 1993; Glassick, Huber, and Maeroff, 1997; Shulman, 2000). Most academic leaders and faculty committees who look at these standards will not have trouble accepting their viability. They meet academic expectations for scholarship and mark a productive place to begin.

But they are very general, and as I wrote in Chapter Three, I don't think they provide the specificity needed when a promotion and tenure committee or a department head looks at a collection of work assembled in a dossier or listed on an annual faculty activity report. Does this collection of work merit reward and recognition? Is it exemplary or average? Moreover, these standards fail to capture the unique aspects of pedagogical scholarship. They enable the imposition of disciplinary standards that do not apply to some kinds of pedagogical work. In the analyses of the most common types of pedagogical scholarship found in previously published work presented in Chapters Four and Five, I attempt to draw more specific criteria out of exemplary work. I believe these criteria complement the more general assessment criteria by adding the depth and detail demanded by the different approaches that have been used to explore instructional issues.

In some respects, however, the standards outlined in this book are beyond where most evaluators of pedagogical scholarship start. They can more profitably begin with the literature itself. When I work with a promotion and tenure committee new to pedagogical scholarship or a set of department heads unfamiliar with scholarly work on teaching and learning, I start with a packet of articles representing some of the approaches that commonly appear in this literature. (I've used many of those highlighted and referenced in this book.) I have found that examples very effectively bring all the issues to light. The discussion is no longer academic: before us sits a piece of work—is it scholarly? Why? Why not?

Many of the groups I've worked with quickly reject most of the examples of pedagogical scholarship: they're experience-based, they just offer advice, they're personal and subjective. Into the small pile of accepts goes anything that looks empirical. At this point the discussion must move back to a larger and more theoretical frame. What is the purpose of pedagogical scholarship—beyond helping an individual faculty member get tenure or promoted? How does it relate to the research on teaching and learning occurring in those fields dedicated to advancing instructional knowledge? Is there a need for all pedagogical scholarship to be discovery-based? What kind of knowledge base makes for an informed instructional practice? Once again, it helps to have defined the pedagogical scholarship agenda broadly, because then questions about the kind of resources teachers need can be asked and the role of a viable literature in the growth and development of teachers explored.

At this point in the discussion, I usually see participants picking up articles in the reject pile and looking at them again, considering them from a different perspective. However, I would not be honest if I reported that the light goes on and everyone agrees. Usually, the debate becomes more heated. Disciplinary notions of how knowledge is established and advanced are thoroughly entrenched in most faculty thinking. It takes some time and effort to change that paradigm. If it does not change, then pedagogical scholarship and those who do it are destined to be just as second class as they've always been.

Moreover, those who evaluate pedagogical scholarship should be pushed to think beyond current expectations for scholarly products. Again, those working on scholarship-of-teaching issues have challenged us to consider new ways and means of disseminating this work. Must it always be an article in a refereed journal? The opportunities afforded by technology make that a timely question. As we saw in Chapter Six, technology makes possible all sorts of new avenues, venues, and formats. Given the goals and objectives of pedagogical scholarship, some of these actually make much more sense as places for disseminating information than journals.

When it comes to the future for alternative formats and venues, the rubber meets the road when that scholarship is evaluated. If these new approaches don't "count," the door to a distinctive scholarship closes, and definitions of pedagogical scholarship start to narrow and exclude. The best time to present the idea of alternative models is at the beginning, when those evaluating pedagogical scholarship first come to grips with the fact that, historically, pedagogical scholarship has included a wide range of approaches and models, and what it might beneficially embrace in the future could be even wider.

In sum, as an academic leader working with those evaluating pedagogical scholarship, start with the need to set standards—that's an easy sell. Then move to the question of what standards; here I would challenge the assumption that the standards of the disciplines should apply in all cases. Because pedagogical scholarship is different, it merits unique standards. Work with committees and fellow academic leaders to begin the process of establishing new standards. See this as a process—standards need to evolve and change—and recognize that the act of setting standards will stimulate heated discussion—precisely the kind of conversations higher education needs to enhance scholarly work on teaching and learning.

It is a time of promise and possibility for scholarly work on teaching and learning. At the end of Chapter Three I compared previously published pedagogical scholarship to an old house, constructed across time by dedicated builders who have worked without blueprints and few resources. In recent years the neighborhood has changed. Growth and development are occurring all around, and we are faced with a decision: Do we preserve what we have as a historic landmark? Do we restore, transform, and make this old house viable? Or do we tear it down? I, for one, hope that we don't abandon the old place. Its foundation has stood the test of time, and on it has been constructed a scholarship with unique features. But then, those of us who've lived in the old house are probably hopelessly subjective about this place we call home.

Appendix A: Discipline-Based Pedagogical Periodicals

This appendix contains two listings of periodicals—mostly journals, some magazines—of discipline-based pedagogical periodicals: those written for practitioners in higher education and those for practitioners at all levels of education.

Discipline-Based Pedagogical Periodicals for Higher Education

Academic Medicine

Academic Psychiatry (formerly *Journal of Psychiatric Education*)

Academy of Management Learning and Education

American Journal of Pharmaceutical Education

ASEE Prism (American Society of Engineering Education)

Bioscience Education (only online)

Chemical Educator

Chemical Engineering Education

College Mathematics Journal

Computer Science Education

European Journal of Engineering Education

IEEE Transactions on Education (Institute of Electrical and Electronics Engineers)

International Journal of Engineering Education

Issues in Accounting Education

Journal of Accounting Education

Journal of Architectural Education

Journal of Criminal Justice Education

Journal of Dental Education

Journal of Economic Education

Journal of Education for Library and Information Science (formerly *Journal of Education for Librarianship*)

Journal of Engineering Education

Journal of Financial Education

Journal of Geography in Higher Education

Journal of Legal Education

Journal of Management Education (formerly *Organizational Behavior Teaching Review*)

Journal of Marketing Education

Journal of Nursing Education

Journal of Professional Issues in Engineering Education and Practice

Journal of Social Work Education

Journal of Veterinary Medical Education

Journalism and Mass Communication Educator (formerly *Journalism Educator*)

Mathematics and Computer Education

Medical Education Online

Medical Teacher

Microbiology Education

NACTA Journal (North American Colleges and Teachers of Agriculture, formerly National Association of Colleges and Teachers of Agriculture)

Nurse Educator

PS: Political Science and Politics (incorporated Political Science Teacher)

Teaching and Learning in Medicine

Teaching Philosophy

Teaching Sociology

Discipline-Based Pedagogical Periodicals for All Levels of Education

Advances in Physiology Education

Agricultural Education Magazine

Art Education

American Biology Teacher

Anthropology and Education Quarterly

Biochemistry and Molecular Biology Education (formerly Biochemical Education)

Business Education Forum

Cell Biology Education

Communication Education (formerly Speech Teacher)

Foreign Language Annuals

History Teacher

Journal of Agricultural Education

Journal of Biological Education

Journal of Chemical Education

Journal of Education for Business

Journal of Environmental Education

Journal of Geography

Journal of Geoscience Education (formerly *Journal of Geological Education*)

Journal of Hospitality, Leisure, Sport and Tourism (online only)

Journal of Hospitality and Tourism Education

Journal of Natural Resources and Life Sciences Education (formerly *Journal of Agronomic Education*)

Journal of Statistics Education

Journal of Teaching in Physical Education

Journal of Teaching in Social Work (simultaneously published as *Social Work Education and Curriculum*)

Journal of Teaching Writing

Mathematics Teacher

Physics Teacher

Teaching Geography

Teaching History—A Journal of Methods

Teaching of Psychology

TESOL Quarterly (Teachers of English to Speakers of Other Languages)

Appendix B: Cross-Disciplinary and Topical Pedagogical Periodicals

This appendix contains three lists of journals (and some magazines) with pedagogical material for higher education: cross-disciplinary pedagogical journals; general periodicals with pedagogical content; and theme-based, topical pedagogical journals.

Cross-Disciplinary Pedagogical Journals for Higher Education

College Teaching

Innovative Higher Education

Journal of College Science Teaching

Journal of Excellence in College Teaching

MountainRise (only online)

Teaching in Higher Education

General Higher Education Periodicals with Pedagogical Content

Academe

Change

Educational Record

Liberal Education

Theme-Based, Topical Pedagogical Journals for Higher Education

Active Learning in Higher Education

American Journal of Distance Education

Feminist Teacher

Journal of Academic Development

Journal of First Year Experience and Transition to College

Journal of General Education

Journal of Graduate Teaching Assistant Development

Journal of Student-Centered Learning

References

Ackerman, D. S., and Gross, B. L. "My Instructor Made Me Do It: Task Characteristics of Procrastination." *Journal of Marketing Education*, 2005, *27*(1), 5–13.

Allen, G. K., Wedman, J. F., and Folk, L. C. "Looking Beyond the Valley: A Five-Year Case Study of Course Innovation." *Innovative Higher Education*, 2001, *26*(2), 103–119.

Allen, J., Fuller, D., and Luckett, M. "Academic Integrity: Behaviors, Rates, and Attitudes of Business Students Toward Cheating." *Journal of Marketing Education*, 1998, *20*(1), 41–52.

Anderson, G. L., and Herr, K. "The New Paradigm Wars: Is There Room for Rigorous Practitioner Knowledge in Schools and Universities?" *Educational Researcher*, 1999, *28*(5), 12–21, 40.

Andre, R., and Frost, P. J. (eds.). *Researchers Hooked on Teaching: Noted Scholars Discuss the Synergies of Teaching and Research*. Thousand Oaks, Calif.: Sage, 1997.

Angelo, T. A., and Cross, K. P. *Classroom Assessment Techniques: A Handbook for College Teachers*. (2nd ed.) San Francisco: Jossey-Bass, 1993.

Ashbaugh, H., Johnstone, K. M., and Warfield, T. D. "Outcome Assessment of a Writing-Skill Improvement Initiative: Results and Methodological Implications." *Issues in Accounting Education*, 2002, *17*(2), 123–148.

Auster, C. J., and MacRone, M. "The Classroom as a Negotiated Social Setting: An Empirical Study of the Effects of Faculty Members' Behavior on Students' Participation." *Teaching Sociology*, October 1994, *22*, 289–300.

Bacon, D. R., Stewart, K. A., and Silver, W. S. "Lessons from the Best and Worst Student Team Experiences: How a Teacher Can Make a Difference." *Journal of Management Education*, 1999, *23*(5), 467–488.

Bacon, D. R., Stewart, K. A., and Stewart-Belle, S. "Exploring Predictors of Student Team Project Performance." *Journal of Marketing Education*, 1998, *20*(1), 63–71.

Bailey, J. "Students as Clients in a Professional/Client Relationship." *Journal of Management Education*, 2000, *24*(3), 353–365.

Baker, P. J. "Does the Sociology of Teaching Inform *Teaching Sociology?*" *Teaching Sociology*, April 1985, *12*, 361–375.

Balch, W. R. "Practice Versus Review Exams and Final Exam Performance." *Teaching of Psychology*, 1998, *25*(3), 181–184.

Bean, J. C. *Engaging Ideas: The Professor's Guide to Integrating Writing, Critical Thinking, and Active Learning in the Classroom.* San Francisco: Jossey-Bass, 1996.

Beatty, J. E. "Grades as Money and the Role of the Market Metaphor in Management Education." *Academy of Management Learning and Education*, 2004, *3*(2), 187–196.

Becker, W. E. "Quantitative Research on Teaching Methods in Tertiary Education." In W. E. Becker and M. L. Andrews (eds.), *The Scholarship of Teaching and Learning in Higher Education: Contributions of Research Universities.* Bloomington: Indiana University Press, 2004.

Bensimon, E. M., Polkinghorne, D. E., Bauman, G. L., and Vallejo, E. "Doing Research that Makes a Difference." *Journal of Higher Education*, 2004, *75*(1), 104–126.

Billson, J. M. "The College Classroom as a Small Group: Some Implications for Teaching and Learning." *Teaching Sociology*, January 1986, *14*, 143–151.

Black, K. A. "What to Do When You Stop Lecturing: Become a Guide and a Resource." *Journal of Chemical Education*, 1993, *70*(2), 140–144.

Black, T. R. *Evaluating Social Science Research: An Introduction.* Thousand Oaks, Calif.: Sage, 1993.

Boyer, E. L. *Scholarship Reconsidered: Priorities of the Professoriate.* Princeton, N.J.: Carnegie Foundation for the Advancement of Teaching, 1990.

Braskamp, L., and Ory, J. *Assessing Faculty Work: Enhancing Individual and Institutional Performance.* San Francisco: Jossey-Bass, 1994.

Braxton, J. M., Luckey, W., and Helland, P. *Institutionalizing a Broader View of Scholarship Through Boyer's Four Domains.* ASHE-ERIC Higher Education Report, *29*(2). San Francisco: Jossey-Bass, 2002.

Bray, J. N., Lee, J., Smith, L. L., and Yorks, L. *Collaborative Inquiry in Practice: Action, Reflection, and Making Meaning.* Thousand Oaks, Calif.: Sage, 2000.

Brewer, C. L. "William James Talks about Teaching." *Teaching of Psychology*, 2003, *30*(1), 34–37.

Brown, S., Bucklow, C., and Clark, P. "Professionalising Teaching: Enhancing the Status of Teaching, Improving the Experience of Learning and Supporting Innovation in Higher Education." *Journal of Geography in Higher Education*, 2002, 26(2), 159–168.

Bullard, J. "JGHE Biennial Award for Promoting Excellence in Teaching and Learning." *Journal of Geography in Higher Education*, 2002, 26(2), 209–211.

Burke, L. A. "High-Maintenance Students: A Conceptual Exploration and Implication." *Journal of Management Education*, 2004, 28(6), 743–756.

Burkill, S. "Recognizing and Rewarding Excellent Teachers: Towards a Strategy for Geography Departments." *Journal of Geography in Higher Education*, 2002, 26(3), 253–262.

Buttner, E. H. "How Do We 'Dis' Students?: A Model of (Dis)respectful Business Instructor Behavior." *Journal of Management Education*, 2004, 28(3), 319–334.

Calder, L., Cutler, W. W., III, and Kelly, T. M. "History Lessons: Historians and the Scholarship of Teaching and Learning." In M. T. Huber and S. P. Morreale (eds.), *Disciplinary Styles in the Scholarship of Teaching and Learning: Exploring Common Ground*. Washington, D.C.: American Association for Higher Education and Carnegie Foundation for the Advancement of Teaching, 2002.

Carr, J. L. "A Month in the Country: Excerpt." Reprinted in *Academic Medicine*, 2004, 79(5), 488.

Cary, M., and Spelman, D. "Anatomy of a Colleagueship: Collaborations In and Out of the Classroom." In R. Andre and P. J. Frost (eds.), *Researchers Hooked on Teaching: Noted Scholars Discuss the Synergies of Teaching and Research*. Thousand Oaks, Calif.: Sage, 1997.

Centra, J. "Colleagues as Raters of Classroom Instruction." *Journal of Higher Education*, 1975, 46(3), 327–337.

Centra, J. *Reflective Faculty Evaluation: Enhancing Teaching and Determining Faculty Effectiveness*. San Francisco: Jossey-Bass, 1993.

Chin, J. "Is There a Scholarship of Teaching and Learning in *Teaching Sociology*: A Look at Papers from 1984–1999." *Teaching Sociology*, January 2002, 30, 53–62.

Christensen, C. R., Garvin, D. A., and Sweet, A. *Education for Judgment: The Artistry of Discussion Leadership*. Boston: Harvard Business School Press, 1991.

Church, M. A., Elliot, A. J., and Gable, S. L. "Perceptions of Classroom Environment, Achievement Goals and Achievement Outcomes." *Journal of Educational Psychology*, 2001, 93(1), 43–54.

Clough, M. P., and Kauffman, K. J. "Improving Engineering Education: A Research-Based Framework for Teaching." *Journal of Engineering Education*, 1999, 88(4), 527–534.

Cohen, J. "Editor's Note: The Obligation of Teaching and Learning Scholarship." *Journalism and Mass Communication Educator*, 2002, 54(4), 2–3.

Cohen, P., and McKeachie, W. "The Role of Colleagues in the Evaluation of College Teaching." *Improving College and University Teaching*, 1980, 28(4), 147–154.

Connelly, J. E. "Commentary." *Academic Medicine*, 2004, 79(5), 489.

Cooper, J. L., Robinson, P., and Ball, D. (eds.). *Small Group Instruction in Higher Education: Lessons from the Past, Visions of the Future*. Stillwater, Okla.: New Forums Press, 2003.

Cross, K. P., and Steadman, M. H. *Classroom Research: Implementing the Scholarship of Teaching*. San Francisco: Jossey-Bass, 1996.

Cunsolo, J., Elrick, M., and Middleton, A. "The Scholarship of Teaching: A Canadian Perspective with Examples." *Canadian Journal of Higher Education*, 1996, 26(1), 35–56.

Daniel, R. S. "*Teaching of Psychology*, the Journal." In A. E. Puente, J. R. Matthews, and C. L. Brewer (eds.), *Teaching of Psychology in America: A History*. Washington, D.C.: American Psychological Association, 1992.

Darling, A. L. "Scholarship of Teaching and Learning in Communication: New Connections, New Directions, New Possibilities." *Communication Education*, 2003, 52(1), 47–49.

Davidson, C. I., and Ambrose, S. A. *The New Professor's Handbook: A Guide to Teaching and Research in Engineering and Science*. Bolton, Mass.: Anker, 1994.

Deeter-Schmelz, D. R., Kennedy, K. N., and Ramsey, R. P. "Enriching Our Understanding of Team Effectiveness." *Journal of Management Education*, 2002, 24(2), 114–124.

Deiter, R. "A Course Every Department Can (Should?) Teach—Graduating Senior Survey. *NACTA Journal*, 2003, 47(2), 14–17.

Denzin, N. K., and Lincoln, Y. S. (eds.). *Handbook of Qualitative Research*. Thousand Oaks, Calif.: Sage, 1994.

Denzin, N. K., and Lincoln, Y. S. (eds.). *Handbook of Qualitative Research*. (2nd Ed.) Thousand Oaks, Calif.: Sage, 2000.

Diamond, R. M. "Defining Scholarship for the Twenty-First Century." In K. J. Zahorski (ed.), *Scholarship in the Postmodern Era: New Venues, New Values, New Visions*. New Directions for Teaching and Learning, no. 90. San Francisco: Jossey-Bass, 2002.

Diamond, R. M., and Adam, B. E. *Recognizing Faculty Work: Reward Systems for the Year 2000*. New Directions for Higher Education, no. 81. San Francisco: Jossey-Bass, 1993.

Drevdahl, D. J., Stackman, R. W., Purdy, J. M., and Louie, B. Y. "Merging Reflective Inquiry and Self-Study as a Framework for Enhancing the Scholarship of Teaching." *Journal of Nursing Education*, 2002, *41*(9), 413–419.

Druger, M. "The Concept of Creative Scholarship." *Journal of Natural Resources Life Science Education*, 2001, *30*, 124–125.

Druger, M. "A Report on a Survey of JCST Recipients." *Journal of College Science Teaching*, 2003, *33*(2), 6–7.

Ege, S. N., Coppola, B. P., and Lawton, R. G. "The University of Michigan Undergraduate Chemistry Curriculum: 1. Philosophy, Curriculum, and the Nature of Change." *Journal of Chemical Education*, 1997, *74*(1), 74–94.

Eison, J. "Confidence in the Classroom: Ten Maxims for New Teachers." *College Teaching*, 1990, *38*(1), 21–24.

Elbow, P. *Embracing Contraries: Explorations in Learning and Teaching*. New York: Oxford University Press, 1986.

Elbow, P. "One-to-One Faculty Development." In J. F. Noonan (ed.), *Learning About Teaching*. New Directions for Teaching and Learning, no. 4. San Francisco: Jossey-Bass, 1980.

Felder, R. M., and Brent, R. "Navigating the Bumpy Road to Student-Centered Instruction." *College Teaching*, 1996, *44*(2), 43–47.

Feldman, K. A. "Research Productivity and Scholarly Accomplishment of College Teachers as Related to Their Instructional Effectiveness: A Review and Exploration." *Research in Higher Education*, 1987, *26*(3), 227–298.

Feldman, K. A. "Instructional Effectiveness of College Teachers as Judged by Teachers Themselves, Current and Former Students, Colleagues, Administrators, and External (Neutral) Observers." *Research in Higher Education*, 1989, *30*(2), 137–194.

Frederick, P. "Walking on Eggs: Mastering the Dreaded Diversity Discussion." *College Teaching*, 1995, *43*(3), 83–92.

Freeman, P. R., and Schmidt, J. Z. *Wise Women: Reflections of Teachers at Midlife*. New York: Routledge, 2000.

Friedman, H. C. "The Fifty-Six Laws of Good Teaching." *Journal of Chemical Education*, 1990, *67*(5), 413.

Frost, P J., and Fukami, C. V. "Teaching Effectiveness in the Organizational Sciences: Recognizing and Enhancing the Scholarship of Teaching." *Academy of Management Journal*, 1997, *40*(6), 1,271–1,281.

Galbraith, J. K. "How I Could Have Done Much Better." *On Teaching and Learning: The Journal of the Harvard Danford Center*, January 1987, 1–4.

Gallagher, T. J. "Embracing Student Evaluations of Teaching: A Case Study." *Teaching Sociology*, April 2000, *28*, 140–146.

Gallos, J. V. "The Editor's Corner." *Journal of Management Education*, 1994, *18*(2), 135–138.

Gambrill, E. D. "Looking Back and Moving On." *Journal of Social Work Education*, 2003, *39*(2), 2–5.

Glassick, C. E., Huber, M. T., and Maeroff, G. I. *Scholarship Assessed: Evaluation of the Professoriate*. San Francisco: Jossey-Bass, 1997.

Gleason, M. "Why Teach." *Change*, 1982, *14*(7), 8–10.

Glew, R. H. "The Problem with Problem-Based Medical Education." *Biochemistry and Molecular Biology Education*, 2003, *31*(1), 52–56.

Green, D. H. "Student-Generated Exams: Testing and Learning." *Journal of Marketing Education*, 1997, *19*(2), 43–53.

Gregory, M. "If Education Is a Feast, Why Do We Restrict the Menu? A Critique of Pedagogical Metaphors." *College Teaching*, 1987, *35*(3), 101–107.

Griggs, R. A., Jackson, S. L., Marek, P., and Christopher, A. N. "Critical Thinking in Introductory Psychology Texts and Supplements." *Teaching of Psychology*, 1998, *25*(4), 254–266.

Haller, C. R., Gallagher, V. J., Weldon, T. L., and Felder, R. M. "Dynamics of Peer Education in Cooperative Learning Workgroups." *Journal of Engineering Education*, 2000, 89(3), 285–293.

Halpern, D. F., and others. "Scholarship in Psychology: A Paradigm for the Twenty-First Century." *American Psychologist*, 1998, *53*(12), 1,292–1,297.

Hammett, P. "Teaching Tools for Evaluating World Wide Web Resources." *Teaching Sociology*, January 1999, *27*, 31–37.

Hatch, T., Bass, R., Iiyoshi, T., and Mace, D. P. "Building Knowledge for Teaching and Learning: The Promise of Scholarship in a Networked Environment." *Change*, September/October 2004, 42–49.

Healey, M. "Developing the Scholarship of Teaching in Higher Education: A Discipline-Based Approach." *Higher Education Research and Development*, 2000, *19*(2), 169–189.

Healey, M. "The Scholarship of Teaching: Issues Around an Evolving Concept." *Journal on Excellence in College Teaching*, 2003, *14*(2/3), 5–26.

Herreid, C. F. "Case Studies in Science—A Novel Method of Science Education." *Journal of College Science Teaching*, 1994, *23*(4), 221–229.

Hill, N. A. "Scaling the Heights: The Teacher as Mountaineer." *Chronicle of Higher Education*, June 16, 1980, p. 48.

Hiller, T. H., and Hietapelto, A. B. "Contract Grading: Encouraging Commitment to the Learning Process Through Voice in the Evaluation Process." *Journal of Management Education*, 2001, *25*(6), 660–684.

Hobson, S. M., and Talbot, D. M. "Understanding Student Evaluations: What All Faculty Should Know." *College Teaching*, 2001, *49*(1), 26–30.

hooks, b. *Teaching to Transgress: Education as the Practice of Freedom*. New York: Basic Books, 1994.

Houston, M. B., and Bettencourt, L. A. "But That's Not Fair! An Exploratory Study of Student Perceptions of Instructor Fairness." *Journal of Marketing Education*, 1999, *21*(2), 84–96.

Huber, M. T. "Disciplinary Styles in the Scholarship of Teaching: Reflections on the Carnegie Academy for the Scholarship of Teaching and Learning." In M. T. Huber and S. P. Morreale (eds.), *Disciplinary Styles in the Scholarship of Teaching and Learning: Exploring Common Ground*. Washington, D.C.: American Association for Higher Education and Carnegie Foundation for the Advancement of Teaching, 2002.

Huber, M. T., and Morreale, S. P. (eds.). *Disciplinary Styles in the Scholarship of Teaching and Learning: Exploring Common Ground*. Washington, D.C.: American Association for Higher Education and Carnegie Foundation for the Advancement of Teaching, 2002.

Husted, B. L. "Hope, for the Dry Side." *College English*, 2001, *64*(2), 243–249.

Hutchings, P. (ed.). *Opening Lines: Approaches to the Scholarship of Teaching and Learning*. Menlo Park, Calif.: Carnegie Foundation for the Advancement of Teaching, 2000.

Intrator, S. M., and Scribner, M. (eds.). *Teaching with Fire: Poetry That Sustains the Courage to Teach*. San Francisco: Jossey Bass, 2003.

Ironside, P. M. "'Covering Content' and Teaching Thinking: Deconstructing the Additive Curriculum." *Journal of Nursing Education*, 2004, *43*(1), 5–12.

Jacobs, L. C., and Chase, C. I. *Developing and Using Tests Effectively: A Guide for Faculty*. San Francisco: Jossey-Bass, 1992.

Jacobs-Lawson, J. M., and Hershey, D. A. "Concept Maps As an Assessment Tool in Psychology Courses." *Teaching of Psychology*, 2002, *29*(1), 25–29.

Jenkins, A. "Twenty-One Volumes On: Is Teaching Valued in Geography in Higher Education?" *Journal of Geography in Higher Education*, 1997, *21*(1), 5–14.

Karabenick, S. A. (ed.). *Strategic Help Seeking: Implications for Learning and Teaching*. Mahwah, N.J.: Lawrence Erlbaum, 1998.

Keeley, S. M., Shemberg, K. M., Cowell, B. S., and Zinnbauer, B. J. "Coping with Student Resistance to Critical Thinking: What the Psychotherapy Literature Can Tell Us." *College Teaching*, 1995, *43*(4), 140–145.

Kember, D., and Gow, L. "Orientations to Teaching and Their Effect on the Quality of Student Learning." *Journal of Higher Education*, 1994, 65(1), 58–74.

Kennedy, E. J., Lawton, L., and Plumlee, E. L. "Blissful Ignorance: The Problem of Unrecognized Incompetence and Academic Performance." *Journal of Marketing Education*, 2002, 24(3), 245–252.

Knight, R. D. *Five Easy Lessons: Strategies for Successful Physics Teaching*. San Francisco: Addison Wesley, 2002.

Kohn, A. *No Contest: The Case Against Competition*. Boston: Houghton Mifflin, 1986.

Kohn, A. *Punished by Rewards*. Boston: Houghton Mifflin, 1993.

Korn, J. H. "The Teaching Spirit of William James." *Teaching of Psychology*, 2003, 30(1), 44–45.

Korobkin, D. "Humor in the Classroom: Considerations and Strategies." *College Teaching*, 1988, 36(4), 145–158.

Kreber, C. "Conceptualizing the Scholarship of Teaching and Identifying Unresolved Issues." In C. Kreber (ed.), *Scholarship Revisited: Perspectives on the Scholarship of Teaching*. New Directions for Teaching and Learning, no. 86. San Francisco: Jossey-Bass, 2001a.

Kreber, C. (ed.). *Scholarship Revisited: Perspectives on the Scholarship of Teaching*. New Directions for Teaching and Learning, no. 86. San Francisco: Jossey-Bass, 2001b.

Kreber, C. "Challenging the Dogma: Towards a More Inclusive View of the Scholarship of Teaching." *Journal on Excellence in College Teaching*, 2003, 14(3), 27–43.

Kreber, C., and Cranton, P. A. "Exploring the Scholarship of Teaching." *Journal of Higher Education*, 2000, 71(4), 476–495.

Kunkel, K. R. "A Research Note Assessing the Benefit of Presentation Software in Two Different Lecture Courses." *Teaching Sociology*, April 2004, 32, 188–196.

Lagowski, J. J. "Chemical Education: Past, Present and Future." *Journal of Chemical Education*, 1998, 75(4), 425–436.

Lewicki, R. J. "From the Editor: Hail . . . And Farewell." *Academy of Management Learning and Education*, 2004, 3(4), 354–359.

Lewis, S. E., and Lewis, J. E. "Departing from Lectures: An Evaluation of a Peer-Led Guided Inquiry Alternative." *Journal of Chemical Education*, 2005, 82(1), 135–139.

Linkon, S. "Students' Perspectives on Interdisciplinary Learning." In P. Hutchings (ed.), *Opening Lines: Approaches to the Scholarship of Teaching and*

Learning. Menlo Park, Calif.: Carnegie Foundation for the Advancement of Teaching, 2000.

Livingstone, D., and Lynch, K. "Group Project Work and Student-Centered Active Learning: Two Different Experiences." *Journal of Geography in Higher Education,* 2002a, *26*(2), 217–237.

Livingstone, D., and Lynch, K. "Reflections on 'Group Project Work and Student-Centered Learning.'" *Journal of Geography in Higher Education,* 2002b, *26*(2), 213–215.

Lucal, B., and others. "Faculty Assessment and the Scholarship of Teaching and Learning: Knowledge Available/Knowledge Needed." *Teaching Sociology,* April 2003, *31*, 146–161.

Maharaj, S., and Banta, L. "Using Log Assignments to Foster Learning: Writing Across the Curriculum." *Journal of Engineering Education,* 2000, 89(1), 73–77.

Mallard, K. S. "The Soul of Scholarship." In K. J. Zahorski (ed.), *Scholarship in the Postmodern Era: New Venues, New Values, New Visions.* New Directions for Teaching and Learning, no. 90. San Francisco: Jossey-Bass, 2002.

Matthews, H. "Editorial I: Pedagogy, Research and Quality Publishing." *Journal of Geography in Higher Education,* 2002, 26(1), 5–11.

McCabe, J., and Powell, B. " 'In My Class? No.' Professors' Accounts of Grade Inflation." In W. E. Becker and M. L. Andrews (eds.), *The Scholarship of Teaching and Learning in Higher Education: Contributions of Research Universities.* Bloomington: Indiana University Press, 2004.

McKeachie, W. J. *Teaching Tips: Strategies, Research and Theory for College and University Teachers.* (11th ed.) Boston: Houghton Mifflin, 2002.

McKeachie, W. J. "William James's *Talks to Teachers* (1899) and McKeachie's *Teaching Tips* (1999)." *Teaching of Psychology,* 2003, *30*(1), 40–3.

McKinney, K., Saxe, D., and Cobb, L. "Are We Really Doing All We Can for Our Undergraduates? Professional Socialization via Out-of-Class Experiences." *Teaching Sociology,* January 1998, *26*, 1–13.

Meyers, C., and Jones, T. B. *Promoting Active Learning: Strategies for the College Classroom.* San Francisco: Jossey-Bass, 1993.

Miller, B., and Gentile, B. F. "Introductory Course Content and Goals." *Teaching of Psychology,* 1998, *25*(2), 89–96.

Miller, J. E., and Groccia, J. E. "Are Four Heads Better Than One? A Comparison of Cooperative and Traditional Teaching Formats in an Introductory Biology Course." *Innovative Higher Education,* 1997, *21*(4), 253–273.

Millis, B. J., and Cottell, P. G. *Cooperative Learning for Higher Education Faculty.* Phoenix: ACE/Oryx Press, 1998.

Mooney, L. A. "Pitching the Profession: Faculty Guest Speakers in the Classroom." *Teaching Sociology,* July 1998, *26,* 157–165.

Moore, J. W. "Iceberg JCE: Exploring the Invisible Nine-Tenths." *Journal of Chemical Education,* 2004, *81*(10), 1,383.

Mottet, T. P., Beebe, S. A., Raffeld, P. C., and Medlock, A. L. "The Effects of Student Verbal and Nonverbal Responsiveness on Teacher Self-Efficacy and Job Satisfaction." *Communication Education,* 2004, *53*(2), 150–163.

Mourtos, N. J. "The Nuts and Bolts of Cooperative Learning in Engineering." *Journal of Engineering Education,* 1997, 86(1), 35–37.

Murray, H. G., and Renaud, R. D. "Disciplinary Differences in Classroom Teaching Behaviors." In N. Hativa and M. Marincovich (eds.), *Disciplinary Differences in Teaching and Learning: Implications for Practice.* New Directions for Teaching and Learning, no. 64. San Francisco: Jossey-Bass, 1995.

Nelson, C. E. "Doing It: Examples of Several of the Different Genres of the Scholarship of Teaching and Learning." *Journal of Excellence in College Teaching,* 2003, *14*(2/3), 85–94.

Noel, T. W. "Lessons from the Learning Classroom." *Journal of Management Education,* 2004, *28*(2), 188–206.

Norcross, J. C., Dooley, H. S., and Stevenson, J. F. "Faculty Use and Justification of Extra Credit: No Middle Ground?" *Teaching of Psychology,* 1993, *20*(4), 240–242.

Norcross, J. C., Horrocks, L. J., and Stevenson, J. F. "Of Barfights and Gadflies: Attitudes and Practices Concerning Extra Credit in College Courses." *Teaching of Psychology,* 1989, *16*(4), 199–203.

Nummendal, S. G., Bension, J. B., and Chew, S. L. "Disciplinary Styles in the Scholarship of Teaching and Learning." In M. T. Huber and S. P. Morreale (eds.), *Disciplinary Styles in the Scholarship of Teaching and Learning: Exploring Common Ground.* Washington, D.C.: American Association for Higher Education and Carnegie Foundation for the Advancement of Teaching, 2002.

O'Leary, R. "Advice to New Teachers: Turn It Inside Out." *PS: Political Science and Politics,* March 2002, 91–92.

Olson, T., and Einwohner, R. L. "Forming and Transforming the Teaching Self in Different Institutional Environments: Two Teachers' Experiences." *Teaching Sociology,* October 2001, *29,* 403–422.

Palmer, P. J. *The Courage to Teach.* San Francisco: Jossey-Bass, 1998.

Parilla, P. F., and Hesser, G. W. "Internships and the Sociological Perspective: Applying Principles of Experiential Learning." *Teaching Sociology,* October 1998, *26,* 310–329.

Paulson, D. R. "Active Learning and Cooperative Learning in the Organic Chemistry Lecture Class." *Journal of Chemical Education*, 1999, 76(8), 1136–1140.

Perkins, D. "Scholarship of Teaching and Learning, Assessment and the Journal of Geoscience Education." *Journal of Geoscience Education*, 2004, 52(2), 113–114.

Perlman, B., Marxen, J. C., McFadden, S., and McCann, L. "Applicants for a Faculty Position Do Not Emphasize Teaching." *Teaching of Psychology*, 1996, 23(2), 103–104.

Pestel, B. C. "Some Practical Distinctions Between Preaching, Teaching, and Training." *Journal of College Science Teaching*, 1988, 18(1), 26–31.

Pintrich, P. R. "A Motivational Perspective on the Role of Student Motivation in Learning and Teaching Contexts." *Journal of Educational Psychology*, 2003, 95(4), 667–686.

Prados, J. W. "The Editor's Page." *Journal of Engineering Education*, 1996, 85(3), 173.

Prados, J. W. "The Editor's Page." *Journal of Engineering Education*, 1999, 88(2), 139.

Prados, J. W. "The Editor's Page." *Journal of Engineering Education*, 2001, 90(2), 169.

Prince, M. "Does Active Learning Work? A Review of the Research." *Journal of Engineering Education*, July 2004, 223–231.

Puente, A. E., Matthews, J. R., and Brewer, C. L. (eds.). *Teaching of Psychology in America: A History*. Washington, D.C.: American Psychological Association, 1992.

Quinn, J. W. "If It Catches My Eye: A Report of Faculty Pedagogical Reading Habits." *Innovative Higher Education*, 1994, 19(1), 53–66.

Reason, P., and Bradbury, H. (eds.). *Handbook of Action Research: Participative Inquiry and Practice*. Thousand Oaks, Calif.: Sage, 2001.

"Recognizing and Rewarding Excellent Teachers: Towards a Strategy for Geography Departments." *Journal of Geography in Higher Education*, 2002, 26(3), 253–262.

Rubin, D. "Editor's Note." *Communication Education*, 2003, 52(1), ix–xii.

Sandstrom, K. L. "Embracing Modest Hopes: Lessons from the Beginning of a Teaching Journey." In B. A. Pescosolido and R. Aminzade, (eds.), *The Social Worlds of Higher Education*. Thousand Oaks, Calif.: Pine Forge Press, 1999.

Sappington, J., Kinsey, K., and Munsayac, K. "Two Studies of Reading Compliance Among College Students." *Teaching of Psychology*, 2002, 29(4), 272–274.

Saville, B. K. "Reminiscences, Reasons, and Recommendations: An Interview with Charles L. Brewer." *Teaching of Psychology*, 2001, *28*(3), 231–234.

Saville, B. K., and Buskirk, W. "Essential Readings for Teaching of Psychology: Recommendations from the *ToP* Editorial Board." *Teaching of Psychology*, 2004, *31*(1), 2004.

Schön, D. "Knowing in Action: The New Scholarship Requires a New Epistemology." *Change*, 1995, *27*(6), 27–34.

Sharp, J. E., Harb, J. N., and Terry, R. E. "Combining Kolb Learning Styles and Writing to Learn in Engineering Classes." *Journal of Engineering Education*, 1997, 86(2), 93–101.

Shaw, J. B., Fisher, C. D., and Southey, G. N. "Evaluating Organizational Behavior Teaching Innovations: More Rigorous Designs, More Relevant Criteria, and an Example." *Journal of Management Education*, 1999, *23*(5), 509–538.

Shindler, J. V. "'Greater than the Sum of the Parts?' Examining the Soundness of Collaborative Exams in Teacher Education Courses." *Innovative Higher Education*, 2004, *28*(4), 273–283.

Shulman, L. S. "Knowledge and Teaching: Foundations of the New Reform. *Harvard Educational Review*, 1987, *57*(1), 1–22.

Shulman, L. S. "Conclusion: Inventing the Future." In P. Hutchings (ed.), *Opening Lines: Approaches to the Scholarship of Teaching*. Menlo Park, Calif.: Carnegie Foundation for the Advancement of Teaching, 2000.

Smith, P. *Killing the Spirit: Higher Education in America*. New York: Viking, 1990.

Smith, P. A. "Understanding Self-Regulated Learning and Its Implications for Accounting Educators and Researchers." *Issues in Accounting Education*, 2001, *16*(4), 663–700.

Sojka, J., Gupta, A. K., and Deeter-Schmelz, D. R. "Student and Faculty Perceptions of Student Evaluations of Teaching." *College Teaching*, 2002, *50*(2), 44–49.

Spence, L. D. "The Case Against Teaching." *Change*, 2001, *33*(6), 11–19.

Starling, R. "Professor as Student: The View from the Other Side." *College Teaching*, 1987, *35*(1), 3–7.

"Statement of Editorial Policy." *Communication Education*, 2003, *52*(1), 132.

"Statement of Ownership." *College Teaching*, 2005, *53*(1), 13.

Stenberg, S., and Lee, A. "Developing Pedagogies: Learning the Teaching of English." *College English*, 2002, *64*(3), 326–347.

Stenberg, S. J. *Professing and Pedagogy: Learning the Teaching of English*. Urbana, Ill.: National Council of Teachers of English, 2005.

Stringer, E. T. *Action Research: A Handbook for Practitioners*. Thousand Oaks, Calif.: Sage, 1996.

Strommer, D. W., and Erickson, B. E. *Teaching College Freshmen*. San Francisco: Jossey-Bass, 1991.

Svinicki, M. D. "Helping Students Understand Grades." *College Teaching*, 1998, 46(3), 101–105.

Takata, S. R. "The Guided Essay Examination for Sociology and Other Courses." *Teaching Sociology*, April 1994, 22, 189–194.

Terenzini, P. T., and others. "Collaborative Learning vs. Lecture/Discussion: Students' Reported Learning Gains." *Journal of Engineering Education*, 2001, 90(1), 123–129.

Thomas, L. "The Art of Teaching Science." *New York Times Magazine*, March 14, 1982, pp. 14–16.

Tompkins, J. "Pedagogy of the Distressed." *College English*, 1990, 52(6), 653–660.

Tompkins, J. *A Life in School: What the Teacher Learned*. Reading, Mass.: Addison-Wesley, 1996.

U.S. Department of Education, National Center for Educational Statistics, Integrated Postsecondary Education Data System (IPEDS), Winter 2001–02, Table 231.

van Gelder, T. "Teaching Critical Thinking: Some Lessons from Cognitive Science." *College Teaching*, 2005, 53(1), 41–46.

Vance, C. F. (ed). *Mastering Management Education: Innovations in Teaching Effectiveness*. Newbury Park, Calif.: Sage, 1993.

VanderStoep, S. W., Fagerlin, A., and Feenstra, J. S. "What Do Students Remember from Introductory Psychology?" *Teaching of Psychology*, 2000, 27(2), 89–92.

Varner, D., and Peck, S. R. "Learning from Learning Journals: The Benefits and Challenges of Using Learning Journal Assignments." *Journal of Management Education*, 2003, 27(1), 52–77.

Wagenaar, T. C. "Outcomes Assessment in Sociology: Prevalence and Impact." *Teaching Sociology*, October 2002, 30, 403–413.

Walck, C. L. "A Teaching Life." *Journal of Management Education*, 1997, 21(4), 473–482.

Wankat, P. C. "An Analysis of the Articles in the *Journal of Engineering Education*." *Journal of Engineering Education*, 1999, 88(1), 37–42.

Wankat, P. C. "Analysis of the First Ten Years of the *Journal of Engineering Education*." *Journal of Engineering Education*, 2004, 93(1), 13–21.

Wankat, P. C., Felder, R. M., Smith, K. A., and Oreovicz, F. S. "The Scholarship of Teaching and Learning in Engineering." In M. T. Huber and S. P. Morreale (eds.), *Disciplinary Styles in the Scholarship of Teaching and Learning: Exploring Common Ground*. Washington, D.C.: American Association for

Higher Education and Carnegie Foundation for the Advancement of
Teaching, 2002.

Weaver, F. S. "Scholarship for the Teaching Faculty." *College Teaching*, 1986,
34(2), 51–58.

Weimer, M. "The Disciplinary Journals on Pedagogy." *Change*, 1993, *25*(6),
44–51.

Weimer, M. "Learning More from the Wisdom of Practice." In C. Kreber (ed.),
Scholarship Revisited: Perspectives on the Scholarship of Teaching. New Directions for Teaching and Learning, no. 86. San Francisco: Jossey-Bass, 2001.

Weston, C. B., and McAlpine, L. "Making Explicit the Development Toward
the Scholarship of Teaching." In C. Kreber (ed.), *Scholarship Revisited:
Perspectives on the Scholarship of Teaching*. New Directions for Teaching
and Learning, no. 86. San Francisco: Jossey-Bass, 2001.

Whitin, K., and Sheppard, S. "Taking Stock: An Analysis of the Publishing
Record as Represented by the *Journal of Engineering Education*." *Journal of
Engineering Education*, 2004, *93*(1), 5–12.

Wight, R. D. "More than Mere Weather: James's *Talks* to Students about Life."
Teaching of Psychology, 2003, *30*(1), 38–39.

Woods, D. R. "Participation is More than Attendance." *Journal of Engineering
Education*, 1996, *85*(3), 177–181.

Yakura, E. K., and Bennett, C. D. "Finding Common Ground: Collaboration
Across the Disciplines in the Scholarship of Teaching." *Journal on Excellence in College Teaching*, 2003, *14*(2/3), 135–147.

Young, P., and Diekelmann, N. "Learning to Lecture: Exploring the Skills,
Strategies, and Practices of New Teachers in Nursing Education." *Journal
of Nursing Education*, 2002, *41*(9), 405–412.

Name Index

A

Ackerman, D. S., 117
Adam, B. E., xv, 48, 206
Allen, G. K., 126
Allen, J., 109, 112, 116
Ambrose, S. A., 131
Anderson, G. L., 160
Andre, R., 132
Angelo, T. A., 111, 159
Ashbaugh, H., 126
Auster, C. J., 109, 110, 113, 116

B

Bacon, D. R., 98, 100, 101, 109, 113, 116
Bailey, J., 82, 85
Baker, P. J., 30
Balch, W. R., 94, 98
Ball, D., 132
Banta, L., 58, 64
Bass, R., 139
Bauman, G. L., 160
Beatty, J. E., 29

Becker, W. E., 95, 99
Beebe, S. A., 98
Bennett, C. D., xvii
Bensimon, E. M., 160
Bension, J. B., 97
Bettencourt, L. A., 117
Billson, J. M., 70
Black, T. R., 99
Black, K. A., 17, 57
Boyer, E. L., xviii, 3, 61, 70, 166
Bradbury, H., 160
Braskamp, L., 205
Braxton, J. M., 5, 20, 163
Bray, J. N., 160
Brent, R., 77
Brewer, C. L., 28, 33, 133
Brown, S., 35
Bucklow, C., 35
Bullard, J., 35
Burke, L. A., 29
Burkill, S., 35
Buskirk, W., 9
Buttner, E. H., 111

C

Calder, L., 14, 61
Carr, J. L., 128
Cary, M., 128
Centra, J., 205
Chase, C. I., 132
Chew, S. L., 97
Chin, J., 30, 34, 59
Christensen, C. R., 132
Christopher, A. N., 110, 119
Church, M. A., 10
Clark, P., 35
Clough, M. P., 143
Cobb, L., 75, 76
Cohen, J., 61
Cohen, P., 205
Connelly, J. E., 128
Cooper, J. L., 132
Coppola, B. P., 57, 66
Cottell, P. G., 78
Cowell, B. S., 70
Cranton, P. A., 20
Cross, K. P., 61, 111, 159, 181
Cunsolo, J., 20
Cutler, W. W., 14, 61

D

Daniel, R. S., 29, 30, 32
Darling, A. L., 130
Davidson, C. I., 131
Deeter-Schmelz, D. R., 109, 110, 114, 115, 116
Deiter, R., 57
Denzin, N. K., 103, 104, 105, 107
Diamond, R. M., xv, 48, 151, 206

Diekelmann, N., 105, 107
Dooley, H. S., 117
Drevdahl, D. J., 88
Druger, M., 27, 29

E

Ege, S. N., 57, 66
Einwohner, R. L., 82
Eison, J., 69, 70, 74, 76, 77
Elbow, P., 128, 185
Elliot, A. J., 10
Elrick, M., 20
Erickson, B. E., 132

F

Fagerlin, A., 118
Feenstra, J. S., 118
Felder, R. M., 8, 33, 77, 104, 106, 109
Feldman, K. A., 169, 205
Fisher, C. D., 60
Folk, L. C., 126
Frederick, P., 73, 74, 76
Freeman, P. R., 133
Friedman, H. C., 82
Frost, P. J., 34, 132
Fukami, C. V., 34
Fuller, D., 109, 112, 116

G

Gable, S. L., 10
Galbraith, J. K., 82
Gallagher, T. J., 81
Gallagher, V. J., 104, 106, 109
Gallos, J. V., 32
Gambrill, E. D., 9

Garvin, D. A., 132
Gentile, B. F., 109, 110, 114, 116, 119
Glassick, C. E., xv, 48, 206
Gleason, M., 190
Glew, R. H., 81
Gow, L., 10
Green, D. H., 56, 63
Gregory, M., 82, 85
Griggs, R. A., 110, 119
Groccia, J. E., 125
Gross, B. L., 117
Gupta, A. K., 110

H

Haller, C. R., 104, 106, 109
Halpern, D. F., 11
Harb, J. N., 73, 75, 76
Hatch, T., 139
Healey, M., xix, 4, 20, 165
Helland, P., 5, 20, 163
Herr, K., 160
Herreid, C. F., 74, 76
Hershey, D. A., 126
Hesser, G. W., 76
Hietapelto, A. B., 64, 66
Hill, N. A., 82
Hiller, T. H., 64, 66
Hobson, S. M., 70
hooks, b., 133
Horrocks, L. J., 117
Houston, M. B., 117
Huber, M. T., xv, 6, 8, 14, 48, 206
Husted, B. L., 82, 85, 87, 104
Hutchings, P., 166

I

Iiyoshi, T., 139
Intrator, S. M., 189
Ironside, P. M., 108

J

Jackson, S. L., 110, 119
Jacobs, L. C., 132
Jacobs-Lawson, J. M., 126
Jenkins, A., 32, 35, 60
Johnstone, K. M., 126
Jones, T. B., 132

K

Karabenick, S. A., 132
Kauffman, K. J., 143
Keeley, S. M., 70
Kelly, T. M., 14, 61
Kember, D., 10
Kennedy, E. J., 98, 100
Kennedy, K. N., 109, 114, 115, 116
Kinsey, K., 102
Knight, R. D., 131
Kohn, A., 134, 185
Korn, J. H., 28
Korobkin, D., 70, 74, 76
Kreber, C., 3, 20, 150, 193
Kunkel, K. R., 94

L

Lagowski, J. J., 28
Lawton, L., 98, 100
Lawton, R. G., 57, 66
Lee, A., 104, 107
Lee, J., 160
Lewicki, R. J., 35

Lewis, J. E., 101
Lewis, S. E., 101
Lincoln, Y. S., 103, 104, 105, 107
Linkon, S., 59
Livingstone, D., 35
Louie, B. Y., 88
Lucal, B., 29
Luckett, M., 109, 112, 116
Luckey, W., 5, 20, 163
Lynch, K., 35

M

Mace, D. P., 139
MacRone, M., 109, 110, 113, 116
Maeroff, G. I., xv, 48, 206
Maharaj, S., 58, 64
Mallard, K. S., 162, 167
Marek, P., 110, 119
Marxen, J. C., 28
Matthews, H., 29, 34, 35
Matthews, J. R., 133
McAlpine, L., 162
McCabe, J., 111
McCann, L., 28
McFadden, S., 28
McKeachie, W. J., 28, 78, 131, 205
McKinney, K., 75, 76
Medlock, A. L., 98
Menges, R., xxi
Meyers, C., 132
Middleton, A., 20
Miller, B., 109, 110, 114, 116, 119
Miller, J. E., 125

Millis, B. J., 78
Mooney, L. A., 119
Moore, J. W., 137
Morreale, S. P., 6
Mottet, T. P., 98
Mourtos, N. J., 58
Munsayac, K., 102
Murray, H. G., 165

N

Nelson, C. E., 39
Noel, T. W., 127
Norcross, J. C., 117
Nummendal, S. G., 97

O

O'Leary, R., 143
Olson, T., 82
Oreovicz, F. S., 8, 33
Ory, J., 205

P

Palmer, P. J., 84
Parilla, P. F., 76
Paulson, D. R., 56, 64, 66
Peck, S. R., 64
Perkins, D., 59, 61, 161
Perlman, B., 28
Pestel, B. C., 81
Pintrich, P. R., 184
Plumlee, E. L., 98, 100
Polkinghorne, D. E., 160
Powell, B., 111
Prados, J. W., 33, 158
Prince, M., 70, 164
Puente, A. E., 133
Purdy, J. M., 88

Q

Quinn, J. W., 7

R

Raffeld, P. C., 98
Ramsey, R. P., 109, 114, 115, 116
Reason, P., 160
Renaud, R. D., 165
Rice, E., 134
Robinson, P., 132
Rubin, D., 131

S

Sappington, J., 102
Saville, B. K., 9, 33
Saxe, D., 75, 76
Schmidt, J. Z., 133
Schön, D., 53, 54, 58, 162
Scribner, M., 189
Sharp, J. E., 73, 75, 76
Shaw, J. B., 60
Shemberg, K. M., 70
Sheppard, S., 30, 33
Shindler, J. V., 126
Shulman, L. S., xv, 41, 48, 79, 148, 206
Silver, W. S., 109, 113, 116
Smith, K. A., 8, 33
Smith, L. L., 160
Smith, P. A., 130
Sojka, J., 110
Southey, G. N., 60
Spelman, D., 128
Spence, L. D., 82
Stackman, R. W., 88
Starling, R., 82, 85

Steadman, M. H., 61, 159, 181
Stenberg, S., 104, 107, 150, 160, 161
Stevenson, J. F., 117
Stewart, K. A., 98, 100, 101, 109, 113, 116
Stewart-Belle, S., 98, 100, 101
Stringer, E. T., 160
Strommer, D. W., 132
Svinicki, M. D., 69, 70, 75, 77, 134
Sweet, A., 132

T

Takata, S. R., 57
Talbot, D. M., 70
Terenzini, P. T., 126
Terry, R. E., 73, 75, 76
Thomas, L., 184
Tompkins, J., 82, 86, 133

V

Vallejo, E., 160
van Gelder, T., 76
Vance, C. F., 131
VanderStoep, S. W., 118
Varner, D., 64

W

Wagenaar, T. C., 109, 114, 116, 119
Walck, C. L., 82, 86, 87, 104
Walker, C., 67
Wankat, P. C., 8, 30, 33, 62
Warfield, T. D., 126
Weaver, F. S., 4

Wedman, J. F., 126
Weimer, M., xxi–xxii, 21, 96
Weldon, T. L., 104, 106, 109
Weston, C. B., 162
Whitin, K., 30, 33
Wight, R. D., 28
Woods, D. R., 57, 65

Y

Yakura, E. K., xvii
Yorks, L., 160
Young, P., 105, 107

Z

Zinnbauer, B. J., 70

Subject Index

A

Academic leaders, advice for: advancing agenda, 197–204; agenda setting, 193–197; evaluation issues, 204–209

Academy of Management Learning and Education, The, 27, 29, 33, 35, 36, 211

Action research, 160, 161

Advice, good instructional, 75–77

Advice for academic leaders. *See* Academic leaders, advice for

Advice for faculty: advocating pedagogical scholarship, 191–192; commitment to writing, 187–188; fears about publishing, 176–181; goal-setting, 185–186; handling rejection, 190–191; motivation, 169–176; practical first steps, 181–183; pushing the envelope, 188–189; questions to explore, 170; reasons that should motivate, 169–174; scholarship aspirations, 184–185; writing support groups, 186–187, 203–204

Advice-giving literature, 71–74

Advocates for pedagogical scholarship, 191–192

American Association of Higher Education (AAHE), 4

Analysis, areas of, 44–46

Answers to pedagogical problems, 175, 200–202

Applied literature, pedagogical literature as, 142–144

Approaches: analysis of, 44–46; classification system for, 39–40, 46–51; research scholarship, 42–43; wisdom-of-practice scholarship, 40–42. *See also* Research scholarship; Wisdom-of-practice scholarship

Articles: circulating, 199; excellent examples of, 44–45; hybrids, 125–126; innovative

Articles, *continued*
approaches of, 127; three
types of, 124–125; in unusual
formats, 127–129
Aspirations, scholarship,
184–185
Associations: and journals, 25;
online resources from, 138
Audience for pedagogical
periodicals, 26–28
Audience for this book, xiv–xvii
Authors, potential, xv–xvi. *See
also* Advice for faculty
Availability of pedagogical
literature, 198–199

B
"Book of the year" programs,
199
Books, innovative, 131–134

C
Carnegie Academy for the
Scholarship of Teaching and
Learning (CASTL), 4
Categorization: benefits of,
46–48; caveats, 48–51
Changes needed in pedagogical
literature, 157–167
Cited half-life, 35
Classification of approaches:
basis for, 39–40; research
scholarship, 42–44; wisdom-
of-practice scholarship, 40–42
Classroom assessment, 159–160
Classroom research, 159–160,
161

Colleagues: conversations with,
173–174; respect from, 176
College Teaching, 7, 29, 32, 74,
75, 85, 215
Collegiality across disciplines,
165
Columns, monthly, 26
Commitment to writing,
187–188
Content covered in pedagogical
periodicals, 28–31
Courage to Teach, The (Palmer),
84
Course materials and online
work, 137–139
Course releases, 202–203
Credible pedagogical
scholarship, 3, 5–7, 150–151
Cross-disciplinary pedagogical
journals, 7, 22, 215

D
Definition of pedagogical
scholarship, 2, 19–21
Descriptive research:
contribution of, 116–120;
critical assessment of,
111–112; defined, 43, 92;
description of, 109–111;
exemplars, 112–114;
standards for, 114–116
Disciplinary differentiation, as
defining feature, 146–149
Disciplinary pedagogical
literature, relevance of, 13–17
Discipline-based pedagogical
periodicals: for all levels of

education, 21, 213–214; audience for, 26–28; editorial policies of, 24–25; as faculty's first choice, 23–24; for higher education, 21, 211–213; kinds of articles in, 26; organizational arrangements of, 25
Disciplines: looking across, 13–17; relationship between pedagogical scholarship and, 164–166
Diverse literature, pedagogical literature as, 144–145

E

Editorial policies and practices, 24–25
Educational research versus pedagogical scholarship, 2, 20–21
Evaluation issues, 204–209. *See also* Quality issues
Exemplars, reasons for reading, 44–45
Existing pedagogical literature: as applied literature, 142–144; coexisting experience and research in, 144; disciplinary differentiation in, 146–149; as diverse literature, 144–145; and holistic treatment, 145–146; lessons from, 141–142
Experience-based knowledge, how we regard, 161–163
Experience-based (wisdom-of-practice) scholarship:

conclusions on, 89–90; defined, 40; as knowledge in action, 54; personal accounts of change, 40–41, 55, 56–69; personal narratives, 42, 55, 80–89; recommended-content reports, 41, 55, 79–80; recommended-practices reports, 41, 55, 69–79; relevance of, 54–55; versus research scholarship, 50
Expertise, access to pedagogical, 203
Extra credit, descriptive studies on, 117–118

F

Faculty: as advocates of pedagogical scholarship, 191–192; and commitment to writing, 187–188; fears of, 176–181; goal-setting for, 185–186; motivation for, 169–176; as potential authors, xv–xvi; practical first steps for, 181–183; questions that interest, 170; reading habits of, 7–9; reasons that motivate, 169–174; scholarship aspirations for, 184–185; and views on learning, 10; writing support groups for, 186–187, 203–204
Failure, confrontations with, 127
Fear of not getting published, 180–181

Fear of rejection, 190–191
Flaws in pedagogical literature, 12. *See also* Quality issues
Future of pedagogical literature, 33–36

G
Goal-setting, 185–186
Good advice on teaching, 75–77
Guest speakers, impact of, 119

H
High-maintenance students, article about, 29
History of pedagogical periodicals, 31–33
Holistic feature of pedagogical literature, 145–146

I
Impact factor, 34
Innovative books, 131–134
Innovative Higher Education, 127, 215
Instructional awareness, developing, 170–171
Integration and application, scholarships of, 163–164
Interest in scholarship of teaching, 3–5

J
Journal of Chemical Education, 16, 17, 27, 28, 32, 37, 62, 64, 214

Journal of College Science Teaching, 22, 25, 27, 74, 215
Journal of Engineering Education, 30, 33–34, 35, 62, 64, 65, 75, 106, 212
Journal of Geography in Higher Education, 29, 32, 34–35, 60, 212
Journal of Management Education, 16, 29, 32, 33, 60, 64, 85, 86, 113, 212
Journal of Nursing Education, 36–37, 88, 107, 212
Journals, pedagogical: content of, 28–31; defined, 2, 19–21; features of, 24–28; future of, 33–36; history of, 31–33; how to look at, 11–18; lists of, 21–24, 211–216; reasons for looking at, 3–11, 17–18; sections from, 36–38; special features of, 129–131

L
Location of pedagogical scholarship, 21–24

M
Motivation to do pedagogical scholarship, 169–176

N
New Directions for Teaching and Learning, 133–134
Newsletters: audience for, xi–xii; potential of, 134–137

O

Online course materials,
137–139

Open mind, importance of,
11–13

Overlap between approaches, 49

P

Pedagogical scholarship:
content of, 28–31; defined, 2,
19–21; features of, 24–28;
future of, 33–36; history of,
31–33; how to look at, 11–18;
location of, 21–24; reasons for
looking at, 3–11, 17–18;
selected periodicals, 36–38

Pedagogical writing support
groups, 186–187, 203–204

Periodicals, pedagogical:
audience for, 26–28; editorial
policies of, 24–25; future of,
33–36; history of, 31–33;
kinds of articles in, 26; lists of,
21–24, 211–216; organiza-
tional arrangements of, 25;
sections from, 36–38; topics
covered in, 28–31

Personal accounts of change:
contribution of, 67–69;
critical assessment of, 59–63;
defined, 40–41, 55;
description of, 56–58;
exemplars, 63–65; standards
for, 65–67

Personal narratives:
contribution of, 88–89;

critical assessment of, 83–85;
defined, 42, 55; description of,
80–83; exemplars, 85–86;
standards for, 86–88

Positive pedagogical scholarship
agenda, 196–197

Prejudice against teaching,
11–12

Professional associations and
journals, 25

Q

Qualitative studies:
contribution of, 108–109;
critical assessment of,
105–106; defined, 43, 92;
description of, 103–105;
exemplars, 106–107;
standards for, 107–108

Quality issues: areas of analysis,
44–46; sensible stance on,
12–13; standards for journal
articles, 33–35

Quantitative investigations:
contribution of, 101–103;
critical assessment of, 94–98;
defined, 43, 92; description of,
93–94; exemplars, 98–99;
standards for, 99–101

Questions that interest you, 170

R

Reading habits of professors,
7–9

Recommended-content reports,
41, 55, 79–80

Recommended-practices reports: contribution of, 77–79; critical assessment of, 71–74; defined, 41, 55; description of, 69–71; exemplars, 74–75; standards for, 75–77

Re-doing completed pedagogical scholarship, 184

References, absence of, 61–63, 73

Reflexive inquiry, 160, 161

Rejection, handling, 180–181, 190–191

Rejection rates, 25, 33

Research, how we think about, 158–161

Research scholarship: categories of, 43; conclusions on, 120–121; defined, 40, 42–43; descriptive research, 43, 92, 109–120; qualitative studies, 43, 92, 103–109; quantitative investigations, 43, 92, 93–103; teaching quality and, 169–174; versus wisdom-of-practice, 50

Respect from colleagues, 176

Reviewing previously published literature: applied literature, 142–144; areas of analysis for, 44–46; categorization for, 39–44, 46–51; coexisting experience and research, 144; disciplinary differentiation, 146–149; diverse literature, 144–145; exemplars, 44–45; holistic treatment, 145–146; lessons from, 141–142

S

Sabbaticals, 202–203

Scholarship, pedagogical: content of, 28–31; defined, 2, 19–21; features of, 24–28; future of, 33–36; history of, 31–33; how to look at, 11–18; location of, 21–24; reasons for looking at, 3–11, 17–18; selected periodicals, 36–38

Scholarship, research. See Research scholarship

Scholarship, wisdom-of-practice. See Wisdom-of-practice scholarship

Scholarship aspirations, 184–185

Scholarships of integration and application, 163–164

Students, article about high-maintenance, 29

Success, celebrating, 204

Support groups, writing, 186–187, 203–204

Surveys in descriptive research, 110–111

Syllabi, online, 138

T

Teaching of Psychology, 9, 14, 16, 27, 28, 29, 32, 33, 37, 98, 114, 214

Teaching Professor newsletter, xi–xii, 135, 136

Teaching quality and pedagogical scholarship, 169–174

Teaching Sociology, 34, 59, 62, 75, 113, 114, 213

Teaching talk, 199–200

Tenure and pedagogical scholarship, 6, 176, 207

Time to pursue pedagogical scholarship, 179–180

Timeliness of pedagogical scholarship, 3–5

Teaching Tips (McKeachie), 78, 131

Topical pedagogical journals, 22, 216

Topics covered in journals, 28–31

V

Viable pedagogical scholarship, 3, 7–11, 151–155

Visible Learning Project at Georgetown University, 139

W

Wisdom of practice, how we think about, 161–163

Wisdom-of-practice scholarship: conclusions on, 89–90; defined, 40; as knowledge in action, 54; personal accounts of change, 40–41, 55, 56–69; personal narratives, 42, 55, 80–89; recommended-content reports, 41, 55, 79–80; recommended-practices reports, 41, 55, 69–79; relevance of, 54–55; versus research scholarship, 50

Writing, commitment to, 187–188. *See also* Advice for faculty

Writing support groups, 186–187, 203–204